LIGHT FOR THE LAST DAYS

A STUDY IN CHRONOLOGICAL PROPHECY

BY DR. AND MRS.

H. GRATTAN GUINNESS

AUTHORS OF

"THE APPROACHING END OF THE AGE" ETC.

New Edition

EDITED AND REVISED BY THE REV.

E. P. CACHEMAILLE, M.A.

LATE SCHOLAR OF GONVILLE AND CAIUS COLLEGE, CAMBRIDGE

MARSHALL, MORGAN & SCOTT LTD.

LONDON & EDINBURGH

Kessinger Publishing's Rare Reprints
Thousands of Scarce and Hard-to-Find Books!

- •
- •
- •
- •
- •
- •
- •
- •
- •
- •
- •
- •
- •
- •
- •
- •
- •
- •
- •

We kindly invite you to view our extensive catalog list at:
http://www.kessinger.net

PROPHETIC TIMES.

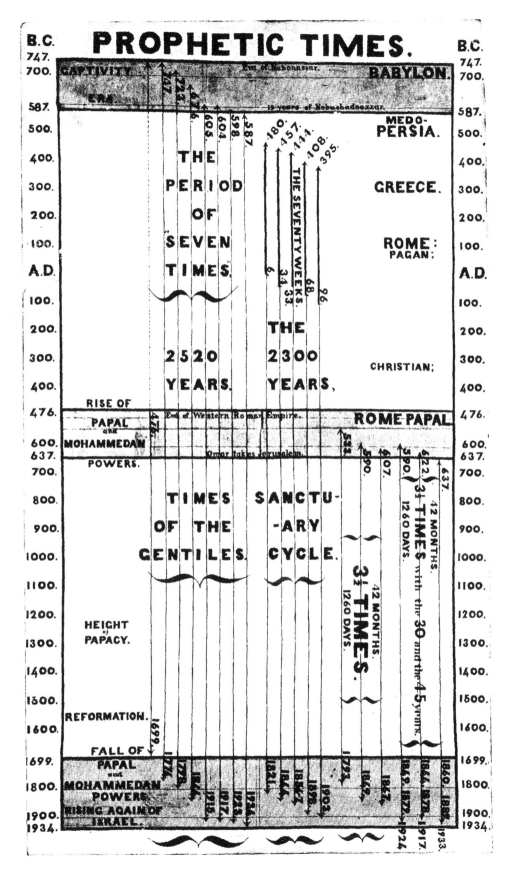

FIRST EDITION . . *July* *1917*
Second Impression . . . *August* *1917*
Third Impression . . . *November 1917*
Fourth Impression. . . *January 1918*
Fifth Impression . . . *March* *1918*
Sixth Impression . . . *April* *1924*
Seventh Impression . *January 1928*
Eighth Impression . . . *November 1934*

MADE AND PRINTED IN GREAT BRITAIN BY
MORRISON AND GIBB LTD., LONDON AND EDINBURGH

PREFACE TO REVISED EDITION

THE late Dr. H. Grattan Guinness' *Light for the Last Days* has been before the public for more than thirty years, and from the first has been recognised and highly valued as a standard work on Chronological Prophecy. Seven editions have been issued, the last appearing in 1893.

Now that a whole generation has passed away since the first appearance of the work, it has been thought well to re-issue it in a form better suited to present requirements. But apart from the necessary alterations due to the lapse of time, very little change has been made in the author's text, except by way of abridgment and condensation, and levelling up of dates. All the essential stands. Some of the later chapters have been omitted, treating as they do of a separate subject—the Millennial Age and the Future Kingdom of God upon Earth.

This has made it possible to reduce the size of the volume without in any way detracting from its usefulness as a Textbook of the Science of Chronologic Prophecy, a science of transcendent interest and importance at the times in which we are living, when so many of the Great Prophetic Periods have already run out, and only a few remain to be terminated in the very near future.

The author brought to his task the qualifications of a mathematician and an astronomer, an equipment of pre-eminent value in dealing with the Chronology of Prophecy. He brought also a deep and sincere belief in the Divine Inspiration and supernatural character of the Prophecies themselves. The result has been a work of permanent value to the student of Prophecy, and of intense interest to the devout reader of the Bible.

The book in its new form is now earnestly commended especially to all ministers of the Gospel, to all whose duty and privilege it is to be teachers of others. Since these great Prophetic Periods seem to be so near their close, let all who love the Lord's appearing see to it that they be not in darkness, that that day should overtake them as a thief.

E. P. CACHEMAILLE.

West Hampstead,
    June 1917

PREFACE TO FIRST EDITION

——◆——

IN the following pages we present, in a detached and
definite form, the historic evidence of the fulfilment
of the main chronologic prophecies of Scripture. The
subject was glanced at in our former volume, *The
Approaching End of the Age*, but owing to the variety
of topics there treated, it was very imperfectly expounded. Here it will be found carefully traced out;
and we feel confident that the more the details are
studied the more clearly will the truth of the entire
system appear.

The demonstration of that system has a double value.
It yields strong confirmation for faith, in the first place;
and affords important practical guidance, as "a light
that shines in a dark place," in the second.

No one who is acquainted with the mental condition
of the great bulk of the intelligent classes in these days
can doubt that a widespread defection from the faith
exists already, and extends continually. Infidelity and
rationalism in countless forms, both open and concealed,
are not only rife in the world, but also in the Church.
A great intellectual change has passed over the minds
of men within this generation, and its effect has been
to a large extent adverse to faith in revelation. Historic
criticism, the philosophical mode of treating ancient
history, which has been applied since the time of

Niebuhr to the books of the Bible, too often rashly and inconsiderately, has done much to produce in the minds of many a state of suspended belief, if not of actual unbelief; while the tendency to hasty generalisation on the part of the rapidly developing natural sciences, which has seemed to place nature, the *work* of God, in opposition to Scripture, His *Word*, has helped to undermine the old foundations.

Truer criticism and truer science are slowly undoing some of the mischief which was all too quickly wrought; but the flood of rationalistic teaching still flows alike from the professor's chair and the periodical press, from the pulpit and the platform. An organised diffusion of infidel principles is proceeding in every class of society, and the young are peculiarly exposed to be injured by it. The less the instruction and experience, the greater the danger of being misled by the specious arguments of scepticism, and the greater the need of confirmation and establishment in divinely revealed truth. The ceaseless warfare being waged against the Word of God should prepare us gladly to welcome every additional evidence of its inspiration.

Of all the various lines of Christian evidence none is so specially adapted to these last days as that based on *fulfilled prophecy*. It is as distinctively adapted to the close of the dispensation as were miracles to the commencement. As the age of miracle recedes, and its occurrence at all is in consequence increasingly called in question, the proofs of supernatural power and wisdom arising from fulfilled prophecy accumulate and become irresistible. Each century of Jewish and Gentile history adds to its amount, and the last two centuries especially have done so very largely.

The prophecies of Daniel stand pre-eminent among all

others in their evidential value. It is an astounding fact, that not only does his brief book give a fore-view of twenty-five centuries of Jewish and Gentile history, including the first and the second advents of Christ, but that it also fixes the chronology of various episodes of the then unknown future, with a simple certainty which would be audacious if it were not Divine. Would any mere man dare to foretell, not only a long succession of events lying far in the remote future, but in addition the periods they would occupy? This Daniel has done, and the predictions have come and are coming to pass.

This great and unquestionable fact can be explained away only on one of three grounds.

1. The accord must be purely accidental and fortuitous; or

2. The events must be manipulated, so as to fit the prophecy; or

3. The prophecy must have been fitted to the events, and thus written after them, though claiming to have been written before.

None of these three explanations can account for the agreement between Daniel's predictions and history, as a moment's reflection will show.

1. It cannot be merely fortuitous. It is too far-reaching and detailed, too exact and varied. Chance might produce one or two coincidences of prediction and fulfilment out of a hundred, not a hundred or more without a single exception. Common sense perceives this at a glance. As far as time has elapsed every single point predicted in Daniel has come true, and there remain but a few terminal points to be fulfilled in the near future.

2. The events were certainly not made to fit the prophecy by human arrangement. The rise and fall

and succession of monarchies and of empires, and the conduct and character of nations, for over two thousand years, are matters altogether too vast to be manipulated by men. Such a notion is clearly absurd. What did Babylonian and Persian monarchs, and Grecian and Roman conquerors, Gothic and Vandal invaders, mediæval kings and popes, and modern revolutionary leaders, all intentionally conspire for long ages to accomplish obscure Jewish predictions, of which the majority of them never even heard?

3. The third and last solution is consequently the only possible alternative to a frank admission of the Divine inspiration of the book, and of the Divine government of the world amid all its ceaseless political changes. Can the prophecy have been written to fit the events? In other words, can it be a forgery of a later date? This is the theory adopted by all the unbelieving critics, who start with the assumption that prophecy in any true sense is impossible. They endeavour to assign to the book a date later than the true one, a date towards the close of the reign of Antiochus Epiphanes, who died in the second century before Christ. They then endeavour to compress all the four empires into the four centuries previous to that date, excluding entirely from the prophecy any allusion to the Roman empire and the first advent of Christ, to say nothing of the second.

Multitudinous have been the attacks made on these lines on the fortress of this Book of Daniel, for scepticism has realised that while it stands impregnable, *a relic of the sixth century before Christ*, all rationalistic theories must fall to the ground, like Dagon before the ark. But the fortress stands firm as ever, its massive foundations revealed only the more clearly by the varied assaults it has repelled. The assailants, German as well as English, have been beaten off time after time by one champion after another, earnestly contending for the faith. As the superficial and shallow nature of the linguistic, historic, or critical objections has been demonstrated, one line of assault after another has been abandoned, till all are alike forsaken. But even if this were not the case, and the later date could be substantiated, it would not in the least warrant the sceptical denial of the existence of prophecy in Daniel. The predictions of the first advent and of the Roman destruction of Jerusalem would be in no wise affected by the later date, nor those of the tenfold division of the Roman empire and of the great Papal and Mohammedan apostasies.

Candour is shut up to the conclusion that real, true, and marvellous foreknowledge is, beyond all question, indicated by the predictions of the book, since twenty-five centuries of history can be proved to correspond with it accurately, in their chronological as well as in all their other features. If this be so, the question of inspiration is settled for honest minds. Nor that alone. For the rule of God over the kings of the earth—the fact that history is working out His Divine purposes, and that all the changing kingdoms of the Gentiles are merely introductory to the eternal kingdom of the Son of man and of the saints—is also established beyond controversy.

It was alleged by the sceptical school that the late origin of Daniel was demonstrated by the presence of Macedonian words, and of impure Hebrew expressions; that its spurious character was proved by its position in the canon, as not among "the Prophets," but among the "Hagiographa"; that it contained historical errors, and irreconcilable contradictions; that it had traces of later ideas and usages; as well as—and this was evidently the head and front of the offending—that the predictions were so clear and definite that they must have been written after the events.

The defence has been twofold. First, a demonstration which leaves nothing to be desired of the utter baselessness of the objections; and secondly, an array of unanswerable arguments in support of the authenticity and date of the book. The contention has given rise to a whole literature, to which we can merely allude in a few sentences. Those who wish to examine into the subject for themselves will find such works as those of Hengstenberg and Dr. Pusey very thorough and candid, as well as learned, giving not the results of investigation only, but the process, and the fullest reference to original documents. Much has since been added by the archæological discoveries in Bible lands.

As the predictions of Daniel lie at the base of the following treatise, we must indicate the nature of the defence, though we cannot do more. Porphyry, in the third century, in his attack on Christianity as a whole, devoted one of his fifteen books to an assault on Daniel. He asserted that it must be the work of a Jew of Palestine, written in Greek in the time of Antiochus; and assigned as the *ground* of his theory the exact correspondence of events with the predictions, asserting that Daniel "did not so much predict future events as narrate past ones," bearing thus a noble testimony to the prophet! His book was by imperial command condemned to the flames, and we know it mostly from fragments preserved in the writings of Jerome. Spinosa, the infidel Jew, was the first modern to renew this old attack; and then Hobbes and Collins, and other English deists. J. D. Michaelis made, however, the first scholarly attempt to undermine confidence in the authenticity of Daniel, and he decidedly *maintained* the genuineness of the greater part of it. The names of more recent opponents are legion, and we need not give them here, but simply indicate the arguments that prove the futility of the objections.

To a Christian mind the highest and most conclusive testimony lies in the fact that our Lord speaks of Daniel as a prophet, and quotes from him. The name by which He most frequently speaks of Himself, "the Son of man," is taken from Daniel vii. 13. Many of His descriptions of His own coming and kingdom are also connected with Daniel's predictions of them.[1] Surely our Lord would not thus endorse an impostor! Josephus tells us that the book was eagerly studied in Christ's days; would He have treated it as Scripture, and allowed His disciples to regard it as such, if it were a forgery?

The apostles uniformly recognise Daniel as a prophet. Peter alludes to his inquiries as to the "times," and states that he was inspired by the Spirit of Christ. Paul in 2 Thessalonians ii. builds his argument on Daniel's prediction of the man of sin and the apostasy. Hebrews xi. 33 alludes distinctly to Daniel and his companions and their heroic deeds; and the whole Book of Revelation is so closely connected with that of Daniel that we might almost call it Second Daniel, or Daniel First Revelation.

The allusions to Daniel as one of the holiest and one of the wisest of men, by his contemporary Ezekiel,

[1] Compare Dan. vii. 13, 14, and 26, 27 with Matt. x. 23, xvi. 27, 28, xix. 28, xxiv. 30, xxvi. 64; John v. 27; Dan. xii. 2. See also His reference in Matt. xxiv. 15 to the "abomination of desolation" mentioned in Dan. xi. 31, xii. 11.

show how *early* he attained his high position in the court of Nebuchadnezzar, and how far the fame of his blameless, holy life had spread, even in his own days. As he most distinctly and repeatedly claims to be the author of his own book, and writes much of it as an autobiography, the very holiness of his character makes the thought of deliberate forgery and falsehood revoltingly inconsistent.

That the book was widely distributed and well-known and revered by the pious in pre-Maccabean times can be demonstrated. The very accurate and reliable First Book of Maccabees makes exact, though brief and simple, reference to the stories in Daniel. The dying words of Mattathias to his sons are recorded, in which he encourages them to fidelity to God amid persecution by recalling various Bible histories, and among the rest that of the Hebrew children in the fire, and Daniel in the lion's den. Hence it is evident the book was known and regarded as Scripture at that time. Further, Josephus makes several remarkable and explicit statements on the subject. Speaking of one of the predictions, he says, " Now this was delivered 408 years before the fulfilment," thus recognising the received date as unquestionable, and as generally admitted to be so in his day.

In a still more conclusive and very interesting passage he asserts that Daniel's prophecy was shown to Alexander the Great when he visited Jerusalem, and that this monarch took the prediction about a Greek who was to overthrow the Persian empire to mean himself, and was encouraged thereby in his enterprise, and very favourably disposed towards the Jews in consequence.

Josephus was indeed much impressed by the remarkable fulfilments of Daniel's predictions, which even in his day were evident. After expounding several of these he says, "All these things did this man leave behind in writing, as God had showed them to him: so that those who read his prophecies, and see how they have been fulfilled, must be astonished at the honour conferred by God on Daniel."[1]

A strong argument in favour of the received date may be drawn from the languages in which the book is written, Hebrew and Aramæan. Both were familiar to the Jews of the Captivity era, and to them *only*; the one was Daniel's mother tongue, the other the language in which he had been educated, and by which he was surrounded for the greater part of his life. Hebrew ceased to be used by the Jews in and from the Captivity, except as a sacred learned language. It had been entirely superseded before the Maccabean days, and no writer of the time of Antiochus could have counted on being understood had he written in that language. Daniel reckons on such a familiar acquaintance with both languages, that it is evidently a matter of indifference to him and to his readers which he uses. "The use of the two languages, and the mode in which the prophet writes in both, correspond perfectly with his real date; they are severally and together utterly inexplicable according to the theory that would make the book a product of the Maccabean times. *The language is a mark of genuineness set by God on the book.* Rationalism must rebel, as it has rebelled; but it dare not now with any moderate honesty abuse philology to cover its rebellion."[2]

Further, the exact knowledge of cotemporary history

[1] *Antiquities,* x. 11. 7.
[2] Dr. Pusey, *Lectures on Daniel.*

evinced in Daniel is such that no writer of the time of the Maccabees could possibly have attained it. Almost every single circumstance mentioned in the book is confirmed directly or indirectly by cotemporary historians, and proved to be absolutely and even minutely correct. In the Maccabean age, as existing remains prove, the utmost ignorance of the history and geography of foreign countries prevailed among the Jews in Palestine, and an exact and comprehensive knowledge of the history of a period so dark and already so remote as the Captivity era, did not exist and could not have existed. And the same may be said of the accurate knowledge exhibited in the book of the institutions, manners, usages, and entire state of things existing in the Babylonian and Medo-Persian times.

Again, it has been remarked that "the complexion of *the prophecies* of Daniel corresponds so exactly with what is related in the historical part of *the circumstances of his life*, that even the most crafty impostor would not have been able to produce this agreement artificially. Daniel occupied high offices of state; he was witness to great revolutions and changes of rulers and empires; and this circumstance is very significantly impressed on his prophecies. The succession of the various empires of the world forms their principal subject. In the representation of the Messianic idea also he borrows his colours from his external relations. Throughout there is apparent a religious as well as a political gift, such as we meet with in no prophet."

Lastly, *the canon of the Old Testament contains the Book of Daniel*, and that canon was closed by Ezra the scribe, and Nehemiah, the second Moses in Jewish estimation, about 400 B.C. Hence the prophecies of Daniel were already at that date recognised as inspired writings. It is true the book does not appear in the list of prophets, because Daniel was not *officially* a Jewish prophet, but a Babylonian statesman. David, also, though a prophet, was officially a king, and thus his writings, like Daniel's, are classed among the Hagiographa, or sacred books, rather than among the prophets. The principle of the Jewish arrangement of the canon was, that sacred writings by men in secular office, and not occupying the pastoral or prophetic position, were put in a class apart from the prophets. Hence Daniel appears not in the list with Isaiah, Jeremiah, and Ezekiel, but rather with David and Solomon, and Mordecai the writer of Esther. But the Jewish rabbis hold his prophetic revelations in the highest esteem, and the Talmud places him above all other prophets.

There is therefore no question at all for candid minds that the book is authentic, and rightly attributed to the time of the Babylonish captivity; and if so, it must be granted by all that it contains prophecy—definite predictions which have been most marvellously fulfilled.

The importance of this conclusion can scarcely be over-estimated, though it seems to be less appreciated by Christians than by sceptics. They regret their inability to wrest a mighty weapon out of the hands of the Church. But we—what are we making of it? What execution are we doing with it? Is it not a pity that it is allowed to so great an extent to lie idle?

If eight or nine centuries of fulfilled prophecy drove Porphyry, in the third century, to feel that we must either admit Divine inspiration or prove the Book of Daniel spurious, ought not the twenty-five centuries of it, to which we in our days can point, be even more efficacious in convincing candid inquirers and confounding prejudiced

b

opponents? The battle of authenticity has been fought and won; no fresh objections can be invented. Archæological discovery may yet find Daniel's name among the Babylonian records; it will certainly produce no evidence against the book which it has already done so much to authenticate. It rests with Christian teachers and preachers to use the miracle of the last days, fulfilled and fulfilling prophecy, for the conviction and conversion of men.

Should this volume increase such a use of "Daniel the prophet," we shall rejoice. It will, we trust, in any case confirm the faith of those who already believe, and brighten the hope of those who are waiting for the kingdom of God.

HARLEY HOUSE, BOW, E.,
     June 1886.

TABLE OF CONTENTS

CHAPTER I

INTRODUCTION. THE DANIEL PARALLEL

CHAPTER II

THE TIMES OF THE GENTILES

CHAPTER III

THE STARTING-POINT; OR, THE CAPTIVITY ERA OF ISRAEL AND JUDAH

CHAPTER IV

THE BISECTION; OR, THE ERA OF THE RISE OF THE APOSTASIES

CHAPTER V

THE TIME OF THE END—WESTERN, OR PAPAL ASPECT

CHAPTER VI

THE TIME OF THE END—EASTERN, OR MOHAMMEDAN ASPECT

CHAPTER VII

THE TIME OF THE END—JEWISH ASPECT, OR THE MODERN
RENAISSANCE OF THE JEWISH PEOPLE

CHAPTER VIII

CHRONOLOGICAL MEASURES OF THE TIMES OF THE GENTILES

CHAPTER IX

LUNAR MEASURES OF THE SEVEN TIMES, RECKONED FROM
THE CAPTIVITY ERA

CHAPTER X

SOLAR MEASURES OF THE SEVEN TIMES

CHAPTER XI

MEASURES OF THE SECOND HALF OF THE SEVEN TIMES

CHAPTER XII

THE SANCTUARY CYCLE

CHAPTER XIII

CHAPTER XIV

CHAPTER XV

CHAPTER XVI

ANSWERS TO OBJECTIONS

CHAPTER XVII

THE CANON OF PTOLEMY

APPENDIX

"Blessed be the name of God for ever and ever: for wisdom and might are His: and He changeth the times and the seasons: He removeth kings, and setteth up kings: He giveth wisdom unto the wise, and knowledge to them that know understanding: He revealeth the deep and secret things: He knoweth what is in the darkness, and the light dwelleth with Him. I thank Thee, and praise Thee, O Thou God of my fathers, who hast given me wisdom and might, and hast made known unto me now what we desired of Thee. . . . But as for me, this secret is not revealed to me for any wisdom that I have more than any living."

"In the first year of Darius . . . I Daniel understood by books the number of the years."—*Daniel, the prophet of Judah and the statesman of Babylon.*

CHAPTER I

INTRODUCTORY

The Daniel Parallel

THE conviction that we are living in days which
have about them a character of finality deepens
in the minds of thoughtful men. From the most
unlikely quarters there come, ever and anon, expressions
of this feeling. The grounds assigned for the senti-
ment or opinion differ; in some cases it is apparently
without foundation; but it prevails.

It is in reality a well-grounded conviction; the Word
of God leaves no room for doubt that we are living in
the last days of this dispensation, and have well-nigh
reached the close of the existing state of things. It
leaves no room to doubt that a change—*a change greater
than any the world has ever seen*—is impending. Bible
readers have a clearer and deeper impression on the
subject than others, though in too many cases even
they would find it difficult to give any solid reason for
their opinion. But students of the prophetic Scriptures
have no such difficulty; to them the fact that these are
in the most literal sense the last days is one capable of
the fullest demonstration, a fact as clearly ascertained
and as easily proved as any other fact of science.

The assertion may sound strange to some, but there
is *a science* of chronologic prophecy—a science of recent

origin, and one as yet too little studied, but one of unspeakable interest and importance.

Our desire in the following pages is to lead lovers of truth to the study of this sacred science. It is not a fashionable one in any circle. It is condemned and decried as speculative folly in some, and totally neglected in others; in others again it is pursued, but only in a desultory manner, by a few. As a rule, it is not publicly taught, even by those who understand it; and the result is that it is scarcely recognised as a science at all.

But if science be a knowledge of facts arranged in order and explained by law, then is there beyond all question a science of chronologic prophecy; and none of the sciences so ardently studied in this twentieth century yield results of greater practical importance. In bygone ages there was a cause why this science made little progress, a reason why it *could not* be understood. But this cause and this reason exist no longer; on the contrary, the time has come when the subject must and will be successfully studied and understood by many; for that such will be the case is distinctly predicted in Scripture.

When, twenty-five centuries ago, God granted to Daniel the revelations which form a large part of the material of this science, the prophet, who failed to understand especially the chronological statements embodied in the predictions given to him, asked further explanation. His request was refused, and he was informed that these predictions were not for the benefit of the then existing generations, but for that of distant future ones. He was directed in the meantime to " shut up the words, and seal the book," and informed that the meaning of the visions was " closed up and sealed " to " *the time of the end* "; that in *that* time " the wise " would understand them, though "the wicked" would never do so. *"None of the wicked shall understand,"* it was said to him; *"but the wise shall understand."* [1]

Now it is clear that none can read a divinely sealed book until God Himself break the seal and throw open the pages. None can penetrate His sacred mysteries till He is pleased to remove the veil that covers them. Chronologic prophecy must, in the very nature of the case, be designed for the benefit of later and not of earlier generations. The prophets themselves did not always understand their own chronological predictions. When the time was near, the period short, and the language in which it was expressed simple and literal, they of course did so; but when the events were distant, the period long, and the prophecy expressed in symbolic language, we are told by the Apostle Peter that, so far from understanding, they "inquired and searched diligently . . . what, or *what manner of time* the Spirit of Christ which was in them did signify," and that it was revealed to them "that not unto *themselves,* but unto *us* they did minister." Hence it is evident that the treasures of chronologic prophecy were committed to earlier ages for the benefit of later ones, and especially of the latest. As the end draws near the mysterious predictions are gradually explained by their own progressive fulfilments, and the light grows stronger and clearer to the close.

The statement that not even "the wise shall understand" chronologic prophecy till "the time of the end,' accounts for all the misunderstandings of earlier ages, and all the partial comprehension of later times, and is an encouragement to the study of it in *these* days; for that we live in "the time of the end" is plain with a

[1] Dan. xii. 10.

moment's reflection. What does the expression in Daniel "the time of the end" mean? Clearly the time of *the end of the events revealed to Daniel*. His prophecies foretold the events of twenty-five centuries, the existence of the Babylonian, Persian, Grecian, and Roman empires, and represent these as occupying the entire interval between the prophet's own days and the day of the resurrection of the dead, and the establishment of the glorious and everlasting kingdom of God on earth. They predict that the last or Roman dominion would exist in two distinct and successive stages, contrasted in many respects, but alike in some, and especially in that they are both phases of the rule of ROME. The first, a stage in which that great city is the fountain of authority and government to an *undivided empire*; and the second, in which it is so, in a different way, to a *tenfold commonwealth* of kingdoms.

Now we know, that not only the three first of these great universal empires have risen, ruled, and passed away as predicted, but that the dominion of Rome pagan was in due time, as foretold, succeeded by that of Rome Papal over the ten Gothic kingdoms of modern Europe; and that this last is now in a state of decadence, its temporal rule having already come to an end in 1870. In other words, we are not only living at a distance of twenty-five centuries from the days of Daniel, but we can trace, during the course of these centuries, the fulfilment of all his predictions except the very last. The Babylonian empire occupied the time of the beginning; the rule of Persia, Greece, Rome heathen, and Rome Papal, occupied the long subsequent course of the period, and the fall of this last power must clearly mark the *close* of the predicted series of events. The promise that in the time of the end "the wise shall understand" *must therefore, if it is ever to be fulfilled at all, be fulfilled in our days*; and there is no room for an "if" as regards any of the promises of the Faithful and True Witness, the God who cannot lie. The time has come at last for the comprehension of the chronological predictions of Scripture, and all who desire to understand them may plead the promise that there shall be light on them in these days.

But let us note well *to whom* light on this great and glorious subject is to be granted in this "time of the end." The promise says to "the wise," and contrasts these, not with the unlearned and ignorant, but with the "wicked"; implying that the qualification required for understanding sacred prophecy is *moral* rather than mental. "The fear of the Lord, *that* is wisdom," says Job, and Solomon calls it "the beginning of wisdom." Godliness, a humble, reverential, teachable spirit, prayerful, holy meditation, and patient observation of God's providential government of the world, would seem to be more essential qualifications for understanding prophetic revelations than mere learning or talent. "Whoso is wise, and will *observe* these things," says the psalmist, after enumerating many of the dealings of God with men, "even *they shall understand* the lovingkindness of the Lord." And similarly we may say, whoso is wise, and will observe the hand of God in history, even they shall understand the meaning of sacred prophecy.

In Daniel's predictions, the saints are continually contrasted with their enemies and persecutors; all through his prophecies, as well as in those of the Apostle John, these two classes are distinguished, and the context shows that *they* are the two classes alluded to by these expressions, "the wicked" and "the wise." The

statement that none of the wicked shall understand
would otherwise be superfluous, for the wicked in general
neither desire nor endeavour to understand, and therefore cannot of course do so. They despise and neglect,
not only the *prophetic* Scriptures, but the Word of God
as a whole. "The wicked" of these verses are pre-
eminently the opponents and persecutors of the saints,
so frequently alluded to in the earlier portions of the
prophecy, and especially those of *the Romish apostasy*,
which figures so largely in all predictions of this Gentile
age. The doctors and teachers of this system *do* study
and profess to understand Daniel's predictions, and they
even presume to expound them to others. This inspired
statement consequently puts us on our guard against any
system of prophetic interpretation which *emanates from
Rome*. Such interpretations must needs be *misunderstandings*, and therefore false and misleading; for it is
written, "none of the wicked shall understand."

Up to "the time of the end" the wicked and the wise
alike would be in darkness on the subject; when that
time arrived "the wise" would receive light, and would
be led to a true comprehension of the meaning of
chronologic prophecy, "the wicked" never. The moral
and ecclesiastical position of these latter forbids the
possibility of their understanding; the true light will
arise, not among the persecutors, but among the persecuted. Hence on this subject we should lean to Protestant
and not to Papal interpretations.

The numerous and wide differences of view among the
students of prophecy are frequently alleged as a reason
for not attempting its study. A moment's thought will
show that under the circumstances this difference was
inevitable. The progress of all sciences is gradual, and
often slow. The transition from total ignorance to

perfect knowledge on any subject cannot, without a miracle, be made suddenly. This promise, that "the wise shall understand," does not contain the condition that they shall do so suddenly, or correctly and completely *at once*. As comprehension was not to take place *till* the time of the end, the dawn of true light *must* have been comparatively recent. What science is there that has never made a mistake or started a false theory in its early days? What science is there that has not been driven, as it grew and developed, to modify some of its first conclusions, and to abandon some of its earlier positions? Recall the history of astronomy, the eldest of the sciences, or of biology, the youngest! Change and modification are involved in growth, nor can they be avoided until full maturity is reached. This objection is therefore simply an expression of impatience with the invariable law that there is no royal road to learning. Time must be allowed for careful and repeated observation, for study, meditation, and research; and patience must be exercised, for it may be many generations before a science is really understood and established on any solid basis.

Moreover, when human selfishness warps the judgment, and produces a strong prejudice, as it does, for instance, in the sciences of political and social economy, opposing theories must be expected. The science of chronologic prophecy bears strongly against three of the most numerous and influential religious communities in existence, — Romanists, Mohammedans, and Jews. How can it then be otherwise than controverted by those belonging to these communities?

If the Government publish the photographs of three notorious criminals, men guilty of high treason and murder, and, holding these in his hand, a detective addresses to a certain trio the accusation, "You are the men," are they likely to agree with his opinion? From the very nature of the case, differences of interpretation *must* exist to the end, between "the wicked" and "the wise"; but the differences of the latter among themselves ought now to be daily diminishing.

As a matter of fact, much real progress has already been made by the godly and learned students of the last three centuries. Though not a few erroneous anticipations have been indulged and false maxims adopted, the main principles of the science are clearly ascertained, and it is now a question of exact application.

This important study has been mainly brought into disrepute by the foolish speculations of some, who, instead of being students of prophecy, become themselves prophets, and presumptuously venture to foretell future events, instead of cautiously comparing history with the statements of Holy Writ. But a broad distinction exists between this foolish and reprehensible course, and that devout and humble study of chronologic prophecy for which we have the highest examples.

Our Lord and Saviour Jesus Christ began His ministry with a statement connected with chronological prophecy; a statement which showed how carefully He had pondered, and how clearly He comprehended Daniel's prediction of the "seventy weeks." Mark records, as the *first* utterance of the ministry of Christ, "*The time is fulfilled*, and the kingdom of God is at hand: repent ye, and believe the gospel." What time was fulfilled? The mysterious "seventy weeks" to Messiah the Prince.

Peter says of this study, that we do well to take heed to it; and John says of it, "Blessed is he that readeth, and they that hear "—the words of the most mysterious of prophetic books,—" and *keep* those things that are written therein,"—the latter clause showing that prophetic study has practical bearings.

Daniel, a scholar and a statesman, one of the wisest and holiest of men, gave himself earnestly, even in his old age, to the study of chronologic prophecy. He was himself a prince among prophets; and yet he disdained not, as he tells us,[1] to devote himself to the study of "books," and especially of the books of Jeremiah, that he might solve to his own satisfaction the chronological problem of the exact period of the termination of the Babylonish captivity. The effect of his studies was to prostrate him in prayer and supplication before God, and to secure for him an additional revelation, the most glorious that up to that time had ever been given—a revelation of the exact interval to the first advent and redeeming work of Christ.

Simeon and Anna were students of chronologic prophecy, and to their light on this subject it was owing that they were found in the temple, waiting for "the Consolation of Israel." The just and devout Simeon was rewarded with a special revelation, that "he should not die till he had seen the Lord's Christ." Do these things look as if prophetic students of the God-fearing, holy living, Bible-loving, sober-minded sort are fools or wise? Nay, is it not an insult to the ALL-WISE to assume that it is folly for His people to study the predictions which He in His wisdom has given, and which He has sealed with this unconditional promise, that the wise *shall* in "the time of the end" understand them?

Twenty-five centuries of history are now casting back the light of their multiplied fulfilments on these sacred

----

[1] Dan. ix.

prophecies. Men require in these last days just such fresh demonstration of the inspiration of Scripture as only fulfilled prophecy can afford. Miracle is doubted or denied; the supernatural is spurned as incredible by this generation, which smiles at the idea of inspiration. But if it be so that the very things now going on in the world were distinctly predicted in Daniel's day, and *even the very dates of the occurrence of* cotemporary events indicated, who can doubt that "holy men of old spake as they were moved by the Holy Ghost"? Such evidence should be, and frequently is, valuable for convincing the most sceptical unbelievers; but if it only serve to root and ground true Christians in their most holy faith, and to render them proof against the attacks of infidelity, it answers no mean end. If it serve, moreover, to quicken hope and practical zeal, and to produce and preserve in the Church a body of disciples who shall be watching and waiting for Christ at His coming, it abundantly accomplishes its purpose.

What is our present chronological position, and our present duty in this matter? It may help us to understand both if we note the parallel between our own position and that of Daniel in the days of Darius the Mede.

The holy prophet had spent in Babylon the greater part of his life, as he had been there during the whole of Judah's captivity. He had risen to high estate in the land of his exile, and was full of years, full of honours, full of wisdom: but his heart remained true to the God and the land of his fathers, true to Jerusalem and the Jewish people; and his mind was consequently full of the—to him—profoundly interesting question, When would their long captivity in Babylon come to an end?

He knew it must be nearly over; for though Judah still hanged her harp upon the willows and sat down and wept by the rivers of Babylon, she yet began to wipe away her tears and to lift up her head, for her redemption was drawing nigh; *she had seen the great city fall*, and the hand of the Persian conqueror was already resting on the pen that was to sign the blessed edict of liberation and return. The day was one of approaching crisis, a great turning point in the history of Israel was at hand, and *Daniel knew it*.

He had not been assured of it by an angel from heaven; he did not *guess* that it was so from political appearances, but he *knew it as the result of study*—a study of "books," as he expressly tells us. Those books included, no doubt, the chronicles of the kings of Israel and Judah, and it may be also the boastful records inscribed on many a Babylonian cylinder and slab. The book which he specially mentions, however, by name is that of the prophet Jeremiah, and the portions of that book which had principally enlightened his mind and influenced his heart were the two chronological predictions recorded in chapters xxv. and xxix. From an earnest study and comparison of these various books the holy prophet gathered that the end of Judah's captivity was close at hand, that the dark week of bondage—a week of decades, seventy years—was well-nigh over, and that already it began to dawn towards the first day of a new "week" in the history of his people.

This glad conclusion was not, however, arrived at so easily as some may suppose. Daniel did not argue, "The captivity was to last seventy years; I have been now about seventy years in Babylon, so it must be nearly over." No study would have been required for such a rough, approximate conclusion as that, no meditation or prayer, no spirituality or communion with God. Daniel's opinion of the crisis at which he lived was evidently the result of all these. His studies had a sanctifying and blessed effect on his mind, leading him to confession, supplication, and prayer, and securing for him an angelic visit, and a further glorious revelation.

He perceived, as he studied the predictions of Jeremiah, and the records of events which had happened when he was a child, that the captivity of his people had not been a sudden catastrophe, *but a gradual process*; that it had been accomplished by stages during a period of twenty years, stages as to the relative importance of which there might be some question. Taking no note of the conquests of the Assyrian monarchs, Pul, Shalmaneser, and Esarhaddon, nor of the various captivities inflicted by them on the ten tribes of Israel, nor even of the overthrow of Manasseh, king of *Judah*, under the last of these three monarchs, but confining his attention exclusively to *the different successive campaigns of Nebuchadnezzar and his generals against Jerusalem*, it was evident that a wide chronological margin—very wide as compared with the whole period of seventy years—existed, *somewhere in which* the initial date of the captivity must occur; but it was not exactly easy to select the precise year. The relative importance of historical events, and especially of contemporary events, is often difficult to discern. The edifice of Jewish monarchy had trembled and tottered for some time before it fell, and when it did fall, it fell in several successive crashes. Which was the critical one?

Was it the third year of Jehoiakim, B.C. 606, when Daniel had himself been brought to Babylon? or was it the following year, B.C. 605, when Judah had for the

first time become thoroughly tributary to Nebuchadnezzar? or was it seven years later, B.C. 598, when in
his eighth year that monarch a second time successfully
attacked Judah and Jerusalem, carrying captive Jehoiachin with his treasures, and all the principal men of
the kingdom? or was it yet again eleven years later
still, B.C. 587, when Zedekiah, the uncle of Jehoiachin,
who had been placed on the throne of Judah as a sort
of Babylonian viceroy, having rebelled against his
master, Nebuchadnezzar, in the nineteenth year of his
reign, once more besieged and took Jerusalem? On
this occasion the city was *finally* broken up, and
Zedekiah, after seeing his sons slain before his face,
and having his own eyes put out at Riblah, was carried
away to languish and die in exile. Later in that same
year Nebuzaradan *burned the temple*, rased Jerusalem
to the ground, and carried off to Babylon the rest of
the people. This was the last stage of the long process
of the decay and fall of Jewish monarchy, and the
record of it terminates with the fateful words, "so
Judah was carried away out of their land."

Now here was *a period of twenty years*, more than
a fourth part of the predicted seventy, *during which
the captivity had been slowly accomplished by stages*!
Daniel had consequently need to pray, and to study
carefully, before he could discern whether the restoration of his people, and of that temple worship for which
his soul yearned, were still twenty years distant, or
even then close at hand.

Moreover, as he pondered the expression, "seventy
years," the question could hardly have failed to occur
to him, What sort of years—sacred years or secular?
The sacred year of the Jews was *lunar*, for the
intervals between the feasts and the fasts of the

Levitical calendar were all strictly *lunar*; but they also used a longer tropical year, as did the Babylonians, while the Egyptians employed a retrograde solar one. The true length of the years intended must therefore have been a point on which Daniel reflected, and that, perhaps, without being able to arrive at any satisfactory conclusion, though he must have perceived that the actual duration of the captivity would vary to the extent of two years, according to the calendar employed.

As he studied, the thought, proved by the result to be a true one, could scarcely fail to be suggested to his mind, that the restoration might probably be *as gradual and as much by stages as the captivity had been*, and so occupy an *era* rather than a *year*. His people had not all come to Babylon at one time; was it likely they would all leave at one time? Jerusalem and its temple had not fallen in a day, nor in a year, but by stages. The temple had been first despoiled of its treasures, and then consumed with fire eleven years later. Was its reconstruction and its rededication to be similarly interrupted? The national overthrow had been gradual; was it not likely that the national restoration would also be gradual? As he pondered, the question would arise in his mind, "If so, which will be *the principal* stage?" Already the first was *past*. Babylon the overthrower had been overthrown; the city still stood, but its power was gone. The Median monarch occupied the palace of Nebuchadnezzar, and the Persian empire had succeeded the Babylonian.

This fact would greatly confirm the faith of Daniel as to the nearness of the restoration of his people, because Jeremiah had said, "This whole land shall be a desolation, and an astonishment; and these nations shall serve the king of Babylon seventy years. And it shall come to pass, *when seventy years are accomplished*, that *I will punish the king of Babylon, and that nation*, saith the Lord, for their iniquity, and the land of the Chaldæans, and will make it perpetual desolations."[1] "Therefore all they that devour thee shall *be devoured*; and all thine adversaries, every one of them, shall go into captivity; and they that spoil thee shall be a spoil, and all that prey upon thee will I give for a prey."[2]

Daniel's studies of chronological prophecy were at a time when one of the salient points of the Divine prediction had already been accomplished. Not only had the time run out, but one part of the thing predicted had happened. How confirmed must his faith have been, and how confident his hopes, though the restoration itself had not come! Yet there were difficulties through which he could not quite see. The promised deliverer was not yet on the throne; Cyrus was *there*, but he was not sole monarch, not yet in a position to make the predicted decree. Darius was the ruling monarch, and prophecy had, two hundred years before his birth, named *Cyrus* as the deliverer. Would Darius soon die then, and Cyrus succeed him? There was probably no immediate prospect of this, but Daniel doubted not that in some way God would make His promise good, fulfilling His own predictions, and that speedily. Cyrus would become supreme ruler, and would restore Israel, and rebuild Jerusalem.[3] Knowing this, he bowed himself in confession and prayer, and in humble supplication that the promise of restoration might come to pass, even as the threats of judgment had done.

[1] Jer. xxv. 11, 12.   [2] Jer. xxx. 16.
[3] Isa. xliv. 26–28 ; xlv. 1–13.

2

Spiritually minded and intelligent students of prophecy occupy in this twentieth century a very similar position. They too understand by books, and especially from the Book of Daniel, that the end of the present state of things must be close at hand. They have studied with reverential care not only the perfected scroll of prophecy, but also the records of God's providential government of the world, from Daniel's days to our own. They have compared history and prophecy, and the actual chronology of the one with the predicted chronology of the other. They have received immense help also through the study of a *third* book, one which throws a flood of light on this latter subject, as from its nature and its authorship it could not fail to do—*the book of nature.* Astronomy has taught them that the great chronometer provided by God for man marks off by its different revolutions *years of three different lengths*: one measured by the sun, one by the moon, and one by the conjoint movement of both orbs; the *solar* year, the *lunar* year, and the *calendar* year. They have found by research that God in His Word employs in prophecy *all these three years* which He has caused the sun and moon to measure, and that the difference between them, small in a single year, becomes so considerable in longer periods, as to have veiled from earlier generations the accurate fulfilment of chronological prophecies.

They have observed that the great episodes of Jewish and Gentile history are measured, both actually and in prediction, by *all these three different years*; and this fact has thrown a flood of light on the whole subject of chronology in relation to prophecy and to history, just such light as it might have been expected that God would graciously grant in the end of the age.

That light, however, is enjoyed as yet by few, because just as there was but one Daniel in the days of Darius the Mede, who endeavoured to understand by books "the number of the years" whereof the Lord had spoken, so there are in these analogous days few who either desire or try to comprehend the more complex chronologic prophecies, contained in Daniel's own book, and in the complementary predictions of Revelation, which alone can illumine the mind on the chronology of the close of the present age.

What had directed Daniel's mind to the study of prophecy at this special time? He was an old man, who might well have excused himself from any such research, on the ground that he had no time for it, and that it would make no difference to him personally whether Judah were restored or not, or when the event should take place; *he*, at any rate, would have to die as he had lived, in Babylon. What led him to the study? We cannot question that it was *the events which were taking place around him*. He had seen the Euphrates, on whose banks he had passed his days, dried up "that the way of the kings of the east might be prepared"; he had seen executed at Babylon the judgment foretold by Jeremiah; and he knew that these events were a sign that the desolations of Judah were accomplished.

Do we not occupy an analogous position? Have we not been watching the drying up of the antitypical Euphrates for many a long year? And have we not beheld the fall of the temporal power of the Papacy, if not as yet the final fall of "Babylon the Great," the apostate Church of Rome? Is it not time then for us to look into these things, and try, as Daniel did, to understand our own chronological position with regard to the approaching second and greater restoration of Israel, marking, as it will do, the end of this Gentile age?

Our desire in the following pages is to help our fellow-Christians to perceive that the chronological prophecies of Scripture are not mysterious, incomprehensible, and comparatively useless portions of the Word of God, but that they are, on the contrary, in these last days, clear and luminous, and of *the utmost practical importance*.

Our statements will be expository rather than controversial. It is high time now that prophetic students of the Protestant Historic School should cease to argue about first principles, and, recognising them as established, go on to their cautious and careful application. The occurrences of the eighteenth and nineteenth centuries have thoroughly tested the firm and solid character of the foundations on which we build; there is no need any longer to question their stability. The multiplied and ever-multiplying proofs of this have set the question practically at rest. Protestant students of the last three hundred years have been following the right tracks. Their mistakes have been only "way-marks in the progress of the Church from that entire ignorance of the times, in which she was purposely left, in the apostolic age, to the full and certain knowledge that the Bridegroom is at hand, which shall prepare her, like the wise virgins, to enter in with her Lord to the marriage feast."

Here, therefore, we take for granted, what has been abundantly proved by many godly and learned writers, and what we have ourselves also in a former

work demonstrated, and assume the following conclusions :

1. That in symbolic prophecy a " day " is the symbol
of a year, and a " time " of 360 years.

2. That Daniel's prophetic visions of the fourfold
metallic Image and of the Four Beasts have been fulfilled in the histories of the Babylonian, Persian, Grecian,
and Roman empires.

3. That " Babylon the Great " in Revelation xvii. is
the Roman Catholic Church.

4. That the little horn of Daniel vii. represents the
Papal dynasty, and the little horn of chapter viii. is, as
to its final form, the Mohammedan Power,—the one
arising out of the Roman empire, and ruling in western
Europe; the other arising out of one of the divisions
of the Greek empire, and ruling in eastern Europe and
in Asia.

To those who recognise these axiomatic truths the
following pages will, we feel confident, prove both
interesting and edifying. They present in a systematic,
concise, and detached form many of the chronological
facts first published in our former work, *The Approaching End of the Age*, with the addition of many
new and most important particulars; and they will,
we trust, help the " wise " to understand better the
nature of the times in which we live, so as to realise
more clearly our present prospects, privileges, and
duties.

Those who have *not* received the above foundation
principles of prophetic science, may nevertheless be
interested by the chronological *facts* here marshalled
in order according to a clue afforded by Scripture. But
for a discussion of the principles underlying the historic
interpretation, we would earnestly refer such to parts

ii. and iii. of the work above alluded to, which treat of these questions, or to other works of a similar character.[1]

Our hope is that, in this time of the end, large numbers of Christians, who have received without personal investigation Futurist views, may be led to examine at any rate the opposite Historic system, to prove all things, and hold fast that which is good.

To trace the hand of God in history, to note how all the ages of His providential government have moved according to a foreseen and foretold order, to watch the last stages of the Divine programme of universal history fulfilling themselves in our sight in these last days, to discern " the signs of the times," and to observe the budding of the fig tree, is to find hope merging in *definite expectation*, and in patient waiting for Christ— a waiting for Him as for one whose footfall may be already heard, one who even now standeth at the door ; it is to lift up our heads, convinced that our redemption, our *full* redemption, the redemption of the body, and of the world itself, draweth nigh.

[1] *The Approaching End of the Age : Viewed in the Light of Prophecy, History, and Science.* Also the writings of Sir Isaac Newton, Bishop Newton, Elliott, Bickersteth, Birks, etc. ; especially *Elements of Scripture Prophecy*, by the last.

"And he informed me, and talked with me, and said, O Daniel, I am now come forth to give thee skill and understanding."—*Dan.* ix. 22.

"Then said he unto me, Fear not, Daniel: for from the first day that thou didst set thine heart to understand, and to chasten thyself before thy God, thy words were heard, and I am come for thy words."—*Dan.* x. 12.

"In the first year of Darius . . . I Daniel understood by books the number of the years, whereof the word of the Lord came to Jeremiah, . . . that He would accomplish seventy years in the desolations of Jerusalem."—*Dan.* ix. 1, 2.

CHAPTER II

The Times of the Gentiles

DANIEL understood, as to the character of the days in which he lived, that the seventy years' captivity was all but over, and that the predicted restoration of Israel and rebuilding of Jerusalem were close at hand. What may *we* "understand by books" as to the chronological character of the days in which we live?

We know that the larger "seven times" of Israel's dispersion and degradation is all but over, and their full and final restoration to Palestine close at hand—a restoration to be accompanied by their repentance and conversion, and by that supreme and long foretold crisis of such profound importance, not to Israel only, but also to the whole world, the manifestation of the kingdom of God on earth.

The restoration for which Daniel prayed *came*, but it proved to be only *partial*, the ten tribes, as tribes, not having been restored at all. It proved also to be only *temporary*; for in consequence of Judah's rejection of their Messiah, it endured but for a few centuries, after which it was succeeded by the present longer and more complete dispersion. Even while it lasted it was not a restoration to complete *national independence*; for during its entire course Jerusalem was *tributary* to one Gentile power or another, and was, as we know, actually under Roman domination at the time of the advent of Christ.

After Messiah was cut off, and by wicked Jewish hands crucified and slain, the wrath of God came upon the people "to the uttermost," and the overthrow of Jerusalem by Titus introduced a judgment incomparably more severe,—their present expatriation and dispersion, the deep affliction and complete subjection to Gentile powers, which have lasted now for more than eighteen centuries.

The continuance and duration of *this whole period of judgment* has its chronological limits assigned, just as the Babylonish captivity had. This last is indeed regarded and treated in Scripture as a part merely of the *one* great and long-continued judgment of "the times of the Gentiles," appointed to last, not for seven *decades* of years, but for *seven years of years*, "*seven times*"—a tremendous national judgment for tremendous national crimes. This is the period to which our Lord alluded in the words, "Jerusalem shall be trodden down of the Gentiles, until the times of the Gentiles be fulfilled." [1]

To some readers this expression may not convey the clear and definite idea which Scripture attaches to it; and as this period lies at the base of all the chronologic prophecies connected with this Gentile age, the duration of which forms the subject of the following pages, we must, before going further, distinctly define its *nature* and its *measures*.

It is the *long period of history which began with the beginning of the succession of the four great Gentile monarchies revealed to Nebuchadnezzar, and which ends with the close of these four empires, and the mani-*

[1] Luke xxi. 24.

festation of the kingdom of God. The "times of the Gentiles" are marked by Jewish loss of dominion and independence, by Jewish subjection to and suffering under Gentile conquerors, by the dispersion of the twelve tribes of Israel, and by the desolation of their land. It is, so to speak, the lifetime of the great four-fold Image of Gentile monarchy shown to Nebuchadnezzar, as well as the period of the Four wild Beasts shown subsequently to the prophet. In other words, it is the joint duration of the rule of BABYLON, PERSIA, GREECE, and ROME.

It is the period during which supreme power on earth is by God Himself committed to Gentiles rather than to Jews, as it is written of Nebuchadnezzar, "Thou, O king, art a king of kings: *for the God of heaven hath given thee* a kingdom, power, and strength, and glory. And wheresoever the children of men dwell . . . He hath made thee ruler over them all." It is the period which elapses between the fall of the throne of Judah, in the days of Nebuchadnezzar, and the restoration of that throne by the establishment of it for ever in the person of Christ, the Son and Lord of David. It is the period extending from the *beginning of the typical* Babylonian Power to the *end of the anti-typical* Power of "Babylon the Great." It is the period of the government of the earth and of Israel by rulers who are like wild beasts in their cruelty and ferocity, as well as in their ignorance of God, who exist only by preying on others, who are evermore warring and slaughtering, and who oppose and persecute the saints of God. It is the period which, according to prophecy, is to be *immediately* followed by the establishment on *earth* of a universal monarchy of a wonderfully different description, by the setting up of the long-predicted, long-prayed for

kingdom of God, the kingdom of the Son of man, of
which Christ so often spoke,—the kingdom in which
God's will is to be done on earth even as it is done in
heaven; the kingdom which shall never be destroyed or
left to other people, but which shall break in pieces and
consume all other kingdoms, and stand for ever;[1] a
kingdom which shall be possessed by "the saints of the
Most High for ever, even for ever and ever," in which
the dominion shall be given to the Son of man, who
comes with the clouds of heaven, whose kingdom is an
everlasting kingdom, and all dominions shall serve and
obey Him.[2]

A great change in God's providential government
took place at the time of the Babylonish captivity. He
ceased to recognise the Jewish monarchy, which He
had established in the days of David and Solomon, on
account of the gross sins of the idolatrous Jews. He
cast them out of their land, deprived them of their
independence, and permitted Babylon to enslave them.
It was not by chance or by mere human prowess that
Assyria overthrew Israel, and Babylon Judah; the hand
of God was in the double catastrophe, and the overthrow was a direct judgment on a disobedient and
idolatrous people. The long period of subjection to
Gentile nations, of which the Babylonish captivity was
only the first section, and which still continues, was
imposed on the Jews as a chastisement for inveterate
and long-continued sin.[3] The full weight of the judgment did not fall on them at first, because they had not
then filled up the measure of their sins; but when they
"killed the Prince of life," a flood of desolation overwhelmed them, and rests upon their nation still.[4] They

[1] Dan. ii. 44.   [2] Dan. vii. 13, 18, 27.
[3] Lev. xxvi.   [4] Dan. ix. 26.

are, however, beloved for the fathers' sakes, and destined, as Scripture abundantly asserts, to be ultimately restored to their land and to their high position of supremacy on earth. When "the times of the Gentiles" run out they will be led to repentance, they will receive their long-rejected Messiah, saying, "Blessed is He that cometh in the name of the Lord!" and the second advent of Christ will bring to them and to all nations those "times of the restitution of all things," of which God hath spoken by the mouth of all His holy prophets since the world began.

These "times of the restitution of all things" are the dispensation next following "the times of the Gentiles." The question of our nearness to the close of this latter dispensation is therefore one of supreme importance and interest. Whereabouts in its course are we, judging from history? The Babylonian empire, the first of the four predicted universal monarchies, rose and fell long since; so did the Medo-Persian, so did the Grecian. The fourth, or Roman empire, would, so it was predicted in the prophecy, exist in two forms, first, as one united empire; then as a commonwealth of ten kingdoms. The first form passed away fourteen hundred years ago, when the old empire built up by pagan Rome fell in the fifth century, under the incursions of the Goths and Vandals. The second, or tenfold form—the commonwealth of nations, bound by a voluntary subjection to the Roman Papacy throughout the middle ages—has already existed for more than twelve centuries. Whereabouts then in the "times of the Gentiles" are we?

Evidently near their close! What are the last forms of Gentile power predicted as dominating during this period? They are symbolised by two "*little horns*," the one described in the seventh, and the other in the eighth chapter of Daniel—two politico-religious dynasties which should exercise a vast and exceedingly evil influence in the latter half of this Gentile dispensation. These two "little horns" symbolise the *Papal* Power in *western*, and the *Mohammedan* Power in *eastern* Europe. The rise, character, conduct, decay, and doom of both these Powers are enlarged upon in the prophecy, as it was natural that they should be, considering the tremendous and most evil influence which they have so long exerted, the one on the Christian Church, and the other both on it and on the natural Israel in Palestine. The *outline* of their history only is given in Daniel, details are added in the New Testament; by Paul, in his epistles, and by John in his Apocalypse.

The Papacy and Mohammedanism rose *cotemporaneously with the ten horns of the Roman beast*; in other words, they originated at the same time as did the kingdoms of modern Europe—that is, *on the fall of the western Roman empire*. They have consequently already lasted for over twelve centuries, and their destruction is to be accomplished by the second advent of Christ Himself, and to be immediately followed by the establishment of the kingdom of God on earth. The reign of these two politico-religious dynasties constitutes the *last* phase of Gentile power presented in prophecy. Both have for more than twelve centuries opposed and blasphemed God and His truth, persecuted His saints, defiled His sanctuary, literal or spiritual, and trodden down the holy city.

It must be remembered that, the object of Scripture being to trace the story of redemption, and the fortunes of the people of God in this world, it dwells exclusively on the history of the nations and powers who have most influenced the Jewish people and the Christian Church.

Hence, while it mentions briefly the career of Babylon, Persia, Greece, and Rome pagan, it enters with far greater fulness into the history of the Papal and Mohammedan Powers, because these are the Powers which have most seriously oppressed, corrupted, or persecuted the natural and spiritual Israels.

In a word, "the times of the Gentiles" occupy the interval between the desolation of the land of Israel by Babylon, and the yet future restoration of the Jews; between the fall of the throne of Judah in the days of Nebuchadnezzar, and the future restoration of that throne in the person of Christ; between the destruction of the temple of God at Jerusalem, and the yet future re-establishment of His worship on Mount Zion. The period is the *great Gentile dispensation*, spoken of by Paul in Romans xi., during which Israel is apparently, though not really, cast off by God in righteous judgment, as an exhibition of Divine *justice*; and during which salvation is come to the Gentiles, as an exhibition of Divine grace; during which blindness in part is happened unto Israel, until "the fulness of the Gentiles" be come in, when "all Israel shall be saved," as it is written.

So much as to the general character and extent of this Gentile age. The question next arises, Does Scripture assign to the period any *definite chronological* limits? The answer might almost be anticipated, when we remember that in previous stages of Jewish history, similar periods of trial had always had their chronological limits foretold. The time of Israel's bondage in Egypt, 400 years; the time of the wandering in the wilderness, forty years; the time of the captivity in Babylon, seventy years,—all were predicted in advance. If to these comparatively brief intervals the wisdom of God saw fit to assign limits, and He permitted these limits to be known to His people, how much more likely it is that He would *assign limits* to this far longer and more terrible dispensation of judgment and suffering appointed to the guilty nation of Israel, and that He would permit those limits to be more or less distinctly understood, at any rate towards the close of the period! On searching the Scriptures we find that this is the case. Chronological limits are distinctly assigned to "the times of the Gentiles" in Scripture, and *in these our days* their actual measures have become evident, *because the fulfilments of the predictions are clearly traceable in history.*

We cannot pause here to prove that the great prophecies of Daniel are for the most part fulfilled and not unfulfilled prophecies; that, starting from near their own epoch, they each give the outline of the history of the people of God, Jewish or Christian, in the world right on to the second advent and the millennial kingdom; that the powers figured as "little horns" in the seventh and eighth chapters of Daniel respectively symbolise the Papal and Mohammedan politico-religious apostasies; and that a day in these predictions stands as a symbol for a year. These basis-truths of prophetic science have been ably demonstrated for some centuries past, and careful, trustworthy works in abundance are available for those who wish to study the subject, such as those of Bishop Newton, the late Professor Birks, Bickersteth, Elliott, and others.

The chronological limits of the times of the Gentiles are given in the same style as the measures of the seventy weeks, or 490 years, to "Messiah the Prince." Moreover, they harmonise in their septiform character, not only with this period, but with all the Levitical measures of the sacred calendar of the Jews, as well as with many other episodes of Jewish history. THEY ARE A GREAT "WEEK," analogous to other weeks on other scales which we find in Scripture, such as the week of *days*; the week of *weeks*, leading to Pentecost; the week of *months*, including all the feasts of the Lord; the week of *years*, leading to the sabbatic year; the week of *weeks of years*, forty-nine years, leading up to the jubilee; the week of *decades*, or of human life, seventy years; and the week of *millenaries*, leading up to the yet future sabbatic millenary. "The times of the Gentiles" constituted a week, each of whose days is a *year of years*, or 360 years, and whose entire duration is therefore 2520 *years*. As we wrote in the *Approaching End of the Age*—

"This is *inferred* from Scripture rather than distinctly *stated* in it; but the inference is so well grounded as to be of almost equal weight with a distinct declaration.

"Though the fourfold Image, which symbolised to Nebuchad-nezzar the succession of Gentile empires which were to fill up this long interval of Jewish rejection, had *no* chronology attached to it, yet we know that those empires, the Assyrian, the Persian, and the Grecian, and the pagan and Papal Roman powers, have, *as a matter of history*, already lasted for *about* 2520 years. Now history is the evolution of the determinate counsel and foreknowledge of God, which *must* therefore have assigned beforehand to 'the times of the Gentiles' at least this duration.

"The symbol of the fourfold Image declared that these Gentile empires were to be succeeded by the kingdom of the God of heaven, but it did not reveal, or even intimate when or after *what lapse of time* this should be. A subsequent vision granted to Nebuchadnezzar did so in mystery. He saw a tree, which he was told symbolised himself, cut down, and its stump left to be wet with the dew of heaven, and its portion with the beasts in the grass of the earth, its heart changed from a man's heart, and a beast's heart given it, until 'seven times' should pass over it. This vision was, as Daniel told the monarch, a prophecy of the seven years' insanity which, as a chastening for his pride, was to overtake him, and which was to teach him to know God, and to own that heavens do rule.

"Now the vision of the tree is not more clearly symbolic of this remarkable incident in Nebuchadnezzar's life, than *that incident itself* is typical of certain moral and chronological features of the succession of Gentile monarchies.

"The leading moral characteristics of all the four great empires, of which Nebuchadnezzar was both head and representative, have been ignorance of God, idolatry, and cruel persecution of the saints. Nebuchadnezzar, prior to this incident, knew not God. He set up a great image, and commanded all men, on pain of death, to fall down and worship it; he cast into the burning fiery furnace the faithful witnesses who refused to obey the idolatrous mandate. How have all his successors, with one consent, followed this example! Idolatry, literal or spiritual, and persecution, pagan or Papal, have marked the whole succession of Gentile monarchies. These episodes in Nebuchadnezzar's life are clearly typical; these features of his character have been stamped indelibly on all his successors; these incidents answer to events on the scale of nations and centuries, with which history makes us familiar. So also does the seven *years'* bestial degradation of the monarch during his insanity answer to the seven years of years of Gentile rule, represented by the fourfold Image and by the Four wild Beasts of a subsequent vision. The king himself represents the succession of imperial sovereignty till the kingdom of Christ shall come; the 'seven times' that passed over *him* similarly represent the whole period of moral and spiritual debasement, and consequent idolatry and persecution, in the Gentile kingdoms, from the times of Nebuchadnezzar till the full redemption of mankind.

"Prophecy assigns to the apostasy of the latter days a duration of 1260 years, and this period is repeatedly spoken of as *half* a week, 'three times and a half.' Where are we to find the other half of this great week? As the apostasy is to be overthrown finally by the advent of Christ, it is clear the other half cannot *follow*, but must *precede*, the half week which measures the existence of that apostasy; that is, it must date *back* from its rise. Now calculating backwards from the rise of the Papal and Mohammedan powers in the beginning of the seventh century, 1260 years *lead up to the days of Babylon*, the point at which we know 'the times of the

Gentiles began.' Thus we see that the entire period occupied by the four great empires represented by the image is the *whole* week, whose *latter half* is the time of the dominion of the Papal and Mohammedan powers.

"During the whole of this period Israel has ceased to be an independent kingdom, and during two-thirds of it Jerusalem has been trodden down by the Gentiles. We conclude, therefore, that the dispensation in whose closing days we live was fore-ordained and appointed by God to run a course of 2520 years, or, in symbolic language, 'seven times'; and that our Lord Jesus Christ had this great week in His mind when He said, 'Jerusalem shall be trodden down of the Gentiles until the times of the Gentiles be fulfilled,' an expression which seems to imply that the period so designated had definite chronological limits.

"Those limits were not intended to be understood *until* 'the time of the end.' Their actual history has now *demonstrated* the scale on which the symbolic period of 'seven times,' or years, is to be enlarged, and that scale is—as in all similar predictions—'a year for a day.' Seven years contain 2520 days, and the period predicted is therefore 2520 years. Arithmetically, this is a very notable number, one peculiarly fit to be the basis of chronologic prophecy. It is altogether unique—a king among numbers. *It is the least common multiple of the first ten numbers*—the first in the entire series of numbers, which is *exactly* divisible without remainder by all the first ten numerals. Thus it is adapted to harmonise several series of periods of different orders and magnitudes in a way that no other conceivable number could do. Is it by chance that this number has been chosen to be the vertebral column of prophetic chronology?"

Now if Daniel had to study books to find out *his* chronological position in the seventy years of the Babylonian captivity, how much more are we likely to have to study, in order to discern *our* position in this much longer period! The problem is not likely to be a *less* perplexing one than that which the holy Daniel pondered.

The Simeons and Annas of our Lord's day had also to study a more difficult question than that of Daniel—

their chronological position in the "seventy weeks," or 490 years, to Messiah; and many must have been their perplexities. There was no difficulty in discerning that they were living in the closing portion of the seventy weeks, or 490 years, for over four centuries had elapsed since the restoration of the Jews from Babylon. They knew that the advent of Messiah the Prince must be *at hand*, but in seeking to ascertain *how near* at hand many questions would arise requiring careful investigation. From what year should they date the commencement of those seventy weeks? From the issue of a decree "to restore and to build Jerusalem." But several such decrees had been issued; Jewish restoration had taken place by stages in a period extending over ninety-two years; which was the principal one? It was generally understood and admitted that the predicted 490 days symbolised 490 years. Now that period, measured from the *first* restoration decree, that of Cyrus, had already run out forty years before, and had failed to bring the Consolation of Israel; so *that* was evidently not the decree intended. Artaxerxes had subsequently made two restoration decrees, at an interval of thirteen years apart; measured from the first of these, the period had forty years yet to run, and measured from the last, fifty-three years. But what the goal? Not the *birth*, but the *death* of Messiah the Prince, who was to be "cut off" prematurely in the midst of the last week of the seventy, or in the middle of the last seven years of the period. Then His *birth* might be looked for at least thirty or forty years previously. Malachi, the last of the prophets, had predicted that he was suddenly to come to His temple, and the prediction might be fulfilled any day. Hence those who loved His appearing would be found watching and waiting, praying and praising in that sacred spot, until their eyes should see God's salvation, the Light to lighten the Gentiles, and the Glory of the people of Israel.

By patient study we too may reach conclusions quite as clear as those of Daniel and Simeon and Anna, and like them be intelligently and joyously waiting for "the Consolation of Israel"; for the chronological measures of "the times of the Gentiles" are evident enough to those who in these days patiently search the Scriptures. We do not for a moment assert that they have always been so; to the earlier generations of the Church they *were*, and they were *intended to be,* so mysterious, that comprehension of them was *impossible*, and only the vaguest guesses could be made as to their true scope and signification. This was a part of God's gracious providence, and was a mark of tender mercy to the early Church. HE knew that well nigh two thousand years of trial and temptation, persecution and suffering, in an evil world and from an awful apostasy, lay before His people; but He did not wish *them* to know it. He never revealed the fact to *them*; the early generation of Christians expected, and were left to expect, the return of Christ in their own day. The first generation of believers took the promise of His speedy return literally, and lived in the hope that they would be "alive and remain" at His coming. But this hope was born of inexperience; it was destined to wither away and be dissipated; the cold logic of facts proved it mistaken, but did not make it while it lasted less sanctifying and cheering.

Blessed be God! there is another kind of hope, born of experience, and founded, not on ignorance, but on knowledge. This hope dawned on the Church, as the other sank beneath the horizon, and it has gradually brightened ever since, and shall not be confounded. As long as ignorance of the appointed times was best for the faith and hope of the Church, it was allowed to endure; but Divine wisdom had taken the precaution of embodying in Scripture *chronological revelations*, in order that, when ignorance ceased to be beneficial, as after the lapse of ages could not but be the case, when gradually increasing knowledge of the real counsels of God would be more sanctifying in its effects, that *then* such knowledge might be gradually attainable. Hence the true duration of this Gentile age was revealed, but *in a mystery*. To have revealed the times *plainly* would have been to shake the faith and damp the courage of the *early* Church; not to have revealed them *at all* would have been to deprive later generations, and especially our own, of a blessed tonic to faith and hope, of a much needed stimulant to courage and patient continuance in well-doing. So the limits of "the times of the Gentiles" were stated in Scripture, but stated in hieroglyphics, which only the lapse of centuries could by slow stages interpret, and which should not become perfectly clear until the long period itself, and even its closing portion, the "time of the end," were already far spent.

Chronological prophecy was intended, as we have seen, for the benefit of *later* generations, and especially of *the last*. The lapse of time only could fulfil it, and the lapse of time only could explain it. The light that it sheds falls not on times near its own, but—as a light-house illuminates the ocean afar, and not the rock on which it stands—on remote future ages.

But while fully granting that a veil of mystery was in ages past allowed to rest on the distant future, so that the early Fathers could only make the most distant approaches to any true understanding of the predictions, and the Protestants of the Reformation era, while coming much nearer the truth, could still see it only dimly and indistinctly, like "men as trees walking"; granting that a hundred incorrect calculations of the "times" have been made in different generations, only a few of the *later* of which have been justified by the event: granting all this, we still ask, is there not good ground for believing that God will fulfil His own word, "and that in the time of the end" *the wise shall understand these sacred predictions?* If they had been designed to be understood by those to whom they were given, they would, of course, have been couched in clearer language. If, on the other hand, they were never intended to be understood at all, *what was the use of giving them?* The style in which they are given, as well as the actual result, prove that they were *not* intended to be understood until history should interpret them, that they were given to one generation for the benefit of other and distant generations. Partial fulfilments began to throw partial light upon them many centuries ago, and the Reformers in their day obtained the true clue. Each additional accomplishment has given additional light, till now that we have reached "the time of the end" all stands out clearly and distinctly.

To Daniel it was said, as regards these sacred times and seasons, "Shut thou up the vision; for it shall be for many days." The words are closed up and sealed *until* "the time of the end." To John, 600 years later, it was said, "Seal *not* the sayings of the prophecy of this book: for *the time is at hand*"—clear evidence that the lapse of time is an element in the comprehension of prophecy. Now, after eighteen centuries more have passed, need we wonder that the true fulfilment can be, not only partially traced, but clearly demonstrated?

But granting that "the times of the Gentiles" are 2520 years in duration, and that they began with the Babylonish captivity, are there no further difficulties attending the solution of the problem of our own chronological position in this long period?

There are very many! The truth never lies on the surface. The Captivity era leaves a broad, historical margin, as in its widest scope including both Israel and Judah it lasted at least 160 years. If we can only reach the general conclusion that somewhere in an analogous period, after the lapse of "seven times," we may hope to behold the dawn of the blessed "times of the restitution of all things," we shall still be left with only a vague conviction that we are living somewhere in "the time of the end." If this was all that chronological prophecy could in these last days do for us, we might almost as well be without it! The general promises of Scripture, such as, "Behold, I come quickly," "the time is short," "the Lord is at hand," etc., would be almost as helpful as chronological predictions, which indicated the end of the age *only within a few centuries*.

Moreover, we must remember the lesson which we have learned from the book of nature, that there are *years of different lengths*: the lunar of 354, the calendar of 360, and the solar of 365 days each. Which scale shall we adopt in measuring the times of the Gentiles? or rather, which seems to have been adopted by the inspiring Spirit in chronological prophecy? Nature measures years on all three scales; and men in different ages have adopted sometimes one and sometimes another. At this present time the Christian almanac is solar, and the Mohammedan lunar; and in the long period which we are considering it makes seventy-five years' difference whether we employ the first of these scales or the last. Here then is an *astronomical* margin of seventy-five years to be added to the *historical* margin of 160 years, and a period of 235 years results, any one of which might be said in a sense to be 2520 years from the commencement of "the times of the Gentiles."

While, therefore, we may fearlessly assert in a broad, general way that we are now living fully twenty-five centuries from the fall of Judah and the rise of Babylon—since those events took place in the sixth century before Christ, and we are living in the twentieth century after—yet this is evidently only a rough and very inaccurate statement, a mere approximation to the truth, which ought not to satisfy us, any more than a similar approximation would have satisfied Daniel. *There is room for further " study of books."* There is more light than this to be obtained by those who care to seek it— glad and glorious light, well worth the trouble of study! To those who seek such light the questions will present themselves :

I. Is it possible to make a rational and well-founded selection of the year or years which form the true starting-points of "the times of the Gentiles ?" And

II. Is there anything to determine the scale by which the period should be measured ?

The reply to the first of these questions is just what the Daniel parallel would lead us to expect. We shall find, as we look into it, that there are *several termini a quibus* leading to *several* corresponding *termini ad quos* There are incipient, central, and final dates of *commencement,* from which respectively, after a lapse of 2520 years, there are corresponding incipient, central, and final dates of *close*; moreover, *the years of crisis* in the fall of Israel and Judah are answered, after "seven times," by years of crisis in the fall of those Powers which have been the great oppressors of the Israel of God, spiritual and literal. The years of crisis in the *rise* of the literal Babylon are followed, at the distance of "seven times," by years of crisis in the *fall* of the spiritual Babylon, and in the *fall* of Islam, the two last forms of Gentile power predicted by Bible prophecy.

The reply to the second question, as to the true *scale*, is again what the Daniel parallel would lead us to expect, that *all three scales are employed*; lunar, calendar, and solar measurements of the great period can all be *distinctly discerned*. Hence chronological prophecy directs our attention to no one date, to no one year, as marking the end of "the times of the Gentiles," *but rather to an era*; an era in which, measured *from* the various commencing dates *by* the various scales, the period is found to run out *again and again*, each close being marked by events, which are distinctly *steps and stages* in *a great historical movement, of a nature directly contrary* to *the movement of Daniel's day. That* was the decline and fall of Judah, and the rise of Gentile Babylon; *this* is the decline and fall of "Babylon the Great," and the gradual rising again of the people of God, Jewish and Christian.

After the lapse of 2520 years from the starting-points of Babylonian dominion, we find *not*, as then, the overthrow of the people of God by their enemies, but the overthrow of those enemies themselves by the hand of God, in order to the deliverance of His people. As at the exodus, and on many a subsequent occasion, the destruction of the oppressor and the liberation of the oppressed coincide. God, who uses wicked men, warriors, conquerors, and tyrants, as rods wherewith to scourge His rebellious people, does not on that account excuse their wickedness. In *their* turn they also are judged; as witness Pharaoh and Egypt, and Nebuchadnezzar and Babylon. The principle of the Divine action is clearly announced over and over again in Scripture, and especially in connexion with the doom of the antichristian Papal power. " He that leadeth into captivity shall go into captivity: he that killeth with the sword must be killed with the sword."

We reach then the conclusion that, in order to understand like Daniel the number of the years in the period in which we are interested, we must study carefully, both in Scripture and in other authentic history open to us, the events of THE CAPTIVITY ERA of Israel and their dates; trying to realise what the story of those times really was, and what was the *relative importance* of the different crises that occurred in the overthrow of Israel and Judah, and in the rise of Babylon.

This on the one hand. On the other, we must study and ponder the events of the "TIME OF THE END," or the days in which we live, the events of the last century and a half, including many which we ourselves remember, and even those which are taking place year by year around us. And we must consider these events, not merely as isolated political changes, but as links in a chain, as *stages in the great movement*, characteristic of the time of the end. We must consider the *moral and spiritual nature* of that movement; we must compare it with the predictions of it in Scripture, and note the style in which it has so far fulfilled those predictions, so as to be prepared to form just conceptions as to the probable nature of the fulfilments of those parts of the prophecy which are still unaccomplished. *The analogy of past fulfilments* is our safest guide as to future fulfilments.

But when we have carefully studied these *two* eras, have we obtained all the light which *can* be obtained as to our own position in the course of "the times of the Gentiles"? Very far from it. In the mouth of two or *three* witnesses shall every word be established. The testimony of the *two* witnesses we have cited is in this case wonderfully confirmed by that of a *third*.

The great "Seven Times" is divided into two halves, and the predictions respecting the *second half* of the week are far more numerous than those respecting the whole period. Bisect a week, and you have three and a half days. Bisect seven times, and you have three and a half times. Bisect 2520 years, and you have 1260 years.

Now *this* last period is more frequently used in prophecy to measure historic episodes than any other. It is mentioned under various names, all conveying the same interval of time; it is sometimes called "forty and two months"; sometimes "1260 days"; sometimes "time, times, and a half"—*some* mysterious designation being always employed instead of the clear statement 1260 years, in order that a veil might rest for a time over the period, and that its true scale might only become clear in the light of its fulfilment.

It is the duration assigned in Scripture to the dominion of the Little Horn (Dan. vii.), to the closing period of Jewish dispersion (Dan. xii.), to the treading under foot of the holy city (Rev. xi.), to the prophecies of the Two Witnesses (Rev. xi.), to the sojourn of the Woman in the wilderness (Rev. xii.), to her flight from the Serpent (Rev. xii.), and to the duration of the eighth or revived seventh Head of the Roman empire (Rev. xiii.). We learn from history that *it has actually been the duration of the realities predicted by these symbols.* It is also the duration of other historical episodes to which it is not attached in Scripture; it measures, as we shall see farther on, the duration of the four pagan empires of antiquity, which occupied the first half of the "seven times," as well as the lifetime of the two little horns, which occupy the second.

Hence we must study, in the third place, *a bisection era,* which throws additional light on the subject, and adds strong confirmation to the results indicated by the *Captivity era* and the *time of the end.* This Bisection era lies centrally in the "seven times," and embraces the history of the fifth and sixth centuries. It was a period full of events of momentous interest to the people of God—events which have had a most mournful and long enduring influence on the Church; events the results of which are all around us this day, and which bear to the judgments which are to close the "times of the Gentiles" the relation of cause and effect. It witnessed the fall of Rome pagan, and the rise of Rome Papal—that great Power which still *claims* the obedience of two hundred millions of mankind. It witnessed also the rise of that false Mohammedan religion, which to this day enslaves a hundred and fifty millions of men in Asia and Africa.

And not only should we study and consider these things for ourselves, but we may also avail ourselves of the study of those who have gone before us, as preserved in books"; for in this science of the interpretation of prophecy, as in all other sciences, they who are rash enough to begin *de novo,* casting aside the results attained by their predecessors, on the ground that they sometimes arrived at wrong conclusions, are not likely to make much headway. The astronomer who should on

the same ground refuse to utilise the researches, observations, and discoveries of all previous astronomers,
would probably reach strangely erroneous results, and
die before he could gain any well-founded comprehension
of the true system of nature. Knowledge grows from
age to age; the stores accumulated by one generation
give a vantage ground to following ones. Rejecting all
that time has proved false, we should avail ourselves of
all that *time has proved true*, and to the amount of
already recognised truth add the result of our own
observations.

In the next chapter we give the conclusions to which
our own study of these three periods has led us,
recognising that our selection of events may in some
instances of course be mistaken. Where several answer
more or less exactly to the terms of the prophecy, it is
not always possible to select with certainty the one
which does so *most* closely; other students may in some
cases reach other conclusions; some whose judgment we
highly esteem have indeed done so. But in any case the
limits are narrow and do not at all affect the main
question.

We shall avoid introducing into the next chapter the
question of chronological relations, reserving that for a
still later one, in order that the impression of the *history*
of these three eras may be left the more clearly and
distinctly on the mind. When we reach the chronological
question, we enter a region where there is much less
room for opinion or for difference of judgment, as the
results depend on astronomically verified data, and exact
arithmetical calculation.

CHAPTER III

THE STARTING-POINT; OR, THE CAPTIVITY ERA OF ISRAEL AND JUDAH

HOWEVER accurately prophecy may have *been* fulfilled, it is impossible we should *perceive* the fulfilment, unless we are acquainted with the history which has fulfilled it. And even when we are familiar with the history, we may yet fail to trace the fulfilment of Divine predictions, from want of a due consideration of the moral and religious bearing of the events which it records; *i.e.* their bearing on the counsels of God with reference to the redemption of the world.

Symbolic prophecy is simply history written beforehand and in hieroglyphics. The whole bulk of it in Scripture is small; hence it is evident that the amount of history with which it is needful to be acquainted in order to understand such prophecy, and have well grounded convictions as to its fulfilment, is not very large. The Atlantic is broad, almost boundless, but the course over it steered by any given steamer is definite and restricted within very narrow limits: so the ocean of history is vast and wide, and every passing year makes it more and more impossible accurately to survey it all; but *the line of events in connexion with which the redemption of mankind has been and still is being wrought out* is comparatively restricted, and even in that narrow line certain points alone are of salient importance in connexion with our present subject.

The line, as we have seen, is that of the history of the Jewish nation and of the Christian Church, and of the Kingdoms and Powers with which they have had to do. It is the line of the Four Great Empires of Daniel ii. and vii. The important periods in this line which it is needful specially to consider here are three:

I. THE CAPTIVITY ERA, introducing "the times of the Gentiles."

II. THE ERA OF THE RISE OF THE APOSTASIES, dividing "the times of the Gentiles" into two parts.

III. THE TIME OF THE END, closing that dispensation.

Before we can profitably consider the *chronological relations* between these three periods, and their respective years of crisis, it is necessary to recall the events of the periods themselves, and their dates. The force and meaning of the chronological facts to which we shall have to call attention later on, depend wholly on the character of the events of the three periods above named, in their relation to the natural and spiritual seed of Abraham. The events themselves are simple matters of fact, and can be verified by reference to reliable historical works on the periods. Scripture itself is the best authority as to the Captivity era, though Ussher, Clinton, Rawlinson, and others may be consulted, and much light has been thrown in recent years on this remote age by the discovery and decipherment of the Assyrian and Babylonian inscriptions, especially the annals of Tiglath-pileser, Sargon, Sennacherib, Esarhaddon, Assurbanipal, and Nebuchadnezzar, etc. A multitude of historians, including Gibbon, Hallam, Milman, Ranke, and Ockley, give full details as to the bisection era; while Alison and many modern authors furnish the facts which we shall have to notice in connexion with "the time of the end." For recent years the annual *Times* summary is a trustworthy guide.

The following sketch will necessarily be brief. It will recall the history to those who are familiar with it, but it will hardly produce any adequate impression of the character of the epochs in question on those who are not so. We should advise such to refer to works like those just named or similar ones, so as to study for themselves, more fully than we can give them here, the important historical episodes mentioned, in order that their true and critical character in connexion with the providence of God may be duly appreciated. It is curious and interesting to note in the tables of contents of many of our great historical classics, that the epochs and divisions adopted by historians are precisely those indicated by chronological prophecy.

THE CAPTIVITY ERA OF ISRAEL AND JUDAH extended over a period of about 160 years. The first deportation of the Israelites from their land took place under Tiglath-pileser, king of Assyria, whose accession is by the Assyrian Canon determined to the year B.C. 745.

Nebuchadnezzar's conquests, extending from B.C. 605 to B.C. 587, over the first nineteen years of his reign, were the *final* stages of the decline and fall of Jewish independence. He was the great and typical monarch of Babylon, but he was neither the first nor the last.

When the prophet said to him, "Thou art this head of gold," he addressed the king *as representing the whole Babylonian empire.* This is evident, because he immediately adds, "After thee shall arise another king, inferior to thee," alluding to the Medo-Persian empire, which succeeded that of Babylon. Now we know that this latter empire did not arise after the death of

4

Nebuchadnezzar *personally*, but only after the fall of his *kingdom* and the death of his fourth successor, Belshazzar. The head of gold therefore represents the Babylonian *empire*, just as the breast of silver represents the Medo-Persian.

Now the *first* king of the Babylonian empire of the Image was NABONASSAR, and the year of his accession is an era of great historical importance, ranking with the greatest eras of history; such as the Greek era of the Olympiads, the Roman A.U.C. era, the Syrian era of the Seleucidæ, the Christian era of the Nativity, the Papal era of Indictions, and the Mohammedan era of the Hegira. Its precise chronological point is also more certainly ascertained than that of any other ancient date, because it is connected with a series of exact astronomical observations, given by Ptolemy in the work containing his celebrated Canon; it is certain not only to a year, but to a day and to an hour: it is *noon of February 26th*, B.C. 747.

This most important era marks the commencement of the Babylonian empire, and therefore the commencement of " the times of the Gentiles."

Six years later, in B.C. 741, the future date of the destruction of the ten tribes was announced beforehand by Isaiah. Ahaz, the wicked king of Judah, had been terrified by a warlike alliance formed against him by the king of Israel and the king of Syria, a powerful monarch named Rezin. The avowed object of their confederacy was to overthrow the dynasty of David and Solomon, and to place on the throne of Judah a stranger and an alien, " the son of Tabeal." Isaiah was directed to calm the fears of Ahaz by promising him deliverance, and reminding him of the unalterable purpose of God, that of the royal line of Judah, and of the kingly house of David, Christ was to be born ; that the sceptre was not to depart from Judah till Shiloh came. A virgin (of the house of David) should conceive and bear a Son, whose name was to be called Immanuel. Ahaz was therefore not to fear.

Judah's national existence could not cease till SHILOH came ; it might pass under an eclipse, as it did later on, but it must be restored, till the true Son of David should appear. Ahaz was informed that both his enemies would speedily be destroyed. As to Israel, the prophecy was a brief and a literal one, " *Within threescore and five years shall Ephraim be broken, that it be not a people.*" The national existence of the ten tribes, who were at that moment conspiring against Judah, would, it was predicted, terminate within sixty-five years.

Their captivity did actually take place, in several stages, within those limits. A careful study of the records given in the books of Kings and Chronicles shows that the first deportation of Israelites from their own land occurred as far back as the reign of Pekah, king of Israel, when TIGLATH-PILESER, king of Assyria, reduced the ten tribes to tribute, and carried the Reubenites, Gadites, and half tribe of Manasseh, from the other side of Jordan, into captivity. A second stage of the process was when Samaria was first besieged by SHALMANESER, in B.C. 723. The city fell after a three years' siege (B.C. 721), and Shalmaneser carried Israel away captive into Assyria, and placed them "in Halah and in Habor by the river of Gozan, and in the cities of the Medes."[1]

The next critical date in the Captivity era is that of

[1] 2 Kings xv. 29 ; 1 Chron. v. 26. See also the inscriptions of Tiglath-pileser II., in *Assyrian Discoveries*, by George Smith, pp. 276–286. The annals of this king are in a very imperfect and

the invasion of Judæa by Sennacherib, B.C. 713. The association of this memorable incident with Hezekiah's faith and prayer, and with the signal deliverance which God wrought for his people, the large space in the sacred narrative given to a description of it, compared with that devoted to other stages of the overthrow, makes this episode of the decline and fall of Judah one of special interest.

It occurred in the interval between the first destruction of Israel by Shalmaneser, and its final ruin by Esarhaddon, and it brought Judah to the *verge* of ruin, from which she was saved by a marvellous miracle. We read that " in the fourteenth year of Hezekiah did Sennacherib king of Assyria come up against all the fenced cities of Judah, and took them " (2 Kings xviii. 13). Hezekiah was distressed at the ruin of his kingdom, and, conscious of his inability to oppose the forces of the Assyrian invader, he asked for terms of peace, offering to recognise Sennacherib as his sovereign lord. An enormous ransom of 300 talents of silver and thirty talents of gold was demanded, to pay which Hezekiah had to exhaust both the treasury of the temple and his own coffers. Having obtained this treasure, Sennacherib broke his treaty engagements, and continued to ravage the country, till of all the strong places of Judah *Jerusalem alone remained untaken.* Even the capital was so greatly reduced, that the foe offered 2000 horses, if Hezekiah could find riders for

---

broken condition, but much of the deepest interest to Biblical scholars can still be made out from them. The names of Azariah and Jehoahaz, kings of Judah, of Menahem, Pekah, and Hoshea, kings of Israel, of Rezin of Damascus, and of Hiram of Tyre, occur in the records, which fully confirm the Biblical accounts of the campaigns of Tiglath-pileser in Syria.

them! Proud and haughty blasphemies were hurled against the helpless defenders of the holy city by Rabshakeh and other generals of Sennacherib. Hezekiah's heart sank within him; but he spread the king's letter before the Lord, sought the intercession of Isaiah, and betook himself to prayer. God heard and answered; promised that the host of the Assyrian king should not even *attack* the city, but that He would Himself defend it, for His servant David's sake. It was an awful emergency, and a great deliverance. Silently and swiftly the vast army was annihilated. The following account of his exploits by the great conqueror himself is inscribed on one of the Assyrian cylinders :—

"And Hezekiah king of Judah did not submit to my yoke: forty-six of his strong cities I captured, 200,150 people, small and great, male and female, with horses, mules, asses, camels, oxen, and sheep without number, I brought out and as spoil I counted. Him, like a caged bird within Jerusalem, his royal city, I had made ; towers round him I raised, and the exit of the great gate of his city I shut. I subjected him to my yoke."

There is, it should be observed, no statement that Jerusalem was taken. When the predicted sixty-five years had fully run out, in the year B.C. 676 (forty-five years after Shalmaneser's capture of Samaria), ESARHADDON, son of Sennacherib, king of Assyria, invaded the land of Ephraim, carried captive another detachment of Israelites, and thus finally destroyed the national existence of the *ten tribes*. They were carried away, never to be restored till "the times of the Gentiles" terminate. Unlike Judah, who, after their captivity in Babylon, enjoyed more than five centuries of renewed national existence, Israel were never again to dwell in their own land. Alien colonists were settled there, and Samaria ceased to be a royal city.

This crisis, B.C. 676, is a specially important one in the course of the Jewish captivity era. But for the prediction of the sixty-five years, we might have supposed that Shalmaneser's invasion was quite as important as that of Esarhaddon; but the latter was divinely indicated beforehand as a terminal year in the historical movement, and the former must consequently be regarded as a minor stage in the process.

Esarhaddon's son and successor, Assurbanipal, carried captive at a later period Manasseh, king of Judah some of the commanders of his army having made an inroad into Judæa, and God having delivered its wicked monarch into their hands for a time (B.C. 650–648). After some years in Babylon, Manasseh, however, repented of his sins. "When he was in affliction, he besought the Lord his God, and humbled himself greatly before the God of his fathers, and prayed unto Him. and He was entreated of him, and heard his supplication, and brought him again to Jerusalem unto his kingdom. Then Manasseh knew that the Lord He was God." This happened some time before his death, and during the interval the sincerity of his repentance was proved by his abolition of idolatry, and re-establishment of the worship of the true God. He could not, however, undo the evil he had done in Jerusalem ; the final doom of Judæa, and overthrow of the throne of David, is especially attributed to "the sins of Manasseh, according to all that he did ; and the innocent blood that he shed: for he filled Jerusalem with innocent blood ; which the Lord would not pardon,"[1] His son and successor, Amon, was also a wicked king ; but the glorious reign of Josiah, a time of revival, followed, and the national existence of Judah was prolonged yet awhile.

[1] 2 Kings xxiv. 3, 4.

As soon as the Babylonian empire was fully developed by the destruction of Nineveh, and had reached its height in the days of Nebuchadnezzar, the more serious disasters of Judah began. While still acting for his father, Nabopolassar, Nebuchadnezzar, in a war with Egypt, was victorious over Necho its king. This was the war in which Josiah king of Judah, foolishly engaging, was slain. The life of this good king seemed the last barrier that kept off the long predicted judgments from his people. A world of miseries followed his death, which was so bitterly mourned by the Jews, that the year of its occurrence became proverbial as a year of lamentations, "the lamentation of Hadadrimmon in the valley of Megiddo," the spot where Josiah was slain.[1]

His three sons all succeeded him. Jehoahaz was deposed by the king of Egypt, who placed on the throne his elder brother Jehoiakim. In the beginning of this king's reign Jeremiah, by the command of God, earnestly exhorted the people to repentance, and, standing in the court of the temple, denounced against them the seventy years of the Babylonish captivity, if they should not repent. Urijah also prophesied in a similar strain, and such was the enmity exhibited against him in consequence, that he had to flee to Egypt to save his life. He was captured, brought back to Jerusalem, and murdered; and Jeremiah narrowly escaped a similar fate. The prophet Habakkuk also had reason to complain of the stubbornness of the Jews, and was answered by God that He was about to punish them, and to bring on them the Chaldæans, " that bitter and hasty nation," which should march through the breadth of the land, and possess the dwelling-places that were not theirs

[1] 2 Chron. xxxv. 22.

as if it were their own inheritance. "I will do a work in your days, which ye will not believe, though it be told you."[1] Baruch the prophet wrote in a book from the mouth of Jeremiah, "all the words" that the Lord had spoken to him concerning Israel and Judah, from the time of Josiah even unto that day. He read them in the house of the Lord, in the audience of all the people assembled at the Feast of Tabernacles, and was himself exceedingly overwhelmed and amazed with horror at the judgments which he was commissioned to denounce. Jeremiah comforted him, and assured him his own life should be spared in the midst of the Babylonian troubles about to burst on Judah.[2]

Nebuchadnezzar, who was at this time associated with his father in the kingdom, had overthrown the Egyptians at the battle of Carchemish, when he first besieged Jerusalem; and God gave the wicked city and its impenitent king into his hands, as He had foretold He put Jehoiakim in chains, to carry him away to Babylon, but does not seem to have fulfilled his intention; for on Jehoiakim's submission, and promises of subjection, he left him in his own house, where he reigned for three years as a tributary vassal to Babylon, and then rebelled. This brought down bands of the Chaldæans and others, who came against him, and after a four years' struggle he fell, and, according to the word of the Lord, was "buried with the burial of an ass," thrown out and cast forth beyond the gates of Jerusalem.[3] "Surely at the commandment of the Lord came this upon Judah, to remove them out of His sight, for the sins of Manasseh, according to all that he did; and also for the innocent blood that he shed; for he filled Jerusalem with innocent blood; which the Lord would

---

[1] Hab. i. 5.　　[2] Jer. xlv.　　[3] Jer. xxii. 18, 19.

not pardon." [1]   This overthrow in the fourth year of Jehoiakim, when Nebuchadnezzar invaded Judæa, and rendered the king tributary, B.C. 605, is the first *terminus a quo* of the "seventy years" of the Babylonish captivity, as is proved by the issue of the restoration decree of Cyrus, seventy years later.   It was the year in which the king and people of Judah first lost their *independence* and became *subject* to Babylon.   It is consequently the beginning of the "Seven Times" of Gentile power.   One or two years later Nebuchadnezzar had the vision of the Great Image, of which it was said to him, "Thou art this head of gold."

Jehoiakim was succeeded by his son Jehoiachin, then only eighteen, who reigned but three months; he also "did that which was evil in the sight of the Lord, according to all that his father had done," and a second time Nebuchadnezzar besieged Jerusalem.   The king and his family, his servants, his officers, and all his courtiers surrendered themselves to the Babylonian monarch, who carried them to Babylon, with ten thousand of the principal men of the land, and seven thousand mechanics, "all that were strong and fit for war," together with the treasures of the temple and of the king's house, *leaving only " the poorest sort of the people of the land."*

Ezekiel the prophet was among this party of captives (as Daniel had been among the previous party), and consequently he always reckons from this year, "*the year of our captivity*," as he terms it in his prophecy.   It was the year B.C. 598, and *a very important* and *principal* year of crisis in the Captivity era, a year marking the height of Nebuchadnezzar's power.   It was also the year of the birth of that monarch who was to be the

---

[1] 2 Kings xxiv. 3, 4.

destroyer of Babylon and the deliverer of Israel, Cyrus the Persian. In the Persian language, this name signifies "the sun," and Cyrus is in some respects a type of the "Sun of righteousness," who shall yet arise with healing in His wings, to deliver Israel in a far more glorious sense.

One more fatal stage of overthrow and captivity awaited Jerusalem. Judah had been destroyed, and its noblest sons and daughters, including most of the priests, languished in exile. But the temple of Solomon still stood, though bereft of its treasures and its glory. After the fall of Jehoiachin, Zedekiah, his uncle, not his legal heir, had been placed by Nebuchadnezzar on the throne at Jerusalem, nominally as king, but virtually as Babylonian viceroy; a position he occupied for eleven years.

Like his predecessors, this man did evil in the sight of the Lord, and by his rebellion against Nebuchadnezzar, to whom he had taken an oath of subjection, he provoked the final stage of Judah's destruction. The result was that in the year B.C. 589, nine years after the fall of Jehoiachin, the city was a third time besieged.

Jeremiah had forewarned the people of the total destruction that was coming, but they would not hearken. When the Chaldæan armies actually approached the walls, they were in the end of the observances of the sabbatical year, when according to Mosaic law liberty was to be proclaimed to all servants. In the fear engendered by the siege the people complied with this Divine statute, and liberated their slaves; but when Pharaoh-Hophrah approached for their succour, and the Babylonians for a time raised the siege, they took back their Hebrew slaves again, and made them serve as before, contrary to the covenant into which they had entered. For this sin they were severely reproached by Jeremiah, who told them that God would "proclaim liberty to the sword, to the pestilence, and to the famine against them," and that the siege should be renewed by the Chaldæans, and their city taken and destroyed by fire. And so it came to pass. In the second year of the siege the city fell. Zedekiah and all the men of war fled by night, but were pursued and overtaken; the king was brought before Nebuchadnezzar at Riblah; his children were slaughtered before his eyes, which were then put out, and, loaded with chains, he was carried away to Babylon, fulfilling thus the remarkable prophecy, that with his eyes he should see the *king* of Babylon, but that he would never see the *city*, though he would die there (Ezek. xii. 13).

Then followed the supreme act of destruction. Nebuzaradan, captain of the guard, made his entry into Jerusalem on a Sabbath day, set fire to the king's palace, to all the mansions of Jerusalem, *and to the temple*! That sacred temple—in which the glory of Jehovah had been manifested, which Solomon had erected, Hezekiah and Josiah restored, which had stood for between four and five centuries, the scene of Jewish sacrifice and the centre of Jewish worship, the "holy and beautiful house" in which so many generations had praised God—perished in the flames. A second temple was afterwards reared on its site, but was "as nothing" to Solomon's temple in its glory. After having been wonderfully enlarged and improved by Herod, it also perished in the flames kindled by the Roman soldiery of Titus.

Five centuries later a Christian church crowned the sacred site. When Omar the Saracen captured Jerusalem, it became a Mohammedan mosque, and for twelve

centuries that mosque, and the adjoining one erected by
Omar, which bears his name, have defiled the sacred hill
of Moriah, where Abraham offered his son, his only son.
But all these events lay in the distant future on that
fateful day when Jerusalem finally fell before Babylon,
B.C. 587. The walls of the city were razed to the
ground, and the rest of the Jewish people were deported
to Babylon, and continued there for the remainder of
the seventy years, while the land kept Sabbath.

This period of 160 years, extending from B.C. 747 to
B.C. 587—that is, from the first of Nabonassar to the
nineteenth of Nebuchadnezzar—may well therefore be
called the *Captivity era*. It was a period during which
the Jewish monarchy was falling, and Babylonish or
Gentile monarchy rising triumphant over it, as well as
over Egypt and other countries. In 2 Kings xxiv. 7 we
read, "The king of Babylon had taken *from the river of
Egypt unto the river Euphrates all that pertained to
the king of Egypt*," as well as all that pertained to the
king of Judah. He had virtually rendered himself
supreme.

There is no doubt either about the above events or
their dates; they are not drawn from the Bible alone.
The records on the stones in the British Museum confirm the statements of Scripture. On one of these, for
instance, we read Shalmaneser's vainglorious description
of his conquests :

"I am Shalmaneser, king of multitudes of men, prince and hero,
king of all the four zones, the marcher over of the whole world!
In my first year I crossed the Euphrates in its flood to the sea of
the setting sun; my weapons on the sea I rested; to Mount
Amanus I went up; logs of cedar wood and pine wood I cut; an
image of my royalty I erected, of large size I constructed it . . .
In my eleventh year cities too of countless number I captured in
the land of the Hittites. . . . I forced under my dominion the land

which would not bow to me, I broke the pride of kings ; being king I have had no equal among the kings from the first day of my accession ; being a warrior, I did not withdraw from battles and fights ; all countries I crushed ; I asked from them the symbols of submission ; I besieged and occupied the town of Samaria ; I brought into captivity 27,280 persons ; I took them to Assyria, and instead of them I placed men to live there whom my hand had conquered. I instituted over them my lieutenants as governors, and imposed on them tribute like the Assyrians."

After naming a number of other places which he had subdued, he adds of one of them, " Those who remained, I pulled them out of their dwellings, and placed them in the town of Samaria." And Sennacherib says :

"Hezekiah, king of Judah, did not submit to my yoke ; forty-six of his cities, strong fortresses, and cities of their territory which were without number, I besieged, I captured, I plundered, I counted as spoil. I made Hezekiah himself like a caged bird in the midst of Jerusalem, the city of his royalty. Garrison towers over against him I raised ; his cities which I had plundered from the midst of his country I separated, and made them over to the kings of Ashdod, Askelon, Ekron, and Gaza. I diminished his land. In addition to previous taxes, I imposed on them a tribute. The fear of the approach of my majesty overwhelmed Hezekiah himself, and the soldiers whom he had called to enter Jerusalem, his royal city ; he consented to the payment of tribute ; the treasures of his palace, his daughters, the women of his palace, male and female musicians, he sent to Nineveh, the city of my power. . . . On my return I seated Esarhaddon, my son, on the throne of his dominion, and entrusted him with authority."

Such were the *facts* of this melancholy CAPTIVITY ERA. Its moral features are most solemn and instructive. Though long threatened and distinctly foretold by revelation, it was not expected, or feared, or even deemed credible. When the judgments had actually begun, they were not accepted as from God, nor did their early stages awaken conscience, produce repentance, or lead to serious apprehension. The warnings of the prophets were despised, treated either with ridicule or resentment and produced only persecution to those who uttered them. The words of Jeremiah, recorded by Baruch, were read to King Jehoiakim; but though he had witnessed one Babylonish overthrow, and had himself been bound and all but carried away captive, and was even then tributary to Nebuchadnezzar, yet he turned a deaf ear to the word of the Lord, and dared *to burn the book* that contained the Divine denunciations. The dungeon was awarded to Jeremiah as his due, and his life was preserved with difficulty by his friends. False prophets who cried peace, peace, when there was no peace, were heard and heeded, and the true witness was despised and rejected.

A vain alliance with idolatrous Egypt was eagerly sought, though it had been foretold that it would prove but as a staff of reed, wounding the hand of him who leant on it: its only result was that Egypt and Judah had to share one and the same sad fate. Jehoahaz, Jehoiakim, Jehoiachin fell one after another, yet Zedekiah learned no lesson! When the Chaldæan armies had ravaged the country, and were actually within sight of Jerusalem, he repented, like Pharaoh, for a moment; but no sooner was the danger averted than he afresh defied the Lord.

Even at the very last, when God set before them life and death, confirming His oft-repeated assurance that the city would be miserably destroyed, together with all those who chose to abide in it, but confirming also His promise of life and safety to those who voluntarily surrendered to the Chaldæans, Zedekiah and his people would not heed, but rushed madly on their tragic fate.

The terrible doom denounced was only too well

deserved. Boastful self-exaltation, inveterate and multiplied idolatry, rebellion against every law of God, secular and sacred, corruption and cruelty, violence and blood, refusal to amend, refusal to believe, slaughter of the faithful witnesses, and Pharaoh-like hardening of the heart against the first stages of the Divine judgment,—these were the iniquities that brought down the righteous wrath of God until there was "no remedy."

No remedy! No "healing," as the margin has it; no possibility of healing the inveterate sore of Judah! Of Zedekiah, who reigned in Jerusalem for the last eleven years of its existence, the Divine record is, that he only "did that which was evil in the sight of the Lord his God, and humbled not himself before Jeremiah the prophet speaking from the mouth of the Lord. And he also rebelled against King Nebuchadnezzar, who had made him swear by God: but he stiffened his neck, and hardened his heart from turning unto the Lord God of Israel." And as to his subjects, it is said:

"Moreover, all the chief of the priests, and the people, transgressed very much after all the abominations of the heathen; and polluted the house of the Lord which He had hallowed in Jerusalem. And the Lord God of their fathers sent to them by His messengers, rising up betimes, and sending; because He had compassion on His people, and on His dwelling-place: but they mocked the messengers of God, and despised His words, and misused His prophets, until the wrath of the Lord arose against His people, till there was no remedy. Therefore He brought upon them the king of the Chaldees, who slew their young men with the sword in the house of their sanctuary, and had no compassion upon young man or maiden, old man, or him that stooped for age: He gave them all into his hand. And all the vessels of the house of God, great and small, and the treasures of the house of the Lord, and the treasures of the king, and of his princes; all these he brought to Babylon. And they burnt the house of God, and brake down the wall of Jerusalem, and burnt all the palaces thereof with fire, and

destroyed all the goodly vessels thereof. And them that had
escaped from the sword carried he away to Babylon ; where they
were servants to him and his son until the reign of the kingdom of
Persia : to fulfil the word of the Lord by the mouth of Jeremiah,
until the land had enjoyed her sabbaths : for as long as she lay
desolate she kept sabbath, to fulfil threescore and ten years"
(2 Chron. xxxvi. 14–21).

Now these various stages of the captivity of Israel
and Judah occupied a period of 160 years. We must
therefore measure the Gentile dispensation, at the close
of which we live, *not from any one year exclusively,*
but from *this era of* 160 *years in length,* and from its
various years of crisis. Considering that the whole
period embraces twenty-five centuries, this historical
margin of 160 years is not so wide a one, *in proportion,*
as the historical margin which Daniel had to consider
when he sought to ascertain where the starting-point of
the seventy years' Babylonish captivity should be placed.

If the opening era of this Gentile age occupied 160
years, we may expect that the closing era, from the
early *incipient* stages of its characteristic movements
to their *final* stage, will at least do the same. It is
likely indeed to do more ; for it is evident that lunar as
well as solar measurements of the year are employed in
the chronological predictions of Scripture ; so we must
be prepared for an *astronomical* margin as well as an
historical one. The difference between solar and lunar
years in "seven times" (or 2520 years) amounts to as
much as seventy-five years ; if we add this astronomical
75 to the historical 160, we have a *period of 235 years,*
in which the closing events of the age—reversing those
of the Captivity era—may be looked for. Some of these
would be likely to fall out at the *lunar* close of the
period, dated from the *earliest* starting-point others at

the *solar* close, dated from the *latest*; and others again at various intermediate points.

A *series* of commencing dates would, in any case, give rise to a *series* of terminal ones, extending over an equal period; and as from each starting-point the time may be measured by a short scale, or by a medium scale, or by a long scale, the terminal era will, in all probability, be lengthened. That

CHRONOLOGICAL PREDICTIONS ARE FULFILLED IN LUNAR AS WELL AS IN SOLAR YEARS

is proved by the case of the celebrated prophecy of "seventy weeks" to Messiah the Prince;[1] a prophecy which is perhaps more fundamental than any other in the Bible, as evidence that Jesus of Nazareth was the promised Messiah of Israel. It will be well, before we go further, to point out the evidence of this fact, as it is very remarkable and important, and amounts to a demonstration.

That chronological prediction was given to measure the interval from the rebuilding of Jerusalem to the first advent of Christ. For fifteen hundred years the children of Abraham had been looking for his promised "Seed," in whom they and the whole world were to be blessed. Cyrus was a *type* of the great Deliverer who formed the goal of Jewish expectations, but only a type; and soon after Cyrus overthrew Babylon, before he had issued his great restoration decree, it was revealed to Daniel that "seventy weeks" had yet to elapse before MESSIAH would appear. The event proved, as might have been expected, that weeks of *years*, not *days*, were intended—a period of 490 years; and it is undeniable that this prophecy was fulfilled both on the solar and

[1] Dan. ix. 27.

5

lunar scales, *and on the latter with most marvellous exactness.*

The starting-point was to be *a decree to restore and to build Jerusalem,* and the terminus was to be "*Messiah the Prince.*" Now there were two restoration decrees issued by Artaxerxes, and they were thirteen years apart. Either of them may be taken as the starting-point, as each involved a measure of rebuilding of Jerusalem and of re-establishment of Jewish polity and national existence. The two decrees are associated with the two names of Ezra and Nehemiah, and the second of the two—that given to Nehemiah—answers *most* fully to the terms of the prophecy. The first was given by Artaxerxes in the seventh year of his reign,[1] B.C. 457, and the second in the twentieth year of his reign, B.C. 444. The 490 years ran out on the *solar* scale from the first date, in A.D. 34; and, more accurately, on the lunar scale from the second date, A.D. 32–3. In both cases the last or seventieth week of years included most of the ministry of Christ, His death, resurrection, and ascension; together with the formation of the Church by the descent of the Holy Ghost at Pentecost, and the early proclamation of the gospel in Palestine.

But the prophecy states that the Messiah was to be cut off *before* the close of the seventy weeks (or 490 years), "*after*" the sixty-ninth had elapsed, and *before* the seventieth fully ran out; that is to say, *in the course of the seventieth week.* He was to be cut off "in the

---

[1] It has been contended by some that the decree of the seventh of Artaxerxes must not be taken into account, because it makes no explicit mention of the *city,* as the later decree does. But the same might, with even more force, be alleged against the still earlier decree of Cyrus, which speaks exclusively of the temple (Ezra i.). Yet in Isaiah xlv. 13 God says of Cyrus, two hundred years before he was born, "He shall build My *city.*"

midst of the week," *i.e.* of the last supreme week—the one week which is marked off from its fellows; the week which stands pre-eminent, not only among the seventy, but among all the weeks the world has ever seen; the week of seven years which witnessed the miracles, the death, the resurrection, and the ascension of the Son of man and Son of God. In the middle of this terminal week of the seventy, Messiah would, according to the prophecy, be "cut off," and by the shedding of His own blood would confirm the new covenant with "many"— not with the nation of Israel, but with many, both Jews and Gentiles. He would also cause all Jewish sacrifice and oblation to cease by putting away sin for ever "by the sacrifice of Himself."

This chronological prediction was fulfilled on the solar scale from the *first* edict of Artaxerxes, and on the lunar scale *to a day* from the *second*. A simple calculation shows this. Seventy weeks are 490 years, but sixty-nine and a half weeks are only 486½ years; *this* is therefore the number of the years predicted to elapse *between Artaxerxes' decree and the death of Christ.* Nehemiah commenced his journey to Jerusalem in accordance with the decree given in the twentieth of Artaxerxes, during the Passover month, the month of Nisan, B.C. 444; and our Lord was crucified at the same season, the Passover, A.D. 29. From Nisan, B.C. 444, to Nisan, A.D. 29, 472 ordinary solar years only elapsed, not 486½. *But 472 solar years are exactly 486½ lunar.* Hence sixty-nine and a half weeks of lunar years, from Passover to Passover, *did* extend between Artaxerxes' decree in the twentieth year of his reign, and the crucifixion, or cutting off, of "Messiah the Prince," A.D. 29. Thus the prophecy was accurately fulfilled, even to a day, *on the lunar scale.*

Now if the most important of *all* events was chronologically predicted *in lunar form*, as well as in solar, it is clear we may expect other periods also to run out on both scales.[1]

Now the long period we have to consider—the "seven times" of Gentile dominion, the lifetime of the fourfold metallic Image—if measured on this lunar scale, comprises 2445 ordinary years only, and not 2520, the difference in that period amounting to seventy-five years.

We have said that these "seven times" extend from the gradual fall of Israel and Judah to their gradual restoration in the time of the end, that they measure the long period of Jewish dispersion and subjection to Gentile powers. This is true as a general statement, but accuracy requires that a distinction be made between Israel and Judah at this point.

[1] The prophecy asserts that the death of Messiah would be followed by the destruction of the second temple (the temple just about to be rebuilt by order of Cyrus), by a fresh cessation of the daily sacrifice (just about to be recommenced), and by a longer and more terrible judgment than the Babylonish captivity (just about to terminate); that Judah's crowning sin in rejecting her Messiah would bring down God's severest judgments upon her, which would rest upon the Jewish nation till, "the times of the Gentiles" being fulfilled, Rome, the great desolator, should itself be desolated and judged,—an event which, as we learn from other Scriptures, will take place at the second advent. *No chronology, however, is attached to this last event,* the object of the prophecy of the "seventy weeks" being to measure the time up to the *first*, and not up to the *second* advent of Christ. Chronological measures, terminating in this *latter*, had been previously given to Daniel in connexion with his earlier visions (Dan. vii.).

The reason why the first advent of Christ is not alluded to in either of the great prophecies of the "times of the Gentiles" (Dan. ii. and vii.) is, that it is too important an event to appear as a *mere incident* of the history of the fourth, or Roman, empire. *It has an entire prophecy dedicated to itself and its consequences.*

The Divine grant of the LAND is to *all* the seed cf Abraham;[1] the grant of the THRONE is to the tribe of Judah and house of David exclusively;[2] and the restoration of the glory of God to the TEMPLE is distinct from either. In chronologic measurements this distinction is important.

Seven times of dispersion *have* passed over Israel or the ten tribes; for 2520 years they have been driven from the land given by God to Abraham and his seed for ever. But not so Judah. Their *exile and dispersion* did not begin till the Roman war, A.D. 70–135, seven or eight hundred years later. In what sense then has "seven times" passed, or all but passed, over them? In the sense of *the loss of their peculiar and distinctive privileges*, the loss of their *regal honours* and pre-eminence, the loss of *the throne*, the loss of national independence. *That* dates from the Captivity era, though their complete expulsion from the land of their fathers did not take place until 1800 years ago. The throne of Judah has been vacant since the days of Nebuchadnezzar, and is to be vacant for "seven times." It is entailed, however, in the tribe of Judah, and in the family of David, to whom God sware "with an oath that He would raise up Christ to sit upon His throne."

The critical dates in this Captivity era which we have mentioned are the following :—

B.C.
747. Era of Nabonassar, king of Babylon.
741. First chronological prophecy of Israel's desolation.

[1] Gen. xii. 7, xiii. 14, 15, 17, xvii. 8.
[2] 2 Sam. vii. 13, 16.

B.C.

738. First deportation of Israelites under Tiglath-pileser, king of Assyria.

727. Shalmaneser's accession.

723. His campaign against Israel and Judah.

713. Sennacherib's invasion of Judah.

676. Esarhaddon's deportation of the ten tribes.

650–647. Captivity of Manasseh, king of Judah.[1]

606–5. Nebuchadnezzar's overthrow of Jehoiakim in the first year of his reign.

598. Nebuchadnezzar's overthrow of Jehoiachin in the eighth year of his reign.

587. Nebuchadnezzar's overthrow of Zedekiah, with final destruction of the city and temple, in the nineteenth year of his reign.

The captivity era lies chronologically thus:

160 years.

B.C. 747——————————————————————————————————————B.C. 587

---

[1] The exact date of Manasseh's captivity is not given in Scripture, but it can be gathered from the Assyrian annals of Assurbanipal. It is fixed, by the rebellion of Saulmugina, in the year B.C. 650–648, as it was Manasseh's connexion with that movement which occasioned his deportation to Babylon. Saulmugina was a younger brother of Assurbanipal, and had been appointed both by him, and previously by their common father Esarhaddon, governor of Babylon, then a dependency of Assyria. He raised a dangerous and nearly successful revolt against his brother, in which Manasseh, as well as many other tributary kings, was compromised. The rebellion was crushed with revolting cruelty. See *Assyrian Eponym Canon*, p. 162.

CHAPTER IV

The Bisection; or, the Era of the Rise of the Apostasies

WE must proceed now to recall the events connected with the rise of the two Powers whose rule is in prophecy viewed as occupying the second half of the "times of the Gentiles."

The first half was occupied by the succession of four pagan empires, all of which ruled in turn over Israel, and held Jerusalem; and the last of which was officially responsible for the crucifixion of Christ, the destruction of Jerusalem and the Jewish nationality, as well as for the ten cruel persecutions of the primitive Church, ending with that of Diocletian.

When imperial Rome in the west passed away, the commonwealth of kingdoms which constitute modern Europe rose up, and has existed ever since, united for the first twelve centuries of its existence by a common bond of subjection to Rome Papal, the rule of Rome being thus the characteristic feature in both the latter part of the first, and the whole of the second half, of this great period. During the second or tenfold stage of the Roman world, the bond has, it is true, been a *religious* instead of a *political* one, but it has been none the less real. The prophecy foretold precisely what has come to pass, that when the Roman empire ceased to exist as *one*, it should continue to exist as *ten*; that, losing its pristine strength and unity, it should be broken up into a commonwealth of nations, bound together by a common connexion with and subjection to Rome, a subjection different in character from the previous one, inasmuch as it would be consistent with political independence, but one even more injurious, since it would at last bring down Divine judgment on the Roman or Latin earth.

That the number of these kingdoms, *ten*, would not be invariable or constant is implied by the statement that there would spring up amongst them a " Little Horn," which would make the number eleven, and that three others would be plucked up before this " Little Horn," when, of course, there would be only eight left for a time. Fresh " horns," or kingdoms, however, would take the place of the uprooted ones, for at the end of the history the number is presented as still ten. Hence the number of the kingdoms was to be generally, but not rigidly or unvaryingly, ten. There would as a rule, throughout the whole period, be ten kingdoms, occupying the sphere of the western empire of Rome; the number would be elastic, sometimes more, sometimes less, but always *about* ten. Alexander's empire was represented by *one* notable " horn," and the dynasties that arose out of its broken fragments by *four* " horns." But Daniel foretells that Rome was to break up into a larger number, and that *ten* different kingdoms would appear upon the scene, and occupy, even to the end, the territory belonging to Rome, still having that great city as in some sort their centre and bond of union.[1]

[1] These ten kings should be looked for in the territory of the western empire of Rome only. "The ten horns of the fourth empire must none of them be sought for in the realms of the third,

European history from the fifth century onwards presents us with the fulfilment of this remarkable prediction, all the more remarkable because it foretold a state of things which had never existed in the world at the time when the prophecy was given, and which never did exist till a thousand years afterwards. Babylon, Persia, Greece, and Rome in its first phase, all sought and obtained *universal* dominion, and could brook no rival power. The prophecy foretold that in the distant future another state of things should arise, and that, co-existing side by side, a family of about ten kingdoms should divide the heritage of Rome, and, though no longer in subjection to it as the provinces of an empire, should yet, as independent kingdoms, continue to own a voluntary and spontaneous allegiance to Rome; they should "have one mind, and give their power and strength" to the Papacy, for the greater part of their existence, though in the end they should turn against it.

That this is a *fulfilled* prediction is evident from the fact, that never since the fall of the old Roman empire has Europe been united under one monarch, nor has it

second, or first, but exclusively in *the realm of the fourth*, or in the territory peculiar to ROME, and which had never formed part either of the Grecian, Medo-Persian, or Babylonian empires." The master mind of Sir Isaac Newton perceived this long ago. He says : "Seeing the body of the third beast is confined to the nations on this side the Euphrates, and the body of the fourth beast is confined to the nations on this side of Greece, we are to look for all the four heads of the third beast among the nations on this side the Euphrates, and for all the eleven horns of the fourth beast among the nations on this side of Greece." Therefore we do not reckon the Greek empire seated at Constantinople among the horns of the fourth beast, because it belongs to the body of the third.

ever been divided into thirty or forty kingdoms. On the contrary, amid incessant changes, the number of the kingdoms of the European commonwealth has, as a rule, averaged ten. Machiavelli, without the slightest reference to this prophecy, mentions, as the kingdoms occupying the western empire at the time of the fall of Romulus Augustulus, the last emperor of Rome, the Lombards, the Franks, the Burgundians, the Ostrogoths, the Visigoths, the Vandals, the Heruli, the Sueves, the Huns, and the Saxons—ten in all. And it is beyond all question that, amid countless fluctuations, the kingdoms of Europe have, from their birth in the fifth century to the present day, *averaged about ten in number*. A census taken at different intervals reveals the fact that the number has sometimes risen as high as thirteen or fourteen, and sometimes fallen as low as eight or nine, and that it has incessantly oscillated between these extremes. And the division is as apparent now as ever; plainly and palpably inscribed on the map of Europe this day, it bears its silent testimony to the fulfilment of this great prophecy. The Franco-Prussian war and the unification of Italy once more distinctly developed the normal number of the kingdoms of western Europe in the territory of old Rome. Italy, Austria, Switzerland, France, Germany, England, Holland, Belgium, Spain, and Portugal—ten and no more, ten and no less. Divided consequently at the point where the prophecy itself divides the history of Roman rule, we find that the bisection takes place A.D. 476, when the last of the Cæsars fell, and the tenfold commonwealth of modern Europe commenced.

The northern nations, Norway, Sweden, Denmark, and Russia; and the eastern nations, which territorially belong to the Greek and not to the Roman empire (though subject to it in its golden days), do not, of course, enter into the calculation of the kingdoms occupying the territory of Rome proper. There is as permanent a distinction between the geographical spheres of the four empires as between their chronological period. Neither overlap each other; *i.e.* the body of each "beast" is distinct from his dominion for a time over the other "beasts." Each empire actually governed all in its day of dominion, but it had nevertheless its own proper sphere, Dan. vii. 12, "They had their *dominion* taken away, yet their *lives* were prolonged." Persia remains distinct from Greece, and Greece from Rome.

It is in the midst of these ten kingdoms that we are to look for the rise of the Great Apostasy. "I considered the horns," says Daniel, "and, behold, there came up among them another little horn." It is stated also in the seventeenth chapter of Revelation (where fuller details of later stages are given) that these ten horns are ten kings, which receive authority as kings "*with the beast*," or Papal Antichrist, for one hour; then "give their power and authority to the beast." The initial rise of the Papacy consequently must be looked for in the latter part of the fifth century; and the records of that age show only too plainly that already the characteristics of antichrist had begun to be manifested in the bishops of Rome. The high ecclesiastical rank attached from the earliest days to the Roman bishop arose from his position as *bishop of the imperial city*, which had so long been the metropolis of the world.

Roman Catholic and Protestant writers alike recognise the importance of this epoch in connexion with the rise of the Papacy.   Cardinal Manning, for instance, writes :

"To the least discerning mind it must be manifest that God had some purpose of His Divine wisdom in the migration of Constantine and of the empire from Rome to Byzantium.   What could be more improbable than that an emperor should forsake an imperial city of a thousand years? . . . The Byzantine emperors ceased to be proprietors of Italy and of Rome. . . . Now *the abandonment of Rome was the liberation of the pontiffs.*   Whatsoever claims to obedience the emperors may have made, and whatsoever compliance the pontiffs may have yielded, the whole previous relation—anomalous, and annulled again and again, was finally *dissolved.* . . . The providence of God permitted a succession of irruptions, Gothic, Lombard, and Hungarian, to desolate Italy, and to efface from it every remnant of the empire.   The pontiffs found themselves alone, the sole fountains of order, peace, law, and safety ; and *from the hour of this providential liberation,* . . . the chains fell off from the hands of the successor of St. Peter, as once before from his own.   *No sovereign has ever reigned in Rome since, except the vicar of Jesus Christ.* . . . [This was written before 1870.]

"The throne of sovereignty was vacant by the visitation of God. . . . A power had grown up in Rome, far more imperial over the reason and will of man than the iron despotism of the Roman empire. . . . This interior and supernatural power of direction and government over the actions and hearts of men flowed from one centre, and was embodied in one person, the bishop of Rome. . . The floods which swept all the other authorities away threw out into bolder relief and more conspicuous prominence *the supreme pastoral authority of the vicars of Jesus Christ.*   To whom else should the people go ?   They alone had, not only the words of eternal life, but the sole and supreme moral power to support and to reorganise the shattered society of Rome. . . . *The possession of the pontiffs commences with the abandonment of Rome by the emperors.* . . . The rebellion against the vicar of Jesus Christ is in the same order as the rejection of his Master. . . . God has instituted His kingdom upon earth, and fixed the head and centre of it in Rome, as of old in Jerusalem. . . . I showed you how, by an indirect but Divine providence, our Lord liberated His vicar on earth, in the plenitude of His spiritual sovereignty, from all civil subjection—first by the translation of the seat of empire to the East, and then by the eventual *extinction of the Roman empire in Italy.* . . . The world has been waiting at least for twelve hundred years for the fall of the civil sovereignty of Rome, to see if the test of Gamaliel would have effect, 'If this counsel be of man, it will come to nought.' "

Shortly after these sentences were written, it did come to nought. Again the cardinal writes:

"The conversion of the empire to Christianity, and then its removal into the far East, freed the vicar of Christ from temporal *subjection*; and then, by the action of the same providence, he was clothed with the prerogatives of *a true and proper legal sovereignty*, for that state and territory and people were committed to his charge. . . . From that hour, which I might say was fifteen hundred years ago, or, to speak within limits, I WILL SAY WAS TWELVE HUNDRED, THE SUPREME PONTIFF HAS BEEN A TRUE AND PROPER SOVEREIGN, exercising the prerogatives of royalty committed to him by the will of God over the people to whom he is father in all things, both spiritual and temporal. . . . *In the person of Pius IX. Jesus reigns on earth, and 'He must reign, till He hath tup all enemies under His feet.'* "

The blasphemous pretensions of these passages are not more clear than their indication of *the point* at which we should place the first rise of the Papacy— the rise of that Antichrist, who, sitting in the temple of God, or Christian Church, was to claim to be as God, and to be so regarded, obeyed, and worshipped by men. Cardinal Manning thus strongly describes the deadly wound which old, imperial Rome received in the fifth and sixth centuries:

"When the Church went out into the world, it found there a vast empire, which covered it with a perfect organisation, social and political. It had one chief city, reigning over the whole world; it had one emperor, whose will was the fountain of all law, one senate, one legislature, one code of laws. It had one political organisation, uniting all nations, and one vast military system, holding all people in subjection. It had one great chart, and one centre, the *milliarium aureum*, the golden milestone, which stood by the arch of Severus, upon which were marked all the distances throughout the world-wide empire of Rome. It was ruled by the most perfect and minute legislation which had ever governed the natural order of the world.

"Perhaps you may think that it was this organisation of which the Church took possession. No; before the Church assumed its civil mission to create modern Europe, the seven vials from heaven were poured out upon that empire, and the seven trumpets blew, and the four winds of heaven were let loose, and the great angel cast the mighty stone into the sea, and said, 'Babylon the Great is fallen'; for that great empire was ravaged, desolated, and pillaged by the invasion of barbarians, by hordes from every quarter, until there remained of all its structures scarcely anything but mutilated ruins of its greatness, its aqueducts, its military roads, the Flavian amphitheatre, and the Pantheon. Before Almighty God sent His Church out into the world on its civil mission, the whole of that vast empire was burnt up as by fire and deluged by blood. Italy became a desolation, and Africa was abandoned to itself, and Britain was cast off, and Spain was forgotten: for the empire departed to Constantinople; the Byzantine emperors were feeble and helpless; they were harassed by the assaults of the oriental tribes, and Italy they were no longer able even to protect. This is what all historians tell us. There was a time when even Rome itself is said to have been without a living inhabitant, when foxes ran over the Palatine Hill, and their bark alone was heard in the golden house of Cæsars. Such was Rome, this mighty Rome, which once had some two millions of inhabitants, and twelve miles of diameter, stretching from the Mediterranean Sea to the Sabine Hills; it has gone to desolation. And for centuries after this it was ever and again the object of attack. It was besieged, it was sacked, it was ruined again and again. All its civil power had departed, and its sovereignty existed no more.

"It was into such a world as this that the Church was sent forth to do its work. Christian Europe is *not the remains of the old Roman empire; it is a new creation.*"

For some time previous to this crisis, the mystery of iniquity had been working in the Church. In an earlier part of the fifth century another claim to supremacy on the part of the bishops of Rome had been urged—*the authority of the keys, the successorship of Peter.* As early as the Council of Chalcedon, A.D. 449, and then in the Council of Ephesus, A.D. 451, these claims were distinctly made. The headship of Christendom and the world was claimed by Pope Leo, A.D. 457; and Gelasius, Bishop of Rome, A.D. 494, strenuously asserted this prerogative, styling himself the vicar of the blessed Peter, and saying in a letter to the emperor, "There are two authorities by which the world is governed—THE PONTIFICAL AND THE ROYAL, the sacerdotal order being that which has charge of the sacraments of life, and from it must be sought salvation. Hence in Divine things *it becomes kings to bow the neck to priests*, especially to *the head of priests*, whom Christ's own voice has *set over the universal Church.*" The haughty assumption was followed up by his next successors; "so evidently," says Mosheim, "was the foundation laid, even thus early, of the subsequent Papal supremacy."

The event then which marks the commencement of the era we are considering is *the fall of Romulus Augustulus*, A.D. 476—the end of the ancient, and the beginning of the modern; the end of the empire, the beginning of the ten kingdoms; the end of the mere *secular* power of Rome, and the point at which its *spiritual* power began to be paramount. The Apostle Paul distinctly intimates this point as that of the *commencement* of the apostasy in 2 Thessalonians ii., where, speaking of the then existing pagan Roman empire, he says: "He who now letteth will let, until he be taken out of the way (or, that which now hindereth will hinder, until it be removed); *and then* shall that Wicked be revealed, whom the Lord shall consume with the spirit of His mouth, and shall destroy with the brightness of His coming." From this initial point of the incipient rise of the Papacy to the time when all Europe bowed down before its pretensions, and the Papal Antichrist sat firmly on his seat at Rome, is the period which we call THE ERA OF THE RISE OF THE APOSTASIES. The further principal stages by which the Christian Church fell before Babylon the Great, anti-typing thus the fall of Israel before the ancient Babylon, were:

I. The point at which the saints were delivered into the hand of the Roman Pontiff by the famous decretal letter of the Emperor Justinian, in March, A.D. 533 constituting the Bishop of Rome "head of all the holy Churches and of all the holy priests of God." The emperor also in this decree recognises him as his own head and as judge of the faith, and appeals to him for his approbation before publishing to the Roman world a formal statement of Christian faith; and he represents the unity of all the Churches *as converging to Rome as its centre*.

II. The accession of Gregory the Great, A.D. 590, is another marked stage in the rise of the Papacy. This man, who "stands at the meeting place of ancient and mediæval history, did more than any other to set the Church forward upon the new lines on which henceforth it must travel to constitute a *Latin Christianity*."[1] Gibbon speaks of his "temporal reign," and others of his "sacerdotal monarchy." He was contemporary with the Emperor Phocas.

III. Seventy-five years after Justinian's edict there was issued another equally notable one by this Phocas, a centurion, who rebelled against the Emperor Mauritius

[1] Archb. Trench, *Lectures on Mediæval Church History*.

usurped his throne, and subsequently slew four of the late emperor's sons, as well as his brother, and tortured and beheaded his widow and her daughter. In the year A.D 607 this cruel monster issued a decree conceding to Boniface III. the headship over all the Churches of Christendom, and even over that of Constantinople. This event is memorialised by the PILLAR OF PHOCAS, still standing at Rome, bearing the inscription: "Die prima Mensis August. Indict. Und. ac Pietatis ejus Anno Quinto. Pro innumerabilibus Pietatis ejus Beneficiis." This year constitutes a notable epoch in the rise of the Papal apostasy, especially as it marked also the time at which both the Anglo-Saxon and the Lombard kingdoms (the last of the ten) gave in their formal submission to the religious supremacy of Papal Rome. Clovis I., king of France, had been the first to do so, in A.D. 496, and so received the title, transmitted through fourteen centuries to the French kings, his successors, of "eldest son of the Church." In the days of Phocas there had already "appeared, on the part of the western princes, indications of submission and subserviency to the Roman pontiff in all that concerned religion and the Church, as of inferiors to a superior, of children to a father, of common mortals to one who, like the great Druid of their ancestral paganism, was the chief mediator, and the administrator of Divine wrath and favour."[1]

Anti-heretical decrees were also at this time first promulgated, and legal intolerance of the true faith of the saints furnished means for future persecution and oppression.

IV. In A.D. 663 Pope Vitalian enjoined the exclusive use of the LATIN tongue in the offices of Divine worship

[1] Elliott, *Horæ*, vol. iii. p. 149.

6

throughout Christendom, and thus completed the development of the *Latin, or Roman, Church.* Thus far as to the Papacy, or great apostasy of the *West.*

MOHAMMEDANISM, or the great apostasy of the *East,* rose also towards the close of this period. It was in A.D. 622 that the so-called "flight" of Mahomet took place, an event which forms the era of the Hegira, the *terminus a quo* of the Mohammedan calendar to this day. He fled from Mecca to Medina, where he was received as a prophet and prince. The conquering career of his Saracenic followers commenced the year of his death, A.D. 632. The Caliph OMAR led his army into Syria in the course of that year; in August A.D. 634 Damascus was taken. At the battle of Yermouk the eastern Roman armies were overthrown, and the fate of Syria determined; and in the year A.D. 637 JERUSALEM was captured after a four months' siege. The Patriarch Sophonius, who was governor of the city at the time, had to surrender to Omar; and all the other towns in Syria followed his example. The conquest was completed in 638, and the Mosque of Omar was erected on the site of the temple.

Mohammedanism is one of those great movements which have impressed a new and lasting character on a vast number of the nations of the world. No power known to history ever wielded the sceptre over a wider sphere than this has done. In less than a single century Arabia, Palestine, Syria, Armenia, Asia Minor, Persia, part of India, Egypt, Numidia, Tripoli, Tunis, the Barbary States, Morocco, the African coast as far down as the Niger, Spain, Sicily, Candia, Cyprus, and other islands of the Mediterranean, and even parts of Italy itself, had fallen under Saracenic sway; and that sway extended, not only to civil government, but to religious faith as well. Everywhere the corrupt and idolatrous form of Christianity prevalent succumbed before the onslaught of the vigorous monotheistic faith of Islam. Gibbon, the historian, writes:

"At the end of the first century of the Hegira the caliphs were the most potent and absolute monarchs of the globe. Their prerogative was not circumscribed, either in right or in fact, by the power of the nobles, the freedom of the commons, the privileges of the Church, the votes of the senate, or the memory of a free constitution. The authority of the companions of Mahomet expired with their lives, and the chiefs or emirs of the Arabian tribes left behind in the desert the spirit of equality and independence. The regal and sacerdotal characters were united in the successors of Mahomet; and if the Koran was the rule of their actions, they were the supreme judges and interpreters of that divine book. They reigned by the right of conquest over the nations of the East, to whom the name of liberty was unknown, and who were accustomed to applaud in their tyrants the acts of violence and severity that were acted at their own expense. Under the last of the Ommiades the Arabian empire extended two hundred days' journey from east to west, from the confines of Tartary and India to the shores of the Atlantic Ocean. And if we retrench the sleeve of the robe, as it is styled by their writers, the long and narrow province of Africa, the solid and compact dominion from Fargana to Aden, from Tartary to Surat, will spread on every side to the measure of four or five months of the march of a caravan. We should vainly seek the indissoluble union and easy obedience that pervaded the government of Augustus and the Antonines; but the progress of the Mohammedan religion diffused over this ample space a general resemblance of manners and opinions. The language and laws of the Koran were studied with equal devotion at Samarcand and Seville, the Moor and the Indian embraced as countrymen and brothers in the pilgrimage of Mecca, and the Arabian language was adopted as the popular idiom in all the provinces to the westward of the Tigris."—Gibbon, *Decline and Fall*, p. 318.

Does any one inquire why these two powers, the

Papal and the Mohammedan, should occupy so prominent a position in the predictions of Scripture as regards this Gentile dispensation? The reply is easy. No power ever exercised on earth has proved, on the whole, so injurious to mankind and so antagonistic to the redeeming purposes of God, as the Papacy. Its reign has been long, its sphere has been wide, its power has been vast. It has usurped the headship of the Christian Church, and the titles and prerogatives of Deity. It has corrupted the gospel, suppressed the Bible, and turned Christianity into a mere baptized heathenism. Idolatries and false doctrines have been inculcated and promulgated throughout Christendom by its instrumentality. For centuries it made war with the saints, and overcame them. Millions of evangelical martyrs have been slain by its authority. It has injuriously affected countless myriads of human beings, during its course of more than 1200 years, thirty or forty generations having suffered under it, either in the way of corruption or persecution. In a word, it has vindicated its title to be considered that system of supernatural and soul-destroying error, that dire and dreadful apostasy revealed by prophecy as THE principal power of evil, to arise between the first and second advents of Christ.

" How worthy of such conspicuous mention in the sacred oracles, of such solemn denunciation by the Holy Ghost,—how worthy of such pre-eminent fame (or rather infamy !) among the gigantic evils that have afflicted mankind,—how deserving of every dark designation bestowed, and of the dread doom denounced, has THE PAPACY proved itself to be ! The self-styled vicar of Christ has been His worst enemy in the world ; the crowned priest on the Papal throne has been the undoing of the Church on earth. The system which asserts salvation impossible beyond its borders has destroyed the spiritual and temporal well-being of untold multitudes of men. Unutterably disastrous as have been its direct effects,—its millions

of slaughtered saints, its myriads of deluded disciples,—its indirect
effects have been hardly less terrible. By its priestly assumptions
and pious frauds ; by its notorious cupidity and mercenary practices ;
by its gross perversions of the truth and unblushing corruptions of
morality ; by its reason-revolting dogmas, childish superstitions,
and endless old wives' fables ; by its uniform opposition to social
progress, and its habitual alliance with political tyranny,—it has
brought all religion into contempt, and filled Catholic Christendom
with scorners, infidels, and atheists."—*Approaching End of the
Age*, p. 225.

Could sacred prophecy have passed by unnoticed this
gigantic and universally influential power, which ruled
the whole of Christendom with despotic sway, and with
inconceivably evil results, for more than a thousand
years ? No ; to lead the people of God to shun all
connexion with it, ample and repeated descriptions of
it are given, and unparalleled denunciations are made
against it. And as to the power of Islam, when it is
remembered that, not only did it exterminate Christianity in northern Africa, leaving but a feeble and
ignorant remnant of the Coptic Church in Egypt, but
that the professing Christians of the Greek Church fell
by millions before the invasion of its savage and devour-
ing hordes, its myriad horsemen from Central Asia, and
that millions more of subject Christian races have
groaned under its cruel oppression and destructive
exactions ; when we remember that it has put out the
light of the gospel in the lands where it had its birth,
and that, moreover, it has devastated Palestine and
trodden down Jerusalem, carried war and bloodshed
to the gates of Vienna and the northern slopes of the
Pyrenees, threatening the very existence of Christendom ;
when we remember that to this day it dominates
150,000,000 of mankind, involving them in the darkness
of fatal error and antichristian unbelief ;—can we

wonder that the spirit of prophecy should indicate beforehand its rise and its career, and announce its final doom ?

The dates of the chief stages of the rise of these two powers in this bisection era are as follows :—

WESTERN.

A.D.

476. End of western empire of Rome.
494. Council of Rome.   Gelasius.
533. Pope-exalting decree of Justinian.
590. Accession of Gregory the Great.
607. Pope-exalting decree of Phocas.
663. Latinising decree of Pope Vitalian.

EASTERN.

610. Mahomet's announcement of his mission.
622. Hegira Era of Islam.   Flight of Mahomet,
637. Capture of Jerusalem by the Saracens.

CHAPTER V

The Time of the End—Western, or Papal Aspect

WE turn now to consider the closing era of "the times of the Gentiles," called by Daniel "the time of the end." The period must, as we have seen, combine six distinctive peculiarities.

1. It must be removed by *twenty-five centuries from the captivity era*; that is to say, from the fall of Judah and the rise of Babylon, the first of the four great empires.

2. It must be removed by *twelve and a half centuries* from the rise of the western and eastern apostasies, the Papacy and Mohammedanism, each of which lasts "time times, and a half," and perishes at the advent of Christ.

3. It must be a period in which "Babylon the Great" is passing through a series of distinct stages of decline and fall.

4. It must be a period in which the eastern apostasy or Mohammedanism, is undergoing similar experiences.

5. It must be an era during which there takes place *a marked renaissance of the Jewish nation,*—a commencement of that liberation from Gentile oppression and of that material uplifting, which will issue in their restoration to their own land, and recovery of independence.

6. It must also be a period in which the *spiritual Israel, or true Church,* is experiencing a similar but

spiritual liberation from the yoke of the anti-typical Babylon, and uplifting—a time of spiritual revival in the Christian Church, and of widely extended gospel preaching, not in Christendom only, but in heathendom.

Here then are six distinctive and peculiar characteristics of the period as a whole; and if we find them all attaching to the days in which we live, and if careful study reveals the fact that never in the course of twenty-five centuries have all these features similarly characterised *any other period*, we shall then surely have good ground to conclude that we have reached "the time of the end."

As regards the first of these points, that the time of the end must be removed by twenty-five centuries from the Captivity era, we have seen that the Captivity era extended over 160 years, from B.C. 747 to B.C. 587, from the incipient rise of Babylon to the final fall of Judah. The corresponding 160 years after the lapse of "seven times" extend, on the lunar scale, from A.D. 1699 to A.D. 1860; and on the solar scale, from A.D. 1774 *to* A.D. 1934.

B.C. 747	seven times, lunar	A.D. 1699
587		1859–60

B.C. 747	seven times, solar	A.D. 1774
587		1934

We are consequently living (in this year 1917) 218 years from the *earliest commencement* of "the time of the end," and within seventeen years of its *latest close*. This "time of the end" is, from the nature of the case, a longer period than the Captivity era, because the difference between lunar and solar measurement has to be included $(160 + 75 = 235)$. Reckoned from the earliest date on the shortest scale, the 2520 years run out in 1699. Reckoned from the latest date on the longest scale, they do not terminate until A.D. 1934.

The first observation we naturally make is that as seventeen years of the period are still unexpired, it is, of course, impossible for us to discern in history the fulfilment of all the *closing* predictions of the prophecy. This is clearly the case; but we need not wait till it is high water before we decide that the tide is rising; nor do we hesitate to say that it is falling, even though it may not yet have reached low-water mark. Moreover, when we know that the fall of the tide occupies about six hours, and when we have watched it steadily retiring for five, we have little question that the remaining hour will complete the ebb, and reveal low-water mark again.

So in this case. We do not say that "the times of the Gentiles" either have closed, or will close in a few years; nor do we touch any speculative question as to what events the next two decades may bring forth, nor as to the exact point in this "time of the end" which will witness the glorious appearing of the great God and our Saviour Jesus Christ. Time will decide. All we do is to *study the history of that part of the period which has already elapsed,* and to observe if *so far* the general movement seems to be in the predicted direction, and if special and definite fulfilments are perceptible.

The question therefore is, Have the 218 years of this closing era which lie *behind* us, the years from A.D. 1699 to the present time, presented the characteristic features of *the "time of the end"* as above indicated? Have they been years of decay and fall both to the Papal and Mohammedan powers? Have they been conspicuously and undeniably such, so that the fact admits of no question, so that no previous period of their entire history presents anything at all similar or approaching to the course of events throughout this period. *Was there a turn in the tide* of their fortunes at the end of the seventeenth century? and has the subsequent movement been a steadily downward one? Further, is there any sign that the movement is even now arrested? or do things look as if it were absolutely irresistible? Has the world itself observed and noted this phenomenon? or is it a dream of prophetic students only? Is it or is it not a fact so familiar to civilised nations, as that the not distant result is taken for granted, as much as that the sun, when low in the heavens, will quickly sink beneath the horizon?

To ask these questions is to answer them. What historian, what statesman, what newspaper editor, what well-educated person, could hesitate for a single moment to grant that the last two centuries have been a time of special, and previously unparalleled, decay and fall to the Papacy and to the Porte; so that these two great politico-religious dynasties, before whom for so many centuries western and eastern Europe trembled and bowed down in abject submission, are now scarcely practical factors at all in European politics? Has not the king of Italy instead of the Pope ruled at Rome for the last forty-seven years? Is not Italy respected as a power of at least secondary importance, while "the States of the Church" and the patrimony of Peter have long since disappeared from the map of Europe? The Pope is now simply a bishop; he is a monarch no longer. As to the Porte, every one knows that it is an effete kingdom, "a sick man" already at the last gasp! Step by step within the period we are considering *both these dynasties have fallen from their once high estate*, losing first power, then independence, then tribute, and at last, as far as the temporal sovereignty of the Papacy is concerned, *existence itself*. The Porte still remains a temporal power in a small part of Europe, but does any one expect it to do so much longer? Its structure has long been so rotten, and its foundations so shaken, that it would have fallen to pieces like a ruinous old building, but that, in order to avert public danger, it has been propped up and buttressed by external support, until the fences and scaffolding needful for its safe removal can be erected.

The cause and the course of this double decay need not long detain us here, as we write for the educated, who are sufficiently familiar both with the facts and with their philosophy.

Both Popery and Mohammedanism as *religious* systems, as blasphemous apostasies from the true faith, are doomed, according to Scripture, to perish only at the coming of the Lord; but as *political* powers in Europe, their destiny—revealed twenty-five centuries ago—is to perish *before* the advent, in this "the time of the end," an era which to them politically is one of solemn and awful retribution for their deeds of corruption, tyranny, and blood, for their opposition to God and to His truth, and for their persecution of His people. To the world at large this same period is an era of great and growing prosperity, so that when the end comes as "a thief in the night" men will be saying, "Peace and safety," and things go on as in the days of Noah and in the days of Lot. But these two politico-ecclesiastical powers will as such cease to be beforehand.

The doom of the Papacy, as revealed both by Daniel in the Old Testament, and by Paul in the New, is two-fold, consisting of, first, the progress of *slow consumption by the spirit of God's mouth*, and, secondly, of sudden destruction by the brightness of His coming.[1]

Already the first of these has been marvellously accomplished, and that by the means indicated—"the spirit of His mouth"; *i.e.* the Word of God, the circulation of the Scriptures. The Reformation of the sixteenth century gave back to the world the Bible, which had for a thousand years been virtually taken from the Church, and buried in the Latin language. Now wherever an open Bible is found, there Popery loses its power; "The Bible, the whole Bible, and nothing but the Bible," is the watchword of Protestantism; and what has been the result of its circulation in the sphere of Catholic Europe within the last three centuries?

Just prior to Luther's movement, the Pope, in a bull closing the Lateran Council, A.D. 1517, felicitated himself and his bishops, because the unity of the Catholic Church was at the moment untroubled by a single heresy. There was an end of all resistance to Papal tyranny. The long persecuted witnesses of Christ had sealed their testimony with their blood. Not an *avowed* heretic was to be found in Europe! And how stands the matter now? To-day there are no less than *one hundred and fifty millions of Protestants in the world* —a hundred and fifty millions of those whom Rome calls heretics! Germany, Holland, Denmark, Sweden, England, the United States—the greatest and most progressive kingdoms of the world—are *what the Bible has made them*; and the Latin nations of Europe, Italy, Spain, Portugal, and France, are what Popery has made

[1] See Dan. vii. 26 and 2 Thess. ii. 8.

them—Catholic in name only, infidel at heart, and just as much opposed to the temporal sovereignty of the Papacy as Protestants themselves.

The Reformation undoubtedly aimed the first and the most fatal blow at the power of the Papacy in its character as a religious system, for it never recovered from the wound inflicted by that movement. The Protestant States, instead of suffering for their revolt under the anathemas of the Vatican, quickly rose to be the leading powers of Europe. The Pope was ere long obliged to defer to them; and the other European sovereigns who remained in his communion, observing the liberty and the prosperity of the Protestant nations, no longer trembled before the transcendental claims of Rome, no longer feared the Papal curse, or cared for the Papal benediction. The thunderbolts of the Vatican thenceforth produced ridicule and resentment, rather than fear and dread.

The Reformation had also the effect of largely reducing *the sphere of Papal dominion* in Europe. Germany, Switzerland, Norway, England, Sweden, Denmark, Holland, Finland, Iceland, and other countries were henceforth withdrawn from the influence of Rome. The official report at Rome summed up the losses of the holy see in the Reformation movement in these words: " England, Scotland, Denmark, Norway, Sweden, and all the northern countries are alienated; Germany is all but lost; Bohemia and Poland are largely infected; the low countries of Flanders are so far gone that the Duke of Alva's remedies will hardly recover them; and, finally, France is full of confusion: so that nothing appears sound and secure to the Papacy but Spain and Italy."

But the decline and fall of the Papacy had at this time scarcely begun. Its still mighty and terrible power was wielded with deadly force for more than a hundred years after the Reformation, in the vain and cruel effort to crush the Protestants and their faith. The dark chapter of *the Papal reaction* against the Reformation may be dated from about the time of the anti-Protestant Council of Trent, for a century after which the Pope, directly or indirectly, deluged Europe with blood in a desperate attempt to re-establish his supremacy. It has been computed that the Popes of Rome have been the occasion of more wars and slaughter than even Mohammedanism itself.

The two great instruments of this Papal reaction were the Inquisition and the Jesuits; and both were mercilessly wielded. In Bohemia 30,000 Protestant artisans and 200 of the nobility were driven into exile before that kingdom could be re-subjected. In Switzerland, Protestant villages were laid waste with fire and sword; the Thirty Years' War raged among the kingdoms of Europe; the Pope contrived to sow dissension amongst them in order to weaken his enemies by mutual antagonisms. The Spanish Armada was sent against Elizabeth of England, her kingdom having been bestowed by the Pope upon Mary Queen of Scots. The Dutch republic was almost annihilated by the Duke of Alva; deeds of cruelty were perpetrated surpassing in horror any of the darkest period of pagan antiquity. After the Inquisition had exhausted its list of infernal tortures, and the Protestants remained firm in their faith, Alva's campaign added the last touch of horror to their sufferings. Commissioned in 1567 by Philip II. of Spain to exterminate them, he in less than six years put to death no less than 18,000 by the sword, the gibbet, the rack, and the flames. The bloody council established by him soon cast its awful shadow over the land; men, women, and children were burned before slow fires pinched to death with red-hot tongs, starved, flayed alive, broken on the wheel, suffocated, drowned, subjected to all kinds of lingering agonies; and the whole country became one vast sepulchre.

In France the reaction was equally terrible. Civil wars desolated the country, and intervals of severe persecution intervened, and at last the awful massacre of Saint Bartholomew slaughtered at one fell blow a whole hecatomb of martyrs. Murder raged uncontrolled through Paris and the provinces; neither sex nor age nor noble rank was regarded by the murderers. The streets were paved and the gateways blocked up with ghastly heaps of the dead and dying. The small streams were filled with blood, and rolled in red torrents to the rivers. Fifteen thousand Huguenots were slaughtered in Paris alone, and 60,000 throughout the country in the course of one month. The Pope, Gregory XIII., commanded special services and brilliant illuminations in honour of the event, of which he caused a medal to be struck, that Roman Catholics from all parts of the world might thank God for what he considered to be a triumph of Christianity. Jesuit missionaries traversed France in all directions, and within a few years Protestantism in that country fell seventy per cent.

Elsewhere the reaction was equally powerful. The Emperor Ferdinand sought to extinguish civil and religious liberty in Germany, and would have succeeded in doing so, had not God raised up the valiant and godly Protestant hero, Gustavus Adolphus of Sweden, who saved Germany, and rolled back the flood of Papal invasion.

The struggle between the Church of Rome and the

Reformation may be said to have continued in full force up to the time of the Peace of Westphalia, in 1648, when the prolonged agony of the Thirty Years' War terminated. Rome had to some extent been successful in its resistance of Protestantism. It had recovered its supremacy in France, and had imposed its yoke on Austria, Bohemia, and Bavaria; but the other Protestant countries had maintained their ground, and a line of demarcation had at last been drawn, after a century of conflict, between the territories of the two religions. The princes of Europe were never again arrayed against each other in war on religious grounds. Rome was obliged to abandon the dream of universal empire, and the boundaries between Protestantism and Papacy, which exist in our own days, were defined by this treaty. Protestantism became an element in the European system, in spite of the Pope, and ere long the most progressive and important element. The nations of Europe refused thenceforth to engage in mutual slaughter in order to uphold the Papacy. But Rome still retained terrible power to stir up political troubles, to incite monarchs to persecute their subjects, and subjects to rebel against their rulers. Louis XIV. made himself a willing tool in the hands of Rome in France; and so did James II. in England and Ireland. The Jesuits made a desperate effort to subvert civil and religious liberty in England, and this brought about the English Revolution, which established Protestantism firmly in this country. It had, of course, been previously established under the Tudors, but was very nearly overthrown by the desperate efforts of Louis XIV. to reestablish Catholicism by crushing the Protestant nations of Europe, Holland, Germany, and England. The Revolution, which delivered our land from political and ecclesiastical tyranny, by placing William of Orange on the throne, gave the power of England into the hands of that heroic champion of the reformed faith, and he knew how to use his opportunity.

In France Louis XIV. revoked, at the instigation of the Jesuits, the Edict of Nantes, by which Henry of Navarre had secured religious toleration to the Protestants of that country in 1598. Eighty-seven years of toleration had made them numerous, respected, and wealthy, and had the Reformed Church even then been let alone it might have saved France. But in consequence of the determination of Louis to extirpate heresy entirely from his kingdom by the revocation of the Edict of Nantes, which had so long protected them, a most cruel and deadly persecution against them broke out. Large numbers were imprisoned, sent to the galleys, and slaughtered; there was no choice but suffering and death, or treachery to the faith they held; emigration was not permitted, and voluntary exile was therefore a difficult matter. They could not fly, as the Huguenots of former days had done; their exit from the country was prevented by dragoons, and to attempt to leave France was death. In spite of these laws some 400,000 are calculated to have made good their escape, and to have secured refuge in England, Prussia, Switzerland, and America, while an almost equal number perished in the attempt.

This terrible chapter in the history of Papal persecutions was nearly the last. A series of similar dark deeds had extended over about five centuries, the most sanguinary period of Rome's "war against the saints." But the days of her might were drawing to a close, and the end of the seventeenth century may be regarded as the time when the Papacy lost the power, though not

7

the will, to persecute. Some few after-waves of the terrible storm of that Papal war against the truth and those who held it did indeed extend into the first decade of the eighteenth century, but they were local and temporary, though terrible enough in character.

Such was the three years' war of extermination waged against the Camisardes in the Cevennes, whose fair and fruitful hills and valleys were turned into a desolation by the cruel crushing out of its Protestant population. But the PEACE OF RYSWICK, which was signed in 1697 between the Emperor Leopold, Great Britain, the United Provinces, France, and Spain, and which was ratified by William of Orange, marked the end of the sanguinary conflicts between the Protestant and Papal nations of Europe, and secured the recognition of our "glorious Revolution," and of William and Mary as lawful sovereigns of England. It marks the full establishment of civil and religious liberty, and St. Paul's was opened for the great thanksgiving service celebrated on the occasion of the conclusion of this peace. Protestantism was never fully and firmly established in England until this epoch, nor indeed, it may be said, anywhere else.

But if the beginning of the eighteenth century saw— as it undoubtedly did—the end of the period when the Papacy could use the nations of Europe as its tools, the end of its power to persecute the Protestant witnesses for the truth, three-quarters of a century had yet to elapse before the judgments which brought about the more acute stages of its decline and fall began to be poured out on it. The intervening period was full of signs of what was coming; it was the lull before the storm, the gathering time of the forces which were about to explode with terrific violence. About the year 1750 Voltaire began his scoffing attacks on Christianity in France, and for fifty years from that time he and his colleagues in the task of undermining all religious faith in the masses of the people, Rousseau, Diderot, and the Encyclopædists, and others, were indefatigable in their attacks on the only form of Christianity with which they were acquainted—Popery. They succeeded in producing in France an intense hatred and contempt for the priesthood and the Church of Rome. All the Catholic nations, irritated and wearied by the atrocious crimes and terrible immorality of the Jesuits, began one after another to expel them. Savoy did so in 1729, Portugal in 1759, Spain in 1767, France in 1762, Sicily in 1767; in fact, they suffered no less than *thirty-seven* expulsions on account of their intrigues, their immoral doctrines, and evil practices, between 1555 and 1773. In this last year the ambassadors of all nations demanded the abolition of the order itself, and Pope Clement XIV. was obliged to sign a bull for their entire suppression. The act, however, cost him his life.

The Inquisition, the other great pillar of the Papacy, was abolished in Naples, Tuscany, and Parma in 1782, and in 1784 monasteries were also suppressed in Naples. There was not a single kingdom which had confidence in the Roman court, or was willing to fight in its defence, when the French Revolution burst like a hurricane on its head, and for the time swept it away.

From A.D. 1774, the year of the accession of Louis XVI., the unfortunate monarch who lost his crown and life in that Revolution, and whose accession took place in the year following the suppression of the Jesuits, we may date *the commencement of the overthrow of the Papacy under the judgments of the last days.*

France, which ever since the conversion of Clovis and the donations of Pepin and Charleamgne, had taken rank as "the eldest son of the Church," and been the first of Papal nations; France, which had been so prominent in her persecution of the reformed religion, and which had crushed out the new life and extinguished the rekindled gospel light in the massacre of Saint Bartholomew and the revocation of the Edict of Nantes; France, for more than a thousand years the main pillar of the popedom in Europe,—had by this time become anti-Papal to the core. Her people, once so superstitious, had revolted from the tyranny of priestcraft, and become openly and fiercely infidel. All restraints of law and order were then thrown off, and the country plunged into the maddest excesses of revolution and crime.

In the reign of Louis XVI. came to its crisis a tremendous, unparalleled, irresistible movement, which put an end at once to absolute monarchy, aristocracy, and ecclesiastical power in France; and which communicated to the neighbouring nations of Europe the shocks of revolution and the fierce fires of democracy, together with an anti-ecclesiastical mania that has never since been allayed.

The French Revolution is, by common consent, regarded as the commencement of a new era. It could never have assumed the character it did had not the people previously lost all fear of God and all respect for man, had not the national mind been blinded, and the national heart hardened against all claims, human and Divine.

It is needless to dwell on the details here; our readers will mostly be familiar with the tragic facts: how the infidel democracy suddenly uprose in its might, destroyed the Bastile, issued its declaration of the rights of man; assaulted the king and queen by night at Versailles, and, murdering some of their bodyguard, forced them to proceed as prisoners to Paris, the bloody heads carried on pikes before the royal carriage: how the people confiscated all the vast revenues of the Church, all the domains of the Crown, and all the estates of refugee nobles, for the use of the State; subjected to themselves all ecclesiastical, civil, and judicial power throughout the country; murdered the royal guard, and some five thousand leading royalists; dethroned, imprisoned, tried, condemned, and murdered the king and then the queen; declared war against all kings, and sympathy with all revolutionists everywhere: how the "reign of terror" witnessed the slaughter of 1,022,000 persons, of all ranks and ages, and of both sexes, till the streets of Paris ran with blood, and the guillotines could not overtake their work: how thousands were mown down by grape-shot fusillades; drowned in *noyades*, where in loaded vessels hundreds of victims were purposely sunk in the rivers; roasted alive in heated ovens; or tortured to death by other infernal cruelties: how Christianity was publicly renounced, and a prostitute enthroned as "goddess of reason" at Notre Dame, and worshipped by the National Convention and by the mob of Paris, with the wildest orgies of licentiousness—morality as well as mercy having perished with religion—how the most horrid mockery of the solemn rites of Christianity was publicly enacted, an ass being made to drink the sacramental wine: how the Sabbath itself was abolished, and the decade substituted for the week: and how hundreds and thousands of priests were massacred or driven into exile, and the churches and cathedrals turned into stables and barracks. Taken as a whole, the French Revolution was a convulsion, in which the angry passions of men, set free from all restraint, manifested themselves, with a force and fury unprecedented in the history of the world, against monarchical, aristocratic, ecclesiastical, and religious institutions.

Let these things be considered in the light of a mighty and successful revolt against, and overthrow of, absolute monarchical power, and Papal tyranny and usurpation, and it will at once be granted that *nothing similar had ever occurred previously* in the history of the fourth great empire.

Terribly iniquitous had been the career of the monarchical power thus rudely overthrown; and fearfully corrupt the priesthood and religion thus utterly and with abhorrence rejected. A solemn character of retribution attaches to even the worst excesses of the French Revolution. The Papacy in the hour of its agony was exultingly reminded of its own similar cruelties against Protestants. Papists were treated according to the example set by Papists of other days, and the worst barbarities of revolutionary France could not out-Herod the previous barbarities of Papal France.

"The more deeply and earnestly the French Revolution is considered, the more manifest is its pre-eminence above all the strange and terrible things that have come to pass on this earth. . . . *Never has the world witnessed so exact and sublime a piece of retribution.* . . . If it inflicted enormous evil, it presupposed and overthrew enormous evil. . . . In a country where every ancient institution and every time-honoured custom disappeared in a moment, where the whole social and political system went down before the first stroke, where monarchy, nobility, and Church were swept away almost without resistance, the whole framework of the State must have been rotten—royalty, aristocracy, and priesthood must have grievously sinned. Where the good things of this world, birth, rank, wealth, fine clothes, and elegant manners, became worldly perils, and worldly disadvantages for a time, rank, birth, and riches must have been frightfully abused. The nation which abolished and proscribed Christianity, which dethroned religion in favour of reason, and enthroned the new goddess at Notre Dame in the person of a harlot, must needs have been afflicted by a very unreasonable and very corrupt form of Christianity.

"The people that waged a war of such utter extermination with everything established, as to abolish the common forms of address and salutation, and the common mode of reckoning time, that abhorred ' you ' as a sin, and shrank from ' monsieur ' as an abomination, that turned the weeks into decades, and would know the old months no more, must surely have had good reason to hate those old ways from which it pushed its departure into such minute and absurd extravagance. The demolished halls of the aristocracy, the rifled sepulchres of royalty, the decapitated king and queen, the little dauphin so sadly done to death, the beggared princes, the slaughtered priests and nobles, the sovereign guillotine, the republican marriages, and the Meudon tannery, the couples tied together and thrown into the Loire, and the gloves made of men's and women's skins : these things are most horrible ; but they are withal *eloquent of retribution*, they bespeak the solemn presence of Nemesis, the awful hand of an avenging power. They bring to mind the horrible sins of that old France : the wretched peasants ground for ages beneath the weight of imposts from which the rich and noble were free ; visited ever and anon with cruel famines by reason of crushing taxes, unjust wars, and monstrous misgovernment, and then hung up or shot down by twenties or fifties for just complaining of starvation : and all this for centuries ! They call to remembrance the Protestants murdered by millions in the streets of Paris, tormented for years by military dragoons in Poitou and Béarn, and hunted like wild beasts in the Cevennes ; slaughtered and done to death by thousands and tens of thousands in many painful ways and through many painful years. . . .

"In no work of the French Revolution is this, its retributive character, more strikingly and solemnly apparent than in its dealings with the Roman Church and Papal power. It especially became France, which, after so fierce a struggle, had rejected the Reformation, and perpetrated such enormous crimes in the process of rejection, to turn its fury against that very Roman Church on whose behalf it had been so wrathful, . . . to abolish Roman Catholic worship, as she had abolished the Protestant worship ; to massacre multitudes of priests in the streets of her great towns ; to hunt them down through her length and breadth, and to cast them by thousands upon a foreign shore, just as she had slaughtered, hunted down, and driven into exile hundreds of thousands of Protestants; . . . to carry the war into the Papal territories, and to heap all sorts of woes and shames upon the defenceless Popedom. . . . The excesses of revolutionary France were not more the punishment than *the direct result* of the excesses of feudal, regal, and Papal France. . . . In one of its aspects the Revolution may be described as a reaction against the excesses, spiritual and religious, of the Roman Catholic persecution of Protestantism. No sooner had the torrent burst forth, than it dashed right against the Roman Church and Popedom. . . . The property of the Church was made over to the State; the French clergy sank from a proprietary to a salaried body; monks and nuns were restored to the world, the property of their orders being likewise gone; Protestants were raised to full religious freedom and political equality. . . . The Roman Catholic religion was soon afterwards formally abolished.

"Buonaparte unsheathed the sword of France against the helpless Pius VI. . . . The pontiff sank into a dependant. . . . Berthier marched upon Rome, set up a Roman Republic, and laid hands upon the Pope. The sovereign pontiff was borne away to the camp of infidels, . . . from prison to prison, and finally *carried captive into France.* Here . . . he breathed his last, at Valence, in the land where his priests had been slain, where his power was broken, and his name and office were a mockery and a byword, and in the keeping of the rude soldiers of the unbelieving Commonwealth, which had for ten years held to his lips a cup of such manifold and exceeding bitterness. . . . It was a sublime and perfect piece of retribution, which so amazed the world at the end of the eighteenth century: this proscription of the Roman Church by that very French nation that had slaughtered myriads of Protestants at her bidding; this mournful end of the sovereign pontiff, in that very Dauphiné so consecrated by the struggles of the Protestants, and near those Alpine valleys where the Waldenses had been so ruthlessly hunted down by French soldiers; this transformation of the 'States of the Church' into the 'Roman Republic,' and this overthrow of the territorial Popedom by that very French nation, which, just one thousand years ago, had, under Pepin and Charlemagne, conferred these territories.

"Multitudes imagined that the Papacy was at the point of death, and asked, would Pius VI. be the last pontiff, and if the close of the eighteenth century would be signalised by the fall of the Papal dynasty. *But the French Revolution was the beginning, and not the end of the judgment*; France had but *begun* to execute the doom, a doom sure and inevitable, but long and lingering, to be diversified by many strange incidents, and now and then by a semblance of escape, a doom to be protracted through much pain and much ignominy." [1]

The career of Napoleon, in the course of which these things happened to Pius VI., was *a second phase of the French Revolution,* and involved thus the total wreck of the Papal power for a time and the loss of Rome itself to the Popes. His coronation took place in 1804.

A single campaign made Buonaparte master of Italy; Milan, Sardinia, Parma, and Naples were successfully reduced, and all the great cities of the peninsula. The Austrians were defeated, and many of the Pope's territories incorporated with the French dominions. Pius VI. had to pay five millions of livres towards the expenses of the war, and subsequently, when a democratic riot took place in Rome, it was made a pretext for summoning the aged monarch to surrender the temporal government; and on his refusal he was dragged from the altar, and carried a prisoner into Tuscany, the Vatican was plundered, and the Papal States converted into a Roman Republic. The possessions of the clergy and monks were declared national property, and they themselves were cast into prison. "The Papacy was extinct, not a vestige of its existence remained; and among all the Roman Catholic powers not a finger was stirred in its defence. The Eternal City had no longer prince or pontiff, and the decree was already announced that no successor would be allowed in its place" (1798). [2] The

[1] Thomas H. Gill, *The Papal Drama,* Book x.

[2] *Rome, from the Fall of the Western Empire,* by Rev. Canon Trevor. Religious Tract Society.

Pope was forced to sign the Treaty of Tolentino, and was carried captive into France, where he died in exile in 1799.

In 1800, however, the fortunes of war leaving them free to do so, the cardinals were able to elect another Pope, who assumed the name of Pius VII. Napoleon had just returned from his unsuccessful expedition to Egypt, and from selfish motives, perceiving that without religion it was impossible to govern the nation, he entered into negotiations with the new Pope, and once more established the Roman Catholic religion in France, where it had been abolished by the Revolution. The position of the Pope, however, was a very insecure one, and as he firmly refused to fall in with some of Napoleon's views, he in his turn speedily fell a victim. In 1808, the French troops again entered Rome, exiled the cardinals, and kept the Pope a prisoner; and in the following year the Papal States were annexed to the *French* empire, of which *Rome* was declared to be the *second* city !

On this Pius VII. excommunicated Napoleon, and in retaliation the French troops broke into his palace, arrested him, conveyed him across the Alps to Grenoble, while Napoleon revoked the gift of Charlemagne, confirmed the annexation of the Papal States, and detained the Pope a close prisoner. Pius VII. was treated with great severity, his friends taken from him and confined in different dungeons, while he himself was obliged to live on half a crown a day. On his return from Moscow, Napoleon induced the old man to sign the concordat by which he renounced *all claim to Rome for ever, and abandoned the temporal power.*

In 1815 Napoleon fell, and the allies once more restored the Pope, at the same time that they restored the Bourbons. Vain effort to resist the purposes of God!

The restoration lasted but a few years, and even during that brief interval the Papal power was a name, rather than a reality, compared to what it had been in former times. " The Pope sat not on his throne as once before; his power was crippled, his seat unstable; the riches of his Church were rifled, and a mighty precedent and principle of action had been established against him, which could scarcely fail of bearing similarly bitter fruit afterwards."

The year 1830 brought about another thoroughly anti-sacerdotal revolution in France. Charles X., who had acceded to the throne in 1824, had to abdicate, and his ministry had to flee for their lives; while the Duke of Orleans was proclaimed king, under the title of Louis Philippe.

In 1848 a third revolution again constituted France a Republic, tumults broke out in Paris in February, the Tuileries were ransacked, and frightful disorders committed. Louis Philippe was in his turn obliged to abdicate and take refuge in England; and the " Second Republic " was proclaimed.

A fortnight after the fall of Louis Philippe a constitution was proclaimed in Rome, and the city and country were thrown into a state of revolution. Before the end of the year Count Rossi, the Pope's prime minister, was killed, and the Pope had to flee from Rome. He was again deposed from his temporal authority, and an Italian Republic was proclaimed; it was only by the power of the French that the Pope was afterwards for a time restored, when Louis Napoleon had become president of the French Republic. With occasional pauses, and with gleams of passing prosperity now and then, the course of the Papacy has ever since been one of downfall and decay.

The year 1860 was to the Papacy one of sore trouble and dismay. It lost a considerable part of its remaining territories, and had the mortification of seeing a free constitutional kingdom established in Italy. It was the central year of GARIBALDI'S romantic and remarkable exploits on behalf of his cherished ideal of Italian unity. The Pope, inspired with distrust of the French garrison who were upholding him in Rome, organised a mongrel army of his own, consisting of French, Belgian, Austrian, and Irish volunteers.

After liberating Sicily and Naples, and uniting them to the Italian kingdom of Victor Emmanuel, Garibaldi retired from the scene, and the Italian army crossed the frontier of the States of the Church, overran Umbria and the Marches, routed and crushed the Papal forces, and obliged them and General Lamoricière to capitulate in the fortress of Ancona. The Pope, as usual, cursed his foes, but could not conquer them, and his dominion in Italy was henceforth limited to Rome itself.

In 1866 the Romish empire of Austria was worsted by Protestant Prussia at the memorable battle of Sadowa, a battle the results of which were as decisive as those of Waterloo. Austria received a shock from which it has never recovered, and was obliged to cede Venetia, which was annexed to the kingdom of Italy, while Prussia became one of the greatest powers in Europe. In 1868 the Spanish Revolution took place; Queen Isabella fled, and Spain was plunged into years of cruel strife, in the course of which the Jesuits were banished, their monasteries and churches confiscated, and sold or pulled down, and the bones of the martyrs brought to light at the Quemadero.

This same year Pius IX. sent out his famous encyclical letter, *summoning* the Œcumenical Council for 1870. Six archbishop princes, 49 cardinals, 11 patriarchs, 680 archbishops and bishops, 28 abbots, 29 generals of orders, 803 spiritual rulers, representing the Church of Rome throughout the world, obeyed the summons to attend this Vatican council, which solemnly decreed the dogma that the occupant of the Papal chair is, in all his decisions with regard to faith and morals, infallible. Arrangements had been made to reflect a glory around the person of the Pope by means of mirrors at noon, when the decree was made (July 18th, 1870); but the sun shone not that day. A violent storm broke over Rome, the sky was darkened by tempest, and the voices of the council were lost in the rolling of the thunder.[1]

On the very day following this culmination of Papal arrogance and self-exaltation was declared that terrible Franco-German War, in which the French empire of Louis Napoleon—by the soldiers of which the Pope was maintained on his tottering throne—*fell. The temporal sovereignty of the Papacy fell with it.* No sooner had the French troops been withdrawn from Rome, and the French empire collapsed, than the Italian Government announced its intention of entering the Roman States, and did so. On September 20th, 1870, Rome was declared the capital of the kingdom of Italy, and became the residence and the seat of the Government of Victor Emmanuel. The *Times'* summary for that year says: "The most remarkable circumstance in the annexation of Rome and its territory to the kingdom of Italy, is the languid indifference with which the trans-

[1] See *The Pope, the Kings, and the People.* By Rev. W. Arthur, M.A.

fer has been regarded by Catholic Christendom. A change, which would once have *convulsed the world*, has failed to distract attention from the more absorbing spectacle of the Franco-German War. *Within the same year, the Papacy has assumed the highest spiritual exaltation to which it could aspire, and lost the temporal sovereignty which it had held for a thousand years."*

The temporal dominion of Rome Papal has already been consumed. Not a nation in Europe remains under it, and men marvel that they ever did bow beneath it. The *spiritual* power of the Papacy, its idolatrous religion, remains, and will remain to the end; but the *secular power* is a thing of the past.

CHAPTER VI

The Time of the End—Eastern, or Mohammedan Aspect

FROM the date of the fall of Constantinople before the advance of Mohammedan hordes, A.D. 1453, up to the great naval battle of Lepanto, A.D. 1571, the Turkish Power had been continually *advancing* in Europe. The Euphratean flood rose higher and higher, till it reached its highest point under Solomon the Magnificent, in the middle of the sixteenth century. It remained stationary at high-water mark for half a century, and even as late as 1669 Candia was added to the dominions of the Porte. But the last quarter of the seventeenth century was a time of fierce struggle, and of alternate victory and defeat. Wars with Russia and Austria severely shook the Ottoman power, and the war which was closed by the Peace of *Carlowitz*, signed in 1699, broke for ever the aggressive power of the Turkish empire. It closed a twenty years' struggle, in which the Porte had been engaged with Russia and Austria. The conflict had been attended with varying fortunes; but, exhausted at last by the sanguinary defeats inflicted on her by Prince Eugène, the Porte was compelled, in 1699, to lay down her arms, and make peace on most disastrous terms. Louis XIV., urging the Sultan not to accept the terms imposed by its foes, said, "The Turks in all their wars have *never yet* receded; should they do so now, their *prestige* is gone, and their very existence imperilled." And so it proved. For a time Turkey remained, however, a mighty and formidable empire, holding under its cruel and debasing sway numbers of Christian nations.

A long peace with Christendom followed; but when next the shock of war brought the Mussulman forces into the field against Russia and Austria, *victory was again and more decidedly with the Christians.* Crushing defeats were inflicted on the Turkish armies in 1774; the Russians surrounded the vizier and his troops near Shumla, in Bulgaria, and were able to dictate the terms of the humiliating *Peace of Kain ardje*, by which Russia obtained the free navigation of the Black Sea, besides large cessions of territory. Thus commenced that dismemberment of the Turkish empire which has been going on ever since, and a fresh stage of which we seem now to have reached. Never since that date has the Porte been able to take the aggressive against the nations of Europe, or even to stand successfully on the defensive. Its history, as is well known, has consisted of one monotonous series of disastrous wars, humiliating treaties, military and provincial revolutions, insurrections, massacres, cessions of territory, failures of revenue, diminution of population, plagues, bankruptcies, armies destroyed and fleets annihilated, ever-contracting dominions, and ever-increasing debts, and gradual loss of independence; till at the present moment protracted decay verges on total extinction. Europe is driven to recognise that nothing can much longer avert the long predicted and richly deserved doom of Mohammedan rule in Europe—political death.

Ever since the year 1821 the progress of Turkish

decay has been so rapid and alarming as to keep Europe in perpetual anxiety. In that year began the insurrection in Greece, the finest province of the Turkish empire, an insurrection which quickly spread to the Ægean Isles and to Wallachia and Moldavia.

In 1826 Turkey was obliged to surrender to Russia all its fortresses in Asia, and frightful civil commotions distracted Constantinople, ending in the slaughter of the Janissaries, when 4000 veteran but mutinous and unmanageable soldiers were shot or burned to death by order of the Sultan himself in their own barracks in the city, and many thousands more all over the country. The empire had for centuries groaned under their tyranny, and Mahmoud II. was resolved to organise a fresh army on the military system of western Europe, and saw no other way of delivering himself from the tyrannical Janissaries than this awful massacre, which, while it liberated Turkey from an intolerable incubus, at the same time materially weakened her strength. Before a fresh army had been matured, Russia again attacked the Turkish empire, and, backed up by England and France, secured the independence of Greece, after the great naval battle of Navarino, in which the Ottoman fleet was totally destroyed. In 1828 and 1829 Russia again invaded Turkey; her armies crossed the Balkans, and penetrated as far as Adrianople, where a treaty, more disastrous to the Porte than any previous one, was concluded. The freedom of Servia was secured, and no Turk was permitted to reside in future north of the Danube, while Russia obtained one of the mouths of that river, and territory to the south of it. The large Turkish province of Algeria in North Africa was lost to the Sublime Porte, and became a French colony in the following year.

8

In 1832 Turkey was brought to the verge of dissolution in consequence of the successful rebellion of the powerful pasha of Egypt, Mehemet Ali. He attacked and conquered Syria, and defeated the Turkish armies in three great battles, and he would have taken Constantinople had not the western nations intervened. A second rebellion on the part of Egypt took place in 1840, when Ibrahim Pasha defeated the Turks at Nezib. The Turkish fleet was betrayed into the power of Mehemet Ali, and taken to Alexandria; and Europe was obliged again to interfere to protect the Sultan from the rebellion of his vassal, who could at that time have easily overthrown the Turkish empire. In the following year the British admiral took Sidon, Beyrout, and St. Jean d'Acre; and, in order to restore the Turkish rule, which had been completely lost, drove Mehemet Ali out of Syria. Egypt, however, long remained virtually independent; but owing to Turkey joining the Germanic Powers in war against Britain, Egypt was constituted a British Protectorate in December 1914.

In 1844 the Porte was compelled by the Christian nations of Europe to issue an edict of religious toleration, abolishing for ever its characteristic and sanguinary practice of execution for apostasy, that is, for the adoption of the Christian faith. As this was entirely against its will, because against the precepts of the Koran, and contrary to the practice of all the ages during which Mohammedanism had been in existence, it was a most patent proof that *Ottoman independence was gone*, as a matter of fact, though often mentioned still as a plausible fiction of diplomacy, and that henceforth it had to shape its conduct in accordance with the views of its neighbours, the

Christian nations of Europe. It was *a compulsory sheathing of the sword of persecution*, which had been relentlessly wielded for over twelve centuries, *a most marked era in the overthrow of Mohammedan Power.*

The next great stage in the fall of the Moslem power in Europe was the Crimean War, and the Treaty of Paris, which followed it in 1856. This date is one of paramount importance in the process of the decadence of the Ottoman empire. The Crimean War was ostensibly undertaken in defence of Turkey against Russian aggression; and as it was a successful war on the part of the allies, England, France, and Italy, it would seem at first sight that it should be reckoned as a postponement of the fall of Turkey, rather than as a stage of it.

Such, however, is not the case; it was in reality a very decided stage in its loss of independence. The Russian Czar was not alone in seeing that the decay of the Ottoman power had, even at that date, already gone so far that the question as to what should be done with its dominions on its final dissolution pressed for decision. As is well known, he was anxious to be recognised as heir apparent, at any rate to Constantinople; and he was anxious also to secure the position of protector to the Christian races in the Balkan Peninsula and Syria, in order that he might have the power to interfere with Turkish administration in its own dominions, and thus of hastening the long-desired catastrophe. Now the Crimean War was waged, not so much to protect Turkey, as to maintain the principle that the political destiny of these regions should be a matter of *European concert*, and not be settled according to Russian views alone. As the Duke of Argyll says: " The one great question which was really at issue was, not whether Turkey was or was not a sick man, or even a dying man, but whether the Czar had the right to solve that problem by anticipation in his own favour, and to take steps constituting himself sole heir of the sick man's possessions and effects. . . . It was because Turkey, as a Power and as a Government, was decaying, and because sooner or later its place would have to be supplied by some other government, and by the rule of some other people, that it was necessary to take steps in time, to prevent this great change from being made prematurely, in the exclusive and selfish interests of a single Power." [1]

In result, the Turkish empire was placed under the common care of Europe, and the claim of any single Power to settle the destinies of that empire without the concurrence of the rest has since been repeatedly negatived.

In a "Collection of Treaties and other Public Acts, illustrating the European Concert in the Eastern Question," the editor says: "The assumption of the collective authority on the part of the European Powers to supervise the solution of the eastern question, in other words, to regulate the disintegration of Turkey, has been gradual. Such an authority has been exercised tentatively since 1826, *systematically since* 1856. It has been applied successfully to Greece, to Syria, to Egypt, to the Danubian Principalities and the Balkan Peninsula generally, to certain other of the European provinces of Turkey, to the Asiatic boundaries of Turkey and Russia, and to the treatment of the Armenians. The present work will contain the text in full of the treaties and other diplomatic acts which are the title deeds of the

[1] *The Eastern Question*, pp. **2**, **3**. By the Duke of Argyll. Strahan & Co.

States which have thus been wholly or partially *freed by the European concert from the sovereignty of the Porte.*"

Hence 1856 is a critical date in the fall of the Mohammedan power, marking the point of its *entire* loss of independence; the point when it practically passed into the hands of Europe, with a view to its safe and gradual dismemberment. The tottering structure was condemned to come down, and the scaffolding was erected by which it was to be safely demolished.

In 1860 took place the horrible Druze massacre of the Christians in the Lebanon and at Damascus, a massacre connived at, if not planned by, the Turkish Government. The remonstrances of the European consuls in the country were treated with neglect and contempt. The Christians were disarmed by the authorities, and left, like defenceless sheep, to be butchered by their blood-thirsty enemies. Thousands of innocent lives and millions of property were sacrificed, and the total apathy and incompetence of the Turkish Government to maintain order was such that the great Powers of Europe intervened. Syria was occupied by French troops, and an English fleet anchored at Beyrout. The result was the conclusion of the treaty by which northern Syria was placed under a Christian governor, and the welfare of its inhabitants secured by a restriction of the Turkish power, submitted to under European compulsion. The year, in short, witnessed a marked though partial *deliverance of the Holy Land from Mohammedan oppression*; it witnessed the turn of the tide. The condition of Palestine and Syria has ever since been improving, and the contrast of what they are to-day and what they were fifty years ago is remarkable.

Another great crisis in the decay of Turkey was the

Russo-Turkish War of 1877. The horrible atrocities committed by the Turkish soldiery in suppressing an unimportant insurrection in Bulgaria were the immediate cause of this outbreak. Fifteen thousand men, women, and children had been slaughtered in cold blood, with every conceivable circumstance of cruelty and horror, people against whom no crime could be alleged. Their property was destroyed, their villages were burned, and large districts desolated. Christian Europe was horrified. The great Powers would have interfered in concert, but that England, whose supposed interests required the maintenance of the Ottoman tyranny over the subject Christian races, would not join in any effective common action. Russia went to war alone consequently to deliver her co-religionists, and she secured her object by a succession of victories, which broke the Turkish power to pieces, and laid it helpless at her feet. England did interfere then, to prevent her seizing Constantinople, and at the Berlin Conference obliged the victorious Czar to modify the Treaty of San Stefano, and to agree to that of Berlin, by which a large portion of Armenia was ceded to Russia. The Dobrudcha was lost to Turkey, the complete independence of Roumania was recognised, the limits of Servia and Montenegro were extended, and Bulgaria was erected into an autonomous Christian principality. Cyprus was at the same time ceded to England by the Anglo-Turkish Convention, while this country undertook to defend the Turkish possessions in Asia, the Porte promising necessary reforms, subject to British approval.

In 1876 Turkey had become nationally bankrupt; her debt, having been mostly contracted abroad, had reached the amount of one hundred and ninety-five millions, on which sum she was unable even to pay interest. This is as serious a feature in the condition of the country as any of its military reverses or territorial losses.

In 1882 a fresh and very singular stage in the downfall of the Ottoman power and independence was reached. It arose in a military insurrection in Egypt, which was headed by Arabi Pasha; this man and the army obtained a monopoly of power, and the Khedive was forced to accept a national ministry in defiance of the protests of the European controllers of the debt, thus subverting the authority of England and France in connexion with the finances of Egypt. The Sultan encouraged Arabi to defy Christian intervention in the financial and other affairs of Egypt, and tried to seize the crisis as an occasion for enforcing his own authority as suzerain. It was understood throughout Europe that if the western Powers were defeated in this struggle, it would mean a surrender of Egypt to absolute anarchy, and the total ruin of civilisation and European interests in the country. British and French squadrons anchored in the harbour of Alexandria in May. Panic began to prevail among Europeans in Egypt; the military party soon beame totally unmanageable, and the Khedive was a mere tool in their hands. The Europeans in Cairo and Alexandria were obliged to flee the country, and all attempts at pacification, whether on the part of the western Powers, or of the Sultan himself, failed. A Mussulman rising having taken place in Alexandria, in which a large number of Europeans were killed, and their houses pillaged, Arabi also continuing extensive preparations for resistance in defiance of the English admiral's expostulations, Sir Beauchamp Seymour finally bombarded Alexandria in the summer of 1882. The rebels were defeated, and under cover of a flag of truce evacuated Alexandria, not, however, without first setting fire to the European quarters, and letting loose upon it gangs of reckless plunderers. A plan had been laid for the murder of the Khedive, but it was unsuccessful. A brief but brilliant military campaign succeeded, in which the English troops defeated the rebels at Tel-el-Kebir, and victoriously entered Cairo. An army of occupation of 12,000 men was left to keep order in the country, which then became practically an English protectorate.

This campaign was remarkable as an illustration of the diminished fanaticism of Mussulman nations. The Mohammedans of India were in no way affected by the struggle between their rulers and the Egyptians. An Indian contingent was sent to Egypt, with the full approval of the co-religionists of Arabi.

The following are the dates in this time of the end to which we have alluded, as those of the principal stages in the downfall of the Papal and Mohammedan powers:

Western, or Papal Dates.

A.D.

1697. End of the English Revolution.

1750. Voltaire.   Outbreak of infidelity.

1774. Accession of Louis XVI.

1793. Regicide and Reign of Terror.

1798. Napoleon first consul of the Republic.

1808–12. Chief European campaigns of Napoleon.

1830. Anti-Papal revolution, and abdication of Charles X.

1848. Anti-Papal and democratic revolutions in all the Papal countries of Europe.   Republic declared at Rome.

1870. FINAL FALL OF THE TEMPORAL POWER OF THE PAPACY, AND OVERTHROW OF SECOND FRENCH

A.D. EMPIRE. UNIFICATION OF ITALY, WITH ROME AS CAPITAL.

1905. French law for disestablishment of Romish Church in France.

1906. Clergy who fail to comply are placed outside pale of law. Papal representative expelled. Church property confiscated. Stipends of priests stopped.

1910–11. Revolution in Portugal. Separation of Church and State. Expulsion of monks and nuns.

1917. The United States join the Allies against Germany.

EASTERN, OR MOHAMMEDAN DATES.

1699. Treaty of Carlowitz.

1774. Treaty of Kainardje.

1821. Greek Insurrection.

1840. Successful rebellion of Mehemet Ali against the Porte. British intervention in Syria.

1856. Treaty of Paris.

1860. Druze massacre in Syria. The Lebanon placed under a Christian governor.

1878. Conference of Berlin, and Anglo-Turkish Convention.

1882. English occupation of Egypt.

1885. Revolution in Eastern Roumelia.

1897. Autonomy for Crete.

1906–8. Bosnia and Herzegovina lost to Turkey.

1909. Autonomy for Western Arabia. This has involved, in 1916, the very serious loss to Turkey of the holy cities Mecca and Medina.

A.D.

1911.   Italy seizes Tripoli.

1912–13. Bulgaria and other territory lost.

1914.   Turkey joins in war against England and Allies. Loses Egypt and Cyprus.

1917.   British take Bagdad and invade Palestine.

CHAPTER VII

The Time of the End—Jewish Aspect, or the Modern Renaissance of the Jewish People

WE have now seen that two of the features which, according to prophecy, ought to characterise the era of the "time of the end," the fall of the Papacy and Mohammedanism, have been singularly evident during the last two centuries, and especially during the last. It remains to inquire whether the other movement predicted to take place at the same time, the elevation and emancipation of the long oppressed Jewish people, has made equal progress. Has the last century and a half been in any peculiar sense *a time of Jewish renaissance?* Has it presented *a marked contrast to the whole course of Jewish history, during the previous twenty-three centuries of "the times of the Gentiles"?*

What has the history of the Jews been from the time of their restoration after the captivity era to the present day? It should be noted, in the first place, that the restoration of a small remnant to Palestine under the Persian monarchs left, of course, the large majority of the nation—not of the ten tribes only, but of *all* the tribes—scattered among the Gentiles. We can trace to some extent their migrations and movements. In very ancient times, before the Christian era, they had spread themselves in Central Asia, in India, and in China; they had found their way into Africa and into Arabia, and were settled in considerable numbers in Spain, where they were enjoying social consideration, wealth, and influence. Paul desired to visit their numerous synagogues in that country Jews and proselytes were found scattered throughout the Roman empire in the time of our Lord. This earlier "dispersion" differed from the restored remnant of their race, in that they were innocent of the supreme crime of rejecting the Messiah and crucifying the Lord of Glory. Their sufferings consequently have been neither as great nor as long continued as those of their more guilty brethren, whose history especially we are now considering, a history which may be divided into three sections.

1. From the restoration era to the destruction of Jerusalem by Titus, and the close of the Jewish war under Hadrian.

2. From the final dispersion of the nation to the middle of the eighteenth century.

3. From the French Revolution to the present day.

We need not dwell on the first section, save to recall that its six centuries, though a period of revived national existence, did not restore Jewish independence. The Jews were, for the most part, under rulers of their own race, in fulfilment of the prophecy that the sceptre should not depart from Judah until Shiloh came. But the Persians, the Greeks, the Idumæans, the Egyptians, and the Romans, in turn all controlled their destinies, and their sufferings were often great, especially in the time of Antiochus. The severe calamities of this section of their history commenced, however, with the Roman war of A.D. 66, and continued till A.D. 135.

Even before the Christian era they suffered at intervals severely from the Romans, and in A.D. 21 they were banished from Rome, then the world's metropolis. In A.D. 42 they were massacred at Alexandria; in A.D. 50, 30,000 of them were killed in Jerusalem in a tumult with the Romans; and five years later they were again banished from Rome, having been previously restored by Claudius.

But it was in A.D. 66 that the worst sufferings of the Jews under the Romans commenced. Gessius Florus was at that time Roman governor of Judæa, and was a grasping, covetous, cruel ruler. His oppressions led to a widespread revolt, and such was the exasperation of the Jewish people that they made a successful stand in an insurrection against their Roman masters. When the tidings of the defeat of his representative in Judæa reached Nero, in the midst of his fearful debaucheries in Rome, he was alarmed, and sent Vespasian, a general of tried valour and skill, accompanied by his son Titus and by Trajan, the father of the emperor of that name, to reconquer the province of Syria. The command of Upper and Lower Galilee was entrusted by the Jews to Josephus, a famous general of the Asmonean race, more celebrated as the great historian of this war, and of the Jewish people. He sustained with marvellous skill and bravery a siege of forty-seven days at Jotapata, where the Jews made a most desperate resistance. They were at last overpowered by Vespasian, after 40,000 men had been killed and some 1200 taken captive. In another action on the Lake of Gennesaret 30,000 prisoners were made and sold for slaves, while 12,000, unable to bear arms, were put to death. The towns of Galilee one after another yielded to the forces of Vespasian, and awful examples were made of those which resisted, as did Gamala and Gischala.

These were, however, only the beginning of troubles; the courage of the Jews was desperate, amounting almost to infatuation, and sustained by the false hope of supernatural help from the coming of Messiah. During their long four years' struggle with the Romans comparatively few were taken prisoners, though millions fell in fight; but Jewish fanaticism and personal bravery could not cope with the overwhelming resources of Rome and with the high discipline of her armies. The only marvel was that Judæa could hold out as long as it did in the struggle. Twenty thousand were massacred at Cæsarea, while those who escaped the slaughter were seized and sent to the galleys by Florus.

In the spring of A.D. 70 Titus gave orders for the march on Jerusalem. According to Josephus, the city at the Passover contained two and a half millions of people, of whom 1,100,000 perished during the conflicts, sieges, and assaults of the city, or by the hand of the executioner. An immense multitude of prisoners, men, women, and children, were either sold into slavery, crucified, or thrown to wild beasts. Zion was surrounded by a triple wall, defended by ninety towers, and seldom has more difficulty been experienced in taking a city. The siege lasted five months; the Roman cohorts got possession of the city only by sections, and the taking of each wall demanded a fresh siege. During the last two months, when the defence had already become hopeless, Titus tried to persuade the Jews to capitulate; and on their refusal a fearful series of crucifixions of the Jewish prisoners took place by his command around the city. But nothing could shake the confident fanaticism of the Jews, nor damp their expectation of supernatural help at this awful crisis. At last, in desperation, Titus compassed the whole city with a wall and a ditch, at a little distance from the third and last remaining Jewish wall. This work, which might well have occupied three months, was actually completed in three days, owing to the overwhelming numbers and desperate activity of the Romans. Then began the terrible woes of the doomed Jerusalem. The horrors of a famine, in which mothers devoured their own children, were heightened by frightful internal discord and dissension. At length, however, the sanctuary itself was captured; and though Titus had given the strictest orders that the temple should be spared, it was accidentally set on fire and consumed. August 5th, A.D. 70, arose on an awful scene of smoking ruins deluged with blood.[1] The end was come. Many days were devoted by the Roman soldiers to completing the sack of the city and crucifying the remaining inhabitants. Thus were fulfilled the words of Daniel, "The people of the prince that shall come shall destroy the city and the sanctuary; and the end thereof shall be with a flood, and unto the end of the war desolations are determined."

About sixty years later, the Jews had sufficiently recovered from this crushing blow to rise afresh in revolt against the Roman power, and then Hadrian completed the work of their dispersion among all nations of the earth. He made the whole country of Palestine a desolation, expelled all its remaining Jewish inhabitants, forbade the Jews on pain of death even to *approach* Ælia Capitolina, the Roman city erected on the site of Jerusalem. He slaughtered 580,000 Jews in a murderous war which lasted three years and a half, and sold thousands of prisoners at the lowest prices into slavery.

---

[1] The daily sacrifice had ceased in Israel on 13th July, A.D. 70, for lack of persons to offer it.

The rest took refuge in foreign lands, and Palestine was never since inhabited by the children of Israel till quite recently, when great numbers are returning to the land of their fathers.

The first portion of the history of the Jews during "the times of the Gentiles" was therefore for the most part a time of dreadful trouble, and at its close the wrath of God came upon them to the uttermost; their name was struck off the roll of nations, politically and territorially they ceased to be a people. But though without country, metropolis, or temple, they have continued to this day to be as distinct a nation as any on the face of the earth. They had rejected their Messiah, but not their law or their prophets; nor, alas! even those "traditions of the elders," which our Lord so strongly condemned. These they collected with the greatest care, immediately after the triumph of Hadrian, and with much pains and patience embodied as the "oral law" in their Mishna. Behind this wall which they built up they have ever since continued to hide from the light of fulfilled prophecy, making void, not only the law of God, but the predictions of the prophets, that they may keep their own traditions. Their faithful observance of circumcision, of the Sabbath, and of the other ordinances of Moses, and of the Talmudic precepts and ceremonies, preserved them in all the lands of their exile as *one* people, a peculiar people, though dwelling among all nations.

What has been their history since their final dispersion? It is needful to have a clear conception of this in order to be in a position to judge fairly as to current fulfilments of prophecy.

As in the Captivity era, so in this, the predicted judgments did not descend on the Jewish people in full severity at first.   History shows that Divine judgments, as a rule, *advance slowly but steadily on guilty cities and communities*, so that those who are blind to the moral government of God may, if they will, attribute all that happens to second causes.   The judgments on Israel waxed gradually stronger and stronger, only as the long dark night of the Gentile "seven times" wore on.

The interval from Hadrian to Constantine saw the Jewish people in measure prospering and flourishing in the lands of their exile throughout the Roman earth. They were not at first despised and oppressed by their conquerors, but rather the reverse.   They obtained influence over the people, and honour at court in Rome. And, alas! they too often used both for the persecution of Christians.   They looked with a malignant triumph on the disciples of Christ, compelled to assemble in the catacombs to worship the crucified One, while their own synagogues were recognised as under Roman favour, and their schools and colleges increasing in general esteem. They gladly took part in the pagan persecutions of the early Church, as in the case of the venerable Polycarp in the time of the Emperor Marcus Aurelius, showing that the overthrow of their nation and their own exile had in no wise diminished their hatred to Christ and His disciples.   As paganism and superstition lost their hold in the third century, the writings of Moses and the prophets rose in the appreciation of the intelligent, and from a combination of causes the state of the Jews in the three first centuries gave little indication of the advent of the terrible experiences which were to succeed, and to be prolonged more or less over a thousand years. Their rabbis applied to their condition in these early days the words of Daniel, "Now when they shall fall, they shall be holpen with a little help."

9

But the conversion of Constantine changed all this. When the ruler of the Roman world bowed the knee in adoration before the crucified Galilæan, a complete reverse took place in the condition of the Christ-rejecting nation. The Jews then became a condemned and persecuted sect, and sank ever deeper into oppression and misery. They lost the imperial favour and the privileges they had enjoyed, and were excluded from one sphere after another. Military and civic careers were gradually closed to them, though they were still free to observe their own religion, and retain their rights as men and citizens; and their persons and property were as yet secure.

With the fifth century the gloom deepened; and both in the eastern and in the western empire of Rome the treatment of the Jews became worse and worse. The legislation of Justinian put the axe to the root of the tree, by declaring that "civil rights could only belong to those who professed the orthodox faith." The Jews were entirely excluded from his code and his edicts. Restrictions were imposed on them in favour of Christians, and proselytism was punished with death. From this time forward they had no political position of importance in the eastern empire, though in the farther East, beyond its bounds, they continued to flourish till the Saracenic wars. After that time popular hatred and contempt, with bitter persecution, were their portion under the crescent in the East, as well as under the cross in the West. Charlemagne and the entire Carlovingian dynasty sought as far as possible to protect the Jews, but with the downfall of that line of monarchs began the worst troubles of the exiles of Palestine. With the rise of the Norman power, and the feudal system in Europe, commenced a period of *seven centuries of the most cruel oppression and profound degradation* to the Jews in all the nations of Christendom.

The era of the Crusades was the darkest part of this dark night of Israel's tribulation. It brought to them a long continuance of two centuries of the most atrocious massacres and tortures, which aimed at their utter extermination, and were not far from securing it In vain even the Popes exerted their influence to mitigate Jewish miseries and woes; men calling themselves Christians, and setting forth to rescue the holy places from the Turk, commenced their task by the massacre, on their way to Syria, of all the Jews in Europe! That age of chivalry esteemed only two classes of men— military heroes and agricultural serfs. The Jews were neither—they were traders, pariahs of society. Too often their financial transactions were usurious, and excited popular fury, as they still do occasionally on the Continent. The men of those days understood little of finance, and considered all interest usury. The Jews, "doubly detested as the murderers of Christ and as the bloodsuckers of Christian wealth, were in the Middle Ages a special object of severity to the *laws*, both ecclesiastical and civil, of hatred to the *burghers*, and of violence to the *populace*. Even the sovereigns who gave them protection made use of them merely as a sponge, which they allowed to fill with the money of their subjects, that they might squeeze its contents into the royal treasury." [1]

A Jewish calendar, with a chronological table, forming "a summary of Jewish history from the flood to the year 1860," lies before us. We run the eye questioningly over its pages, and what do we find as we review the incidents of this second section of Jewish history there

[1] Dr. Isaac da Costa, *Israel and the Gentiles.*

recorded?   An   unconscious   acknowledgment   from
Jewish pens that every threat of judgment denounced
against Israel in case of continued rebellion and idolatry
by the Moses and the prophets has been fulfilled.   An
acknowledgment that ever since their fall before the
power of Babylon, in the sixth century B.C., they have
been in subjection to Gentile rulers; and that since A.D.
135 they have been dispersed among all nations; that
their history has consisted of one long chain of great
and sore calamities, interrupted only with brief gleams
of passing prosperity.   That they have been exposed to
innumerable evils of every kind: to famines and plagues,
captivities and banishments without number, to social
distress and degradation, to outlawry and the hatred of
their Gentile neighbours, to false accusations and frequent massacres, to exactions and imposts almost exceeding belief, to pillage and torture, to the most painful
forms of social ostracism and injustice; in a word, that
they have been so relentlessly crushed down by their
Gentile masters that existence itself would have been
crushed out of them long since but for the strange
indestructibility with which, in the providence of God,
their race is endowed.   That wonderful, vigorous
vitality, which caused them, even in their profound
misery in Egypt, to multiply till their numbers alarmed
their oppressors, and which, after the return of only
50,000 of them from Babylon, caused them again to
increase to many millions during the five centuries prior
to the first advent, has never forsaken them.   From first
to last their only appropriate emblem is the bush that
"burned with fire, yet was not consumed."   But general
statements fail to impress the mind; let us take some
special incidents, and try to realise the misery the facts
imply.

In A.D. 1020 Canute *banished* all the Jews from England. What is it to be uprooted and banished from your native land? Deprived at a stroke of home and friends and business, and prospects in life, and cast with a helpless family a stranger among strangers.

In A.D. 1068 the only burial place in all England allowed to the Jews was in Cripplegate (where Jewin Street now stands), and Jews from all other parts of the country were forced, at enormous expense and inconvenience, to bring thither their dead. How should we feel if we lived under such a law as that?

In 1096 the Crusaders began what they called the "Holy War," by attempting to murder all the Jews in Europe who would not submit to baptism! The most horrible carnage took place all over Germany, where numbers of Jews destroyed each other, mothers even slaying their own children to avoid the barbarities of the infuriated Christian fanatics. Two hundred Jews who had thrown themselves into the Rhine at Cologne were dragged from the water and inhumanly butchered. Similar atrocities marked the commencement of the second crusade in A.D. 1146, though St. Bernard exerted himself to the utmost to prevent them. About this time commenced the gross *financial* injustice which continued for many centuries to be one principal instrument of persecution. Louis VII. of France released the Crusaders from all their debts to Jews. Henry II. ordered the Jews to quit England, by way of extorting a large sum of money for permission to remain. In A.D. 1181 Philip Augustus seized the Jews in their synagogues, imprisoned them, cancelled all debts due to them, confiscated their property, and ordered them to quit France immediately. When starting on the crusades, Henry II. ordered £60,000 (an enormous sum in those days) to be levied on the Jews to defray his expenses. Murderous riots were raised against these unfortunate people at the coronation of Richard I., when the populace slaughtered every Jew they could find, and after plundering them set fire to their houses. The following year occurred a terrible and similar tragedy in the provinces. The governor of York Castle offered the Jews protection, which they accepted; but they were besieged in the castle, and their resources being cut off, they, at the instigation of their venerable rabbi, in one night slew their wives and children, burnt the property they had with them, drew lots for killing each other, and then set fire to the castle to avoid the more barbarous tortures their persecutors intended.

In England the condition of the Jews was for centuries peculiarly miserable; few things in our history reflect such disgrace on both kings and people. Up to the reign of Edward I., when they were banished the country, they were incessantly victimised in the most cruel and unjust manner. The Jews and their families were in the eyes of the law mere slaves and bondsmen to the king, having no rights whatever.

The laws of Edward the Confessor had established this. "The Jews, and all they possess, belong to the king." The Crown had therefore absolute power to appropriate at any time their persons, their wives and children, and the wealth which with peculiar facility and skill they accumulated. The laws provided that the Jews were not to be taxed like the rest of the nation, "as they are talliable to the king alone as his own bondsmen, and not besides." Apart from any purely *arbitrary* and capricious exertion of power by the Crown over the persons and property of the Jews, there were certain points in which cruel tyranny was *systematically* enforced.   Thus upon the death of a Jew the king asserted his right to the *whole* of the property and effects of which the deceased had been possessed.   If he left a wife or children they were permitted to succeed to the estate only on the payment of heavy and arbitrary fines, amounting to at least one-half of the whole. Upon the conversion of a Jew to Christianity the king, up to the reign of Edward I., *seized all his estate* and applied it to his own use.   Edward I. granted that from henceforth only one-half of the estate should in such cases be taken.   This custom seems to have prevailed in various countries of Europe, as well as in England, and the reason given for it is, that *the sincerity of the conversion might thereby be shown.*   A curious mode for Christians to adopt in order to manifest their desire for the conversion of the Jews!   They oppressed and ill-treated them for *being Jews*, and took away from them all their property on their becoming Christians !

Certain towns were appointed for the residence of the Jews, and certain parts of these towns; and they were not permitted to dwell in any other places.   A special Court of Exchequer was appointed to manage all their financial affairs, so that the king could at any moment become acquainted with any transaction whatever, undertaken by a Jew, as these courts kept copies of all documents.

King John ordered all the Jews of England to be imprisoned until they made a full discovery of all they possessed, after which, by the most cruel tortures, he extorted from them an enormous sum of money.   One man at Bristol was ordered to have a tooth extracted daily until he paid 10,000 marks.   Henry III. demanded 20,000 marks from the Jews in A.D. 1241, and a second time, in 1245, he extorted 4000 more.   Louis

IX. confiscated one-third of the debts due to them throughout his country. Henry III. obliged them to give him 18,000 marks. Philip V. imprisoned the Jews at Paris to compel them to prove all their debts; these he seized, and after obtaining 150,000 francs condemned many to the flames. But it would be impossible to enumerate all the instances of this kind of financial oppression which befell the Jews in Europe in the Middle Ages.

A very common pretext for robbing and murdering the Jews has been to accuse them of some unnatural crime, such as poisoning the rivers to produce cholera or plague, and then to rouse the populace against them. In A.D. 1220, for instance, the body of a girl was found in the Rhine; the Jews of Cologne were accused of having drowned her, and the bishop fined them 4200 pieces of silver. His Jewish physician was accused of poisoning John I. of Portugal, and the Jews were obliged to pay 50,000 crowns. They were often accused of crucifying children for their passover lambs, and of similar enormities; and when the passions of the people were sufficiently roused, massacre and plunder invariably resulted.

The Lateran Council in 1215 ordered the Jews to wear a distinguishing mark, and the death penalty was affixed to a Jew marrying a Christian, or having a Christian servant.

Perhaps the worst calamity which befell these people in the Middle Ages was their banishment from Spain under Ferdinand and Isabella, in A.D. 1492. The edict ran thus: "Seeing that the Jews of our cities induce many Christians to embrace their religion, particularly the nobles of Andalusia, *for this* they are banished under the severest penalties." The penalty was death if found in the kingdom after four months, unless they embraced Christianity. The inquisitor, Torquemada, prohibited Christians supplying them on their journey to the coast with bread, water, meat, or wine. A Jew offered 600,000 crowns in the name of his nation to procure the revocation of this cruel edict; the king and queen were inclined to consent, but the inquisitor Torquemada prevented their doing so. Eight hundred thousand souls on this account had to expatriate themselves from a country where they and their ancestors had resided in safety for centuries; a country whose darkness had been enlightened by their learning, and whose wealth had been increased by their industry. They had to quit the soil they had cultivated, the scenes of their youth, and the graves of their fathers, on a few months' notice, and at the sacrifice of most of their property; and to go forth, not knowing whither they went; and to their honour be it said *they did so* rather than abjure their religion, or forsake the law given on Sinai. Many of them suffered indescribable hardships, and large numbers perished.

Thomas de Torquemada advanced into the royal presence bearing a crucifix. " Behold," he said, " Him whom Judas sold for thirty pieces of silver. Sell ye Him now for a higher price, and render an account of your bargain before God."

The sovereigns trembled before the stern Dominican, and the Jews had no alternative but baptism or exile. For many centuries their fathers had dwelt in this delightful country, which they had fertilised with their industry, enriched with their commerce, adorned with their learning; yet there were few examples of weakness or apostasy. The whole race, in a lofty spirit of self-devotion—we envy not that mind which cannot

appreciate its real greatness—determined to abandon
all rather than desert the religion of their fathers.
They left the homes of their youth, the scenes of their
early associations, the sacred graves of their ancestors,
the more recent tombs of their own friends and
relatives.   They left the synagogues in which they
had so long worshipped their God; the schools where
those wise men had taught who had thrown a lustre
which shone, even through the darkness of the age,
upon the Hebrew name.   They were allowed four
months to prepare for this everlasting exile.   The
unbaptized Jew found in the kingdom after that period
was condemned to death.   The persecutor could not
even trust the hostile feelings of his bigoted subjects to
execute his purpose; a statute was thought necessary
prohibiting any Christian from harbouring a Jew after
that period.   Many were sold for slaves; Christendom
swarmed with them.   The wealthier were permitted
to carry away their movables, excepting gold and silver,
for which they were to accept letters of change, or any
merchandise not prohibited.   Their property they might
sell; but the market was soon glutted, and the cold-
hearted purchasers waited till the last instant to wring
from their distress the hardest terms.   A contemporary
author states that he saw Jews give a house for an ass,
and a vineyard for a small quantity of cloth or linen.
Yet many of them concealed their gold and jewels in
their clothes and saddles; some swallowed them, in
hopes thus at least to elude the scrutiny of the officers.
The Jews consider this calamity almost as dreadful as
the taking and ruin of Jerusalem; for whither to fly,
and where to find a more hospitable shore?

Incidents which make the blood run cold are related
of the miseries which they suffered.   Some of those

from Arragon found their way into Navarre; others to
the seashore, where they set sail for Italy, or the coast
of Morocco; others crossed the frontier into Portugal.
"Many of the former were cast away, or sunk," says a
Jewish writer, "like lead into the ocean." On board
the ship which was conveying a great number to Africa
the plague broke out. The captain ascribed the infection to his circumcised passengers, and set them all
on shore on a desert coast, without provisions. They
dispersed; one, a father, saw his beautiful wife perish
before his eyes, fainted himself with exhaustion, and
waking, beheld his two children dead by his side. A
few made their way to a settlement of Jews. Some
reached the coast of Genoa, but they bore famine with
them; they lay perishing on the shore. The clergy
approached with the crucifix in one hand and provisions
in the other. Nature was too strong for faith; they
yielded, and were baptized. A Genoese, an eye-witness,
describes their landing and their sufferings. He commences with these expressive words: "At first sight
their treatment might seem praiseworthy, as doing
honour to our God; perhaps there was some little
cruelty in it, since we considered them not as beasts, but
as men created by God. It was wretched to witness
their sufferings; they were wasted away with hunger,
especially sucklings and infants; mothers half alive
carried their children famishing with hunger in their
arms, and died holding them. Many expired from cold,
others with squalor and thirst. The tossing about on
the sea, and the unaccustomed miseries of the voyage,
had destroyed an incredible multitude. I speak not of
the cruelty and rapacity with which they were treated
by the captains of the ships. Some were thrown into
the sea by the cupidity of the sailors; some lived to

sell their children to pay for their passage. Many came
into the city, but were not permitted to stay long—by
the ancient laws of Genoa not above three days. They
were allowed, however, to refit their vessels, and to
recruit themselves some days from their fatigues;
except that they could move, and that with difficulty,
you would have thought them dead, they were crowded
on the mole, with the sea on all sides. So many died
that the air was infected; ulcers broke out, and the
plague which visited Genoa next year was ascribed to
that infection." The acts of the clergy, and the compulsory baptism, rest on Jewish tradition.

Into Rome the fugitives were admitted, but they were
received with the utmost inhospitality by their own
brethren, fearful that the increased numbers would bring
evil upon the community. Even the profligate heart of
Alexander VI. was moved with indignation. "This is
something new," he exclaimed; "I had always heard
that a Jew had ever compassion on a Jew." The Pope
commanded the resident Jews to evacuate the country;
they bought the revocation of the edict at a considerable
price. Those who reached Fez were not permitted to
enter the town: the king, though by no means un-
friendly, dreaded the famine they might cause among
his own subjects. They were encamped on the sand,
suffering all the miseries of hunger, living on the roots
they dug up, or the grass of the field, "happy," says one
Jewish authority, "if the grass had been plentiful."
Yet even in this state they religiously avoided the
violation of the Sabbath by plucking the grass with
their hands; they grovelled on their knees, and cropped
it with their teeth. Worse than all, they were exposed
to the most wanton barbarities of the savage people. A
woman, unable to bear the sight of her pining child in

his agony, struck him dead to the earth with a large stone. Many sold their children for bread. The king of the country afterwards declared all such children free. A pirate of Sallee allured a number of youths— one hundred and fifty—on board his ship, with the promise of provisions; and amid the shrieks of the parents on the shore set sail, and sold his booty in some distant port. The captain had intended to murder them all; a merchant on board the ship remonstrated. "How can I otherwise avenge the blood of Christ, whom the Jews slew?" argued the avaricious captain, intent on his plunder. "Christ Himself," was the reply, "allowed His blood to be shed to redeem mankind." It was not thought wrong to cast them out on a wild shore. Another party were landed by a barbarous captain of a ship, entirely naked and utterly desolate, on the African coast. The first who ascended a hill to survey the country were devoured by wild beasts, which came howling down upon the rest of the miserable crew. They plunged into the sea, and stood shivering in the water till the wild beasts retreated; they then crept back to the beach. For five days they remained in this miserable plight, and were rescued by the humane activity of the captain of another vessel, who sent his boat to their relief.

Many of the Spanish Jews naturally sought refuge in the neighbouring kingdom of Portugal, and the king consented to allow them to enter the country on payment of a poll tax; but they were only to pass through to the coast. His successor Emanuel, who was at first inclined to protect the Jews, married the daughter of Ferdinand and Isabella, and was soon influenced to follow her parents' example. He even surpassed them in barbarity. He named a day for all Jews to quit the kingdom, and

appointed certain ports for their embarkation. Before
that time he issued another secret order to seize all
children under fourteen years of age, to tear them from
the arms and bosoms of their parents, and disperse them
through the kingdom, to be baptized and brought up as
Christians. The secret transpired, and lest they should
conceal their children it was instantly put in execution.
Great God of mercy, this was in the name of Christianity!
Frantic mothers threw their children into the wells and
rivers—they destroyed them with their own hands.
One mother threw herself at the feet of the king as he
was riding to church. She had already lost six children;
she implored that her youngest might be spared to her.
The courtiers repelled her with scorn and ill-usage.
The king told them to let her go, "the poor bitch
deprived of her whelps." But though stifled in the
heart of a monarch, the voice of nature still spoke in
that of the people, however bigoted. They assisted the
Jews to conceal their children. By a new act of perfidy,
Emanuel suddenly revoked the order for their embarkation at two of the ports which he had named, and the
delay made them liable to the law. The more steadfast
in their faith were shipped off as slaves; but the spirits
of many were broken, and on condition that they might
receive back their children, and that Government would
not scrutinise their conduct too closely for twenty years,
they submitted to baptism. Yet Pope Alexander VI.
conferred the title "Catholic" on the Crown of Spain for
this cruel act! Some of the exiles took refuge in
Turkey and Africa, some in Portugal, Arragon, Navarre,
and Italy.

So the story goes on; banishment after banishment,
extortion after extortion, massacre after massacre! In
A.D. 1545, 5000 Jews were burned, with their houses,

synagogues, and valuable libraries at Salonica. Fifteen years later, numbers were burned in Germany and banished from Prague, on a false accusation that they had caused the fires which took place in various parts of the empire; the true incendiaries were, however, afterwards discovered, and they were permitted to return. Pope Pius V. ordered the Jews, under penalty of confiscation of property and becoming slaves, to quit the Papal dominions. The Janissaries at Constantinople set fire to the Jews' quarter, burnt down 3000 houses, and obtained property to the value of 50,000,000 of crowns. In 1613 the Jews' quarter in Frankfort was burned, and they were obliged to quit the city, though afterwards permitted to return.

After this date, however, we observe a *diminution* of oppressions and cruelties; such incidents as those we have enumerated did not cease, but they steadily decreased in number and in atrocity. In 1655 a petition was presented by the Jewish people to Cromwell, that they should be allowed to return, with certain privileges and rights, to reside in England. After long consideration in Council, Government were inclined to consent. The judges declared that there was no law which forbade their return, and the divines were much divided in opinion, some asserting that the Scriptures promised their conversion. Cromwell declared that since there was a promise for their conversion, means ought to be used to that end; and that the only means was the preaching of the gospel. How could this means be employed *unless* they were admitted where the gospel is preached? In conclusion, however, any general admission was laid aside "as a thing decried by the clergy"; but after hearing the debates, Cromwell and his councillors gave permission, "toleration and dispensation," to a considerable number of Jews individually to come and live in London, and he granted them permission to build a synagogue.[1]

In the following year, 1656, the burial ground at Mile End, which is still used as a cemetery by the Jews of London, was leased to these people for 999 years, and the same year the first English and Hebrew grammar was published in London.

In 1670, toleration and liberty of conscience were granted to the Jews in Persia, where they had suffered much in former times, and where even as late as the end of the sixteenth century the Jews had been persecuted with much severity. They were banished from Vienna, and also from Oran in Algeria, in 1669, indicted for meeting for public worship in London in 1673, and ordered to quit all the French colonies in 1683, those who did not do so were to be seized and their property confiscated. They were excluded from Russia by Peter the Great in 1687; and even so late as 1685 Jewish merchants were arrested on the Royal Exchange, and " for non-attendance at church"!

Not until the second quarter of the eighteenth century did the tide begin slightly to turn. In 1723 Louis XV. gave the Jews permission to hold real estate in France; and in the same year our own Parliament for the first time acknowledged them as British subjects. In 1740 this privilege of being regarded as British subjects was extended to Jewish sailors who had served two years in our ships of war. Christian VI. of Denmark in 1738 opened all trades to the Jews; and in 1750 Frederick II. of Prussia granted toleration, though on the most intolerant conditions, to those in his dominion.

[1] Bishop Burnet, *History of His own Time*, vol. i. p. 17.

One of the earliest steps towards *real Jewish emancipation* was the passing of the "Naturalisation Bill" in England in the middle of the eighteenth century (A.D. 1753). This Act simply provided that Jews might be naturalised "without receiving the sacrament." It met with the most violent resistance in the House of Commons, but finally passed.

But such was still the inveterate and unreasonable prejudice against the outcast nation, that a loud and fierce opposition against the Act immediately arose throughout the country. Furious pamphlets and sermons assailed it, the streets resounded with popular songs attacking it, and such was the agitation that it had actually to be repealed next year!

In order to give an idea of the extent to which inveterate prejudice, even at this late date, filled the minds of even the educated classes, we give an extract from two sermons of the day. One preacher, who took for his motto Acts xvi. 20, said:

"The Jews have exceedingly troubled our city of late, and they are like 'to trouble it much longer.' The city of London, in Common Council, with great unanimity addressed the House of Commons against the Bill, which passed by a great majority. The Bill is entirely of a religious nature, it must have a malignant influence on our religion. It strikes at the root of our present establishment, and affects the very being of Christianity. The Jews ought to be more concerned to become Christians than Englishmen. God cast them out; we take them in. God expelled them; they come to us expelled, and we naturalise them. What He made their punishment we turn into a reward. . . . The Lord sent them punishments, and therefore it would be prudent to put off naturalising the Jews until He take them away. They who now pretend to be Jews are blasphemers, and shall we naturalise blasphemy? They are the synagogue of Satan, and shall we license Satan's meeting-house? God forbid! The thought fills us with horror. God Almighty keep us from the infatuation, and give us not over to this dreadful guilt!"

There was a curious blending of the temporal and spiritual in some of the alarms.

"With God there is mercy, with the Jews there is no mercy. If this Bill becomes law, *we are Jewish slaves*, and, what is more dreadful, without any hopes of relief from God. For this Bill is in its whole nature a voluntary renunciation of the Providence and protection of God, leaving no room for the continuation of His mercy. . . . Awake, therefore, my fellow Britons, Christians and Protestants! It is not Hannibal at your gates, but the Jews that are coming for the keys of your church doors. Let us, if we have love and zeal for our religion, our king, and our country, pray that we may not be delivered up to *the merciless will of the Jews*, who know no goodness but that which blasphemed and murdered the Lord from heaven; nor desire any glory but that of putting an end to all Christian Churches, kings, and kingdoms."

But "the time of the end" had at last arrived; the long persecutions and miseries of nearly twenty-three centuries were to draw to a close. Neither people nor kings could arrest the change that was coming.

The Emperor Joseph II. of Austria was the first really to emancipate his Jewish subjects. In 1780 he opened the schools and universities of the empire to them; granted them the privilege of taking degrees in philosophy, medicine, and civil law; allowed them to follow any trade or establish manufactories, subjecting them to the same laws as Christians, and to attend fairs in towns where they did not reside, which they had previously been forbidden to do. He delivered them from an odious tax called the body tax, which had imposed upon them the most painful restrictions, forbidding a Jew to wear a beard or to frequent places of amusement, or even to go out of his house on the festival days of the Church; and from other laws which reduced them as far as possible to the level of beasts. In the year 1788, Louis XVI. of France passed a similar edict, appointed a royal commission "to remodel on principles of justice all laws concerning the Jews." Indeed, we may say that the period since *the middle of the eighteenth century* has been one of uninterrupted and rapid emancipation, uplifting, and renaissance to the Jewish people. The following statements of an American professor, Dr. Kellogg, present some of the evidence bearing on this subject.[1]

"It is an indisputable fact that, for now more than a hundred years, the Jews have been steadily rising out of that depth of subjection and debasement in which they had lain for centuries, and that concomitant with this there have appeared among both Jews and Gentiles many other exceptional phenomena predicted by the prophets as to accompany or usher in Israel's final restoration. . . .

"Of these facts the first to be mentioned is the *civil emancipation of the Jews*, which has been one of the remarkable events of the history of our age. The prophetic word, 'oppressed and spoiled evermore,' graphically represents their general history until quite recent times; but a wonderful change has passed, and is still passing, on the condition of the scattered nation. The Lord had said concerning Israel that in the latter days He would break the yoke of the Gentiles from off his neck and burst his bonds (Jer. xxx. 8); and it is a fact which cannot be denied that for the past hundred and thirty years the world had been witnessing a most literal fulfilment of these words.

"The first act in the modern emancipation of the Jews was their *enfranchisement in England in* 1753. Simultaneously two men appeared on the continent of Europe, the one a Jew of Germany and the other a Gentile, a Frenchman, who were destined, in the providence of God, to do more than any other two individuals in preparing the way both of Jewish deliverance and of judgment on the oppressing Gentiles. These men were MOSES MENDELSSOHN and VOLTAIRE. It was in 1755 that Mendelssohn published the first of those writings which soon made him the foremost of the

---

[1] See his admirable little volume, *The Jews; or, Prediction and Fulfilment.*

literary men of his time. About the same time Voltaire, followed by Rousseau and the encyclopædists, began to publish those writings which had so much to do in the bringing about, a generation later, the great French Revolution, *in which awful convulsion the chains fell from the limbs of Israel, wherever the victorious armies of France appeared, and the Jews began once more to be accounted men.* . . .

"Voltaire fiercely hated the Jews, and yet no one did more to prepare the way for their emancipation. The doctrine of the absolute equality of men without regard to race or creed, and the consequent doctrine of the equal rights of all men, so sedulously propagated by Voltaire, Rousseau, and others, involved as its inevitable practical issue the emancipation of the Jews from all exclusive burdens and odious discriminations.

"Professor Grätz, the eminent Jewish historian, in his great work on the history of his people, dates the beginning of the fourth and last of the periods into which he divides Jewish history from A.D. 1750.

"The United States of America were the first nation to embody in their laws the principle that Gentile and Jew were equal in right and privileges before the law, A.D. 1776.

"In 1788 Louis XVI. appointed a royal commission, with Malesherbes at the head, 'to remodel on principles of justice all laws concerning the Jews.'

"So things were going on when the French Revolution, with all its unprecedented terrors, burst upon bewildered Europe. The Lord had said by the prophets that when the hour of Israel's deliverance should come He would make them that had oppressed her drunk with their own blood (Isa. xlix. 24, 26), and that He would then take the cup of trembling out of the hand of Israel and put it into the hand of them that had afflicted her (Isa. li. 22); and so, as every one knows, it came to pass at that time. The great timepiece of the dispensation struck the predestined hour, the great Revolution began, and Europe was straightway filled with fire and blood. Throne after throne went down in flame and judgment, and as the thrones of the Gentiles fell everywhere, there fell with them the chains of ages from the limbs of Israel. In the almost universal massacres in France the Jews alone, it is said, commonly escaped harm, and even in the Reign of Terror passed unhurt, like Israel of old in the days of Egypt's plagues."

The emancipation of the Jews in France was completed in the Revolution, and as the movement spread over Europe, one country after another followed the French example. In 1805 Alexander I. of Russia revoked the edict of banishment, and the Jews flocked back into his empire in such numbers that it is supposed that a third of all the Jews in the world are now found in Russia. In 1806 the Jews were made citizens in Italy and Westphalia, as they had previously been in Holland and Belgium. In 1809 Baden, and in 1813 Prussia and also Denmark, followed the example of the other countries of Europe, and completely emancipated the Jews; and at the Congress of Vienna all the contracting Powers formally pledged themselves to turn their attention to the improvement of the condition of the Jews throughout Europe. Several Acts of Parliament ameliorating their condition, stage by stage, were passed in England in the years 1830, 1833, 1836; but not until the tenth attempt, in 1858, was *full equality* conceded, and the Jews made eligible for election to Parliament. In 1844 was secured from the Turkish Government the firman which pledges to the Jews *protection from persecution throughout the Ottoman dominions, including, of course, the Holy Land.* In 1848, when revolution again shook nearly every throne of Europe to its foundation, the emancipated Jews appeared in the forefront of the movement, leading and ruling where for ages they had been ruled over and oppressed. "In France appeared in the Government the Jews Fould, Crémieux, and Goudchaux; in the provisional government of Venice the Jew Pincherle was a leading member; in Berlin Jacobi was leading the opposition; in the parliament of Frankfort the Jew Riesser was the vice-president; in Austria Fischhof appeared at the

head of the Government after the flight of the court;
while Adjutant Freund, afterwards more widely known
as Mahmoud Pasha, was leading the troops in the
Hungarian insurrection."

In 1867 Turkey gave the Jews for the first time in
centuries the right to own *real estate* in the land of
their fathers. In 1870, in the treaty between Bavaria
and the Confederation of North Germany, which fully
consummated the unification of North Germany,
Bismarck secured for the Jews of Bavaria the same
privileges as they enjoyed in other German States, the
full rights of citizenship; and in this same year, with
the overthrow of the temporal power of the Pope, Jewish
humiliation in Italy was also at an end. In 1878 the
Congress of Berlin made the *full emancipation of the
Jews in Roumania* one condition of the promised
autonomy. It cannot be denied that for the past
hundred years or more the world has been witnessing a
literal fulfilment of the prediction that "the yoke of the
Gentiles shall be taken off the neck of Israel and their
bonds burst." The change in the civil position of the
Jews throughout the largest part of Christendom has
indeed been *one of the most characteristic features of
the history of the nineteenth century.*

In 1860 was formed the Universal Israelite Alliance, "an organisation which has for its object the
promotion and completion of the emancipation of the
Jews in all lands, and their intellectual and moral
elevation, as also the development of Jewish colonisation
in the Holy Land. . . . In the prophecy of Ezekiel we
have, in the vision of the valley of dry bones, and its
interpretation, a very full account of the final restoration
and conversion of Israel (Ezek. xxxvii. 7–14). According to the representation of that vision the restoration

is to take place in *successive and perfectly distinct stages*. Thus the prophet saw that, before the giving of life to the dry bones, which symbolised the house of Israel, before the clothing of them with flesh, sinews, and skin, there was first of all 'a noise and a shaking, and bone came to bone, each bone to his fellow'; that is, he saw in the first place a preliminary organisation, the necessary antecedent of all that followed. If this feature of the vision mean anything, it would seem that it *can* mean nothing else than this, that *a tendency to external organisation* in the scattered nation was to be looked for, *antecedent and preparatory to* their actual reinstatement in their land, and conversion to God, by the power of the Spirit of life." This prediction as to *the beginning of the final restoration* is being very literally fulfilled.

Another point very fully mentioned in prophecy as characterising the restoration era of Israel is that of WEALTH (Isa. lx. 9). The restored Jews are to bring their silver and their gold with them, and this wealth is to be derived *from the Gentiles that oppressed them*; for it is written, "They shall eat the riches of the Gentiles," and again that when their spoilers shall cease to spoil them, then they in turn shall spoil their spoilers (Isa. lxi. 6). Now it is notorious that everywhere in Europe an extraordinary tendency of capital to concentrate in Jewish hands is observable. During the ten years 1854–1864 the Rothschilds alone furnished about 112 millions in loans to England, Austria, Prussia France, Russia, and Brazil, besides many millions to smaller States. All over Germany the relation of the Jews to the finances of the country is causing great anxiety. The anti-Semite petition circulated in 1880 says, "The fruits of Christian labour are harvested by

the Jews; capital is concentrated in Jewish hands."
The Jews are becoming also the actual or virtual
owners of *the soil* through a large part of central and
eastern Europe. A Berlin paper says: "More than a
sixth part of the Jews in Russia live by means of the
liquor trade, and the same is true of Roumania and of
the Slavic lands. With the liquor trade usury goes
hand in hand, and as a result, it is a fact which can no
longer be denied, that the population of the remote
districts of Russia, Austria, Hungary, and Roumania are
only the nominal possessors of the soil, and cultivate
the land for the Jews, to whom they have mortgaged
their estates for their liquor debts. About *a quarter
of the railway system of Russia* is owned by a Jew
called the Russian railway king, Mr. Samuel Solomono-
witz de Poliakoff."

In all the continental countries the proportion of Jews
found in the wage-earning class is exceedingly small,
compared to the number of Gentiles; while in the
capitalist class it is, on the other hand, very large, quite
out of all proportion. A large number of parallel facts
might be cited, and they become more conspicuous continually. In Berlin, where the Jews are only five per
cent. of the population, out of every hundred Protestants
thirty-nine were returned as employers, and out of
every hundred Jews, seventy-one; and it is the same in
Austria. The bourse of Vienna lies mainly in Jewish
hands. In Hungary the Jews have obtained possession
of so many of the old estates as to make a change in
the constitution a necessity. In Roumania and Servia
it has been pleaded that if the Jews are given an equal
chance they will gradually oust the peasantry till they
possess the whole land. "Constantina, Algiers, and
Oran," says the *Télégraphe*, "belong almost entirely to

Jews. The whole trade of Algiers are in their hands, and a large proportion of the people are fallen into the power of the Jews. Here," adds the writer, "appears a dark point full of danger for the future."

THE POWER AND INFLUENCE of the Jewish people have risen, of course, with their political standing and their increase in wealth. They form a very large proportion of the educated classes in Germany, Hungary, Austria, and other countries. They have furnished of late very eminent men, who have taken the foremost rank as scholars and as teachers. Such names, for instance, may be cited as those of Professor Neander and Professor Delitzsch, of the University of Leipzig, and large numbers of others not so well known to Christian readers, because their works consist of anti-Christian Biblical criticism. As linguists, as critics, as philologists, archæologists, political economists, mathematicians, and historians, Jewish names are highly distinguished; while among musicians we have Mendelssohn, Halévy, Meyerbeer, Rossini, Julius Benedict, Grisi, and all the Strauss family. No less than seventy professors' chairs in German universities are held by Jews, and the tide of Jewish influence in education and literature is still rising everywhere. *The control of the Press* also on the Continent has largely fallen into their hands. They occupy seats in the continental chambers of deputies, as well as in our own Parliament. Our own prime minister, Disraeli, was a Jew by race, if not by faith; and one who stood in the first rank of English judges as Master of the Rolls, Sir George Jessel, was also a Jew. On a recent occasion no less than twenty-one Jews were decorated with the order of the Legion of Honour in France, though the Jews in that country number only 60,000 in a population of 37,000,000.

Another remarkable fact in connexion with the signs of renaissance of the Jewish nation is *their rapid increase in number*. This also had been predicted (Isa. lx. 22; Ezek. xxxvi. 37). Basnage, in his *History of the Jews*, 175 years ago, estimated their number to be at that time only about three millions. It already amounts in Europe alone to nine millions, and the Jews are everywhere increasing in a more rapid *ratio* than the Gentile populations in the midst of which they live. They have a very high birth-rate, and an exceptionally low average mortality. "*Twenty* per cent. of the Jews reach the age of seventy years, as against only *twelve* per cent. of the Christians."

The climax of the Jewish renaissance is, as we know, to consist in their restoration as a nation to the land of Palestine,—a climax which has not yet come, but which is perceptibly nearer than it was even half a century ago. No sooner was the law passed which enabled them to hold landed property in Palestine than many Jews began to avail themselves of the right. Up to the year 1841 only 300 Jews were permitted to live in Jerusalem. The number has now risen to over 60,000, and the city is expanding on all sides beyond the walls.

The Palestine Exploration Fund has done a most important work in preparing the work for Jewish restoration. Many thoughtful and judicious writers have suggested that the only way to settle the Eastern Question, so far as Palestine is concerned, is for the Jews themselves to have it back. "Thus as the Ottoman Power moves on to its predestined dissolution, these two questions, What shall be done with the Jews as they are found in various Christian lands? and What shall be done with the land which once belonged to them? force

themselves simultaneously, and more and more impera-
tively, on the attention of the statesmen of Europe."
The Russian persecutions have given a new impulse to
the movement of the Russian Jews towards the Holy
Land, and the *Jewish Chronicle* wrote in 1880, "We
are inundated with books on Palestine, and the air
is thick with schemes for colonising the Holy Land
once more."

The significance of these facts, when considered as a
group, and as a contrast to the condition of the Jews in
Christendom in all preceding centuries, can hardly be
missed by any observer, though it will be most striking
to those who know most of the past history and present
state of the Jewish people.

Hence, while on no one point are the restoration
promises to the Jews fulfilled in any plenary or complete sense, yet it is perfectly evident that a marked
and marvellous change in the experiences of the scattered
nation has already taken place, and that its commencement dates from the eighteenth century; signs of the
movement having appeared as early as 1723, and early
initial stages of it having taken place in 1753, while it
assumed its full proportions at the time of the French
Revolution, and has continued with ever-increasing
energy to the present day. The events which were
predicted by Moses and the prophets, and especially by
Daniel, at intervals of from twenty-five to thirty-five
centuries ago, as ushering in and accompanying the final
restoration of Israel prior to the second coming of Christ,
have been now for the last hundred and fifty years taking
place. The restoration itself has not yet come. This is
evident; but is it not equally evident that its occurrence
is only a question of time, and probably of a short time?
Every stage in the dismemberment of the Ottoman

empire is a stage in the direction of the liberation of Palestine, and the restoration of the Jew.

Confronting the incredulity of our day there are these two great long foretold facts: the people of Judah without a land, and the land of Judah without a people! Yet that land once flowed with milk and honey, and is capable of speedily doing so again; and that people, rapidly increasing in number, and having command of enormous capital, are already reorganised, enlightened, free, and influential, sitting in the senates of the first kingdoms of Europe, wielding the power of the Press in many lands,—a people capable of accomplishing any task they undertake, and a people willing enough to colonise their own country, as soon as they can obtain in their fatherland security for their life and property.

There is in Palestine no strong man armed, keeping his house to oppose any plan for Jewish restoration; the land is feebly held in the fast relaxing grasp of a sick and dying power. What should hinder that at any day the daughter of Judah should arise, shake herself from the dust of her feet, loose herself from the bands of her neck, forget the shame of her youth and the reproach of her widowhood, and return with singing to Zion? Apart altogether from the fact that prophecy says this shall be, and be soon, does not the state of eastern Europe indicate it, as a probable and not distant consummation of movements already far advanced?

To conclude. The rapid glance which we have taken of the twenty-five centuries of Jewish history which have elapsed since the days of Nebuchadnezzar and the beginning of "the times of the Gentiles" shows that—

1. Never since the days when that monarch subdued

the Jews have they been independent of Gentile authority, though for five centuries a remnant of them were restored to a tributary condition in their land.

2. That since their rejection of "Messiah the Prince" total dispersion among the Gentiles has been the lot of their whole nation, and desolation the portion of their land.

3. That the 1000 years of the Middle Ages, and especially the seven centuries from the tenth to the seventeenth centuries, were to them a time of unspeakable degradation and suffering in all lands of their exile.

4. That since the middle of the eighteenth century a complete change has passed over their condition, and they have been everywhere uplifted, emancipated, recognised as equals by all nations, given rights and privileges as citizens, a share in popular representation, seats in councils and senates, a position among the aristocracy, and in the national administration of the countries where they reside; that they have risen to eminence in finance, in literature, in music, in war, in government, in politics, and in education; that their wealth has become enormous, their position secure, their influence great, and their scattered families reunited in one great national organisation.

5. That since the year 1808 efforts have been made to evangelise them, and that in recent years very considerable numbers of them have been converted to Christianity.

6. That during the nineteenth and twentieth centuries the Moslem power, which for 1200 years has occupied and oppressed the land of Israel and the city of Jerusalem, has been decaying with ever-increasing rapidity, the process having now gone so far that it cannot last much longer. On its fall the perplexing question, Who

is to replace the Turks in Palestine? will have to be settled, and the restoration of the Jews is consequently becoming an alternative in practical politics, attracting the attention of some of the great powers of Europe.

We cannot close this section without directing attention to the bearing of these facts on our faith and hope and duty as Christians. Before such a fulfilment of prophecy as Jewish history exhibits what can all the fiery darts of infidelity do? Their story, extending back as it does through 4000 years of history, forms an impregnable fortress for believers in the inspiration of Scripture. What else but Divine foreknowledge and Divine inspiration *can* account for the facts of this strange case?

There exists this day in all nations a scattered people, a people without land or government, without metropolis or temple, speaking all the principal languages of the world, yet regarding the ancient Hebrew as their sacred tongue; one in race, one in faith, one in religious observances; a people who for antiquity of descent are the very aristocracy of the earth, able to trace back their genealogy through 4000 years to one great and good father, as no other people on earth can do; a people who have exerted more influence over subsequent ages than even Greece or Rome, who have been the source of all the monotheism of the world, and but for whom we might this day be polytheistic idolaters like the ancients; a people who have handed down through the ages the sacred books which denounce their own sins, and foretell their own punishment, as well as predicting their ultimate national restoration and salvation. Let unbelievers account for these facts as they may, candour must surely confess that they evidence the hand of God in history and the mind of God in Scripture. Every principal phase of Jewish history was foretold before it came to pass, and has come to pass exactly as it was foretold,—every one except the last; and in this wide analogy of the past we find ground for confident expectation as to the future of Israel.

" Jerusalem shall be trodden down of the Gentiles, *until* the times of the Gentiles be fulfilled."—*Luke* **xxi. 24.**

" When the times of refreshing shall come from the presence of the Lord; and He shall send Jesus Christ, . . . whom the heaven must receive *until* the times of restitution of all things."—*Acts* iii. 19-21.

CHAPTER VIII

CHRONOLOGICAL MEASURES OF THE TIMES OF THE GENTILES

WE must turn now from history to chronology, and we may say of this branch of our subject what Mr. Birks says of his exposition of the two later visions of Daniel: "From the nature of the details of which it is composed, it may perhaps fail to interest general readers; but those who *study it* will find themselves repaid by a more deep and lively sense than ever of the actual providence of the Almighty in this fallen world. Why have we in the Word of God itself so many genealogies and lists of names, of offerings of princes, of journeys in the wilderness, and other passages that seem dry and barren, but to teach us that we must *stoop to details and individual names*, if we would rightly understand the condescension of our God, and the reality of His special oversight of the children of men? Those who are soon weary of these details must pay the cost of their own impatient spirit by a more loose, unreal, and slippery faith. *The tree of faith must throw out ten thousand little roots into the lowly soil of prophetic history, if it is to grow and expand into that noble confidence of hope, which no storms of temptation can uproot or destroy.*"

Here we have to deal with dates and with periods, instead of with names, and these are perhaps even more unattractive to most people, as involving the mental effort of *calculation*; but we venture to assert that those who take the trouble to follow the investigations of this chapter, Bible in hand, will not fail to be at the close more profoundly convinced than ever before of the inspiration of the sacred volume, of the all-embracing providence and foreknowledge of God, and of the near approach of the end of this age. We would earnestly request that our readers verify the chronological calculations of this chapter for themselves. They must indeed do this in order to have any firm, well-grounded conviction on the subject. Merely to read a number of statements as to events, dates, and intervals produces but an evanescent impression on the mind. Our desire is that every student of the subject should be able to say with the men of Samaria, "Now we believe, not because of thy saying"; for we have studied for ourselves, and know that this is indeed the truth.

The *events* should be considered, whether they are indeed as critical and important, in connexion with the historical movements to which they respectively belong, as we represent them to be. The *dates* should be verified where needful, and above all the *calculations* on which our conclusions rest.[1] It is one thing to receive a dogmatic statement, and quite another to investigate the facts for oneself. We would wish our readers to share the feelings of surprise, of awe, and of adoration, which we ourselves have experienced, when earnest prayer, patient, reverent searching of the Scriptures, and study of "books," have from time to time been rewarded by an opening of the eyes to see, one after another, the facts which form links in a chain of

---

[1] The simple operations of addition and subtraction are alone required for this.

evidence, which demonstrates the system of prophetic chronology.

Only gradually and one by one did they come to our knowledge; many a calculation made revealed nothing, but we *believed* that a Divine order pervaded the times of history and prophecy, as it pervades all the other works and ways of God. We knew that appearances were not to be trusted, that the seemingly lawless and erratic movements of planets and comets are in reality regulated by the most exact laws, that the countless apparent anomalies of nature are all capable of classification, and exhibit perfect and wonderful order. We had no doubt that it was the same with these sacred " times," and hence we continued our search, till all became, step by step, clear. And now we invite other Christian students critically to examine the results here presented; for if they are true, every Christian ought to know it, every preacher ought to proclaim it, the world ought to be warned of its fast approaching doom, and the Church ought to be cheered by the assurance of the nearness of her " blessed hope."

Sacred chronology is no barren field to cultivate. The Scriptures contain no unedifying statements, and they contain thousands of chronological ones! Has the Church ever yet received from them any great comfort or consolation   Is not the time come that she should do so? Is she likely to do so without study? Has nature yielded to scientists her potent secrets without long and patient investigation and meditation? Are the material works of God more profound, and more worthy of research, than that WORD which is magnified above all His name, which is " for ever settled in heaven "—that word which is " truth," and which *liveth* and abideth for ever? A living thing has always some-

thing *new* in it; the Bible is no more exhausted than
the rich storehouse of nature! The very truths needed
for our days of doubt and dark infidelity—new and
glorious evidences of the inspiration of Scripture—are
there. Let us be hopeful and diligent, and seek to
develop them to the glory of God.

Before we begin to consider the exact chronological
intervals lying between the events of the three eras of
history we have now treated, it will be well briefly to
summarise the general conclusions we have already
reached.

1. That the fourfold Image of Daniel ii., symbolising
the succession of Gentile monarchies, extends from the
rise of Babylon, and the fall of the throne of Israel and
of Judah, to the yet future establishment of the kingdom
of God on earth.

2. That the appointed duration of this succession of
four Gentile monarchies is "Seven Times," or 2520 years
(seven times 360 years), *a great week*, harmonious with
all the various weeks of the Levitical economy and of
Jewish history.

3. That these 2520 years of "the times of the Gentiles,"
like other periods of chronologic prophecy—and notably
the great prophecy of the "seventy weeks" to Messiah
—may be measured by either the solar, calendar, or
lunar scale, warrant for the employment of each and all
existing both in nature and in Scripture; and that
sometimes the same period runs out on two, or even all
three, of these natural scales.

4. That the difference between these three scales is
such that "seven times" runs out on the lunar scale
seventy-five years earlier than on the solar. This difference between the two measures, or the inequality between
the solar and lunar year, is called EPACT. There is also

an intermediate calendar scale; so that "seven times" may be either 2520, 2484, or 2445 ordinary years, according to the scale employed; and similarly its half, "time, times, and a half" may be 1260, 1242, or $1222\frac{1}{2}$ ordinary solar years. All these three scales are and have been in use among different nations in different ages.

5. That these prophetic periods should be regarded as extending, not merely between certain events, but between certain groups of events; not so much between certain YEARS, as between certain critical ERAS OF HISTORY; the first of these is the *Captivity era* of Israel and Judah, the second is marked by the fall of the western empire of Rome, and by the rise of the *Papal and Mohammedan Powers*; and the last is called in Scripture "the time of the end."

6. That in the course of these eras there occur certain salient *years of crisis*, which are frequently answered by chronologically correspondent years of crisis in a later era, though the *principal* measures are between the eras themselves.

7. That the events foretold by chronological prophecy are exclusively those bearing directly or indirectly on *the history of the redemption of the human race.* Even when apparently mere political changes—such as the rise and fall of the pagan empires, wars, battles, sieges, victories, defeats, treaties, accessions of kings, changes of dynasty, publication of edicts and decrees, etc.—they will yet be found on reflection to be important incidents in the history, either of the typical or of the anti-typical Israel—the people of God, natural or spiritual, the Jewish nation or the Christian Church,— who have been and still are the channel of the world's redemption. Every change in the environment of an

organism has a bearing on the organism itself, and the story of its development cannot be told without reference to the history of its environment.

We must also remind our readers here that the events with which we are now dealing lie in the region of *certain* and not of uncertain chronology. Prior to the era of Nabonassar, there is a measure of uncertainty as to very ancient dates, and as to the intervals between any two given events of antiquity, so that it would be impossible to measure many such intervals accurately.

Bible chronology, calculated as it largely is by the lives of the patriarchs, the administration of judges, and the reigns of the kings, leaves two narrow gaps which can never be bridged over with absolute exactness; one between the death of Moses and the servitude under the Midianites, and the other between the election of Saul and the death of Samuel. The limits of doubt in these two intervals are *very narrow*, but they prevent absolute certainty as to the *exact* length of any interval which includes both or either of these gaps. A near approximation may be made, but accuracy cannot be claimed for any such calculation. After these two gaps, however, Bible chronology is consecutive and certain, and from the era of Nabonassar it is confirmed by astronomy. At that point all becomes perfectly clear and unquestionable; the dates of the Babylonian, Medo-Persian, Grecian, and Roman kings are just as certain as those of the Plantagenets or the Tudors. The exact chronological position of the era of Nabonassar has been accurately determined by the verification of a series of astronomical observations, including eclipses recorded by Ptolemy, the time of whose occurrence was measured by ancient astronomers from this point. In dealing with the dates of the events of the "times of the

Gentiles," we are throughout consequently in *the clear sunlight of authentic chronology*, and we can calculate the chronological distance between any two events of which we possess the exact dates to a day, and in certain cases even to an hour. A fixed astronomical starting-point makes everything clear, and all the intervals which we mention in the following pages are just as easily ascertained as the period which elapsed between the battle of Trafalgar and the battle of Waterloo, or between the accession of William the Conqueror and the present day. It should be noted also as regards the number of events which we have mentioned in the chapter on history, and with whose dates we have now to deal, that though considerable in itself, it is small in comparison with the number that actually took place in the course of these twenty-five centuries of the history of all the important countries of Europe, Asia, and Africa. Moreover, the events which we have selected arrange themselves into *three distinct groups*, and they all happened in three distinct and widely separated eras.

1. The era of the rise of the literal (typical) Babylon.

2. The era of the rise of the mystical Babylon, or antitypical Babylon—called in Scripture "Babylon the Great," Rome Papal.

3. The era of the fall of this latter power, cotemporaneously with the fall of the Moslem power, in these days.

Or to look at these eras from the other side; the events with which we are dealing are connected with—

1. The era of the fall of the natural Israel under Babylon.

2. The era of the fall of the western Church under Rome Papal (Babylon the Great), and of the fall of the

eastern Churches and of Jerusalem and Palestine under the Moslem woe.

3. The present era of the rising again of the Jewish nation and land, cotemporaneous with the fall of the Papacy and the Porte.

Now these historic movements are far removed from each other, and none but Bible students can see any relation between them. Certainly nothing but prophecy indicates any *chronological* relation between them; the predictions of Daniel asserted, twenty-five centuries ago, that there would be such a chronological relation, and that "seven times," or 2520 years, would separate the first from the last, and especially that the Papal Apostasy would last for half that time, or 1260 years; indicating thus that the whole week would be divided into two halves (Dan. vii. 25). The question we now have to study is, *whether the chronological relation predicted in prophecy can be traced in history.*

This is the kernel of our argument—*the chronological relation* between the three eras of which we have treated, and between the years of crisis in the first, and those in the second and third. In considering this question we must needs pass into the regions of clear arithmetical calculation. If we would know whether the "time is fulfilled" and the kingdom of God in glorious manifestation at hand, we must consider, like Daniel, "the *number* of the years whereof the word of the Lord has spoken."

Let it not be for a moment imagined that accurate chronological statements are unworthy of a spiritual revelation, or of Him who gave it. Not only are order and symmetry apparent in every branch of natural science, but harmonious relations of number meet us everywhere among the works of God. Is not chemistry to a large extent a science of number? In the laws of heat, light, sound, and electricity, in music, in botany, in anatomy, and in a host of other sciences, numerical relations are paramount. Now, if God governs *matter* thus, if His material work betrays at every turn that calculation and orderly arrangement have presided over its genesis, how likely is it that His providence should have similar features!

And if history, with its successive eras, and its chronological epochs, be, as it undeniably is, the record of Divine providence, the story of God's moral government of men, may we not expect to find *order* underlying its apparent chaos? If a wonderful and world-wide septiform periodicity has been impressed on nature, organic and inorganic, by its Maker, as it assuredly has,[1] may we not expect to trace something similar in His providential arrangements?

The Bible is full, not only of history, but of chronology It positively bristles with dates and periods, and this is one of the features which most plainly distinguish it from all spurious revelations. "Its doctrines, precepts, promises, and its prophetic imagery and hymns of holy worship, are all inwoven into a narrative of God's moral government, which reaches from Adam to Nero and Vespasian, from the garden of Eden to the city of Rome. This comprehensive history is taken up and completed by a prophecy, no less comprehensive, which stretches onward from Patmos to the New Jerusalem, from the age of the Apostles to an eternity still to come. The Bible may thus be called God's own history of our world, from the first entrance of evil to its final overthrow, and from the dominion of Adam in paradise to the reign of the second Adam, the Lord from heaven. With such

---

[1] See *Approaching End of the Age*, chapter on "The Divine System of Times and Seasons," p. 230.

help it is easy to trace the main outlines of Providence in the six thousand years which have already passed away."

In the Bible alone we can see at once the past and the future of mankind. Other books give parts of the story of which Scripture gives the whole; in it therefore alone shall we find the whole moral and the whole *chronological* plan of God's dealings with the human race. In *its* light alone need we expect to discern the glorious truth, that the apparent chaos of history, with its wars and fightings, conquests and overthrows, rise and fall of kingdoms, is "a mighty maze, *but not without a plan*," even as regards its chronological features.

Moreover, if the Maker of the universe, and Architect of the solar system, be the Author of the chronological prophecy, as well as of the plan underlying history, we may expect to find that all the three years, which the great orbs He has appointed to be time-measurers for man, mark off *as* such, *will be employed as units of measurement.*

These two thoughts ought to abate any foolish prejudice *against calculation* in connexion with chronologic prophecy. Of it as a whole we may say, what inspiration says of a special point, "Here is wisdom; let him that hath understanding *count*" (Rev. xiii. 18).

Proceeding then to count or measure from the extreme limits of the Captivity era—that is, from its earliest and latest dates,—first three and a half, and then "seven times," let us observe, first, the dates to which we are led, and, secondly, the events which took place in the years indicated.

CHAPTER IX

Lunar Measures of the Seven Times, reckoned from the Captivity Era

THE era of Nabonassar, B.C. 747, is the date of the accession of the *first* king of the Babylonian empire; and B.C. 587 is the date of the *last* stage of the fall of Judah under Zedekiah. The two dates mark therefore the beginning and end of the Captivity era. Taking them for our starting-points, we measure 1260 years by the shorter lunar scale, and are led to the years A.D. 476 and A.D. 637.[1]

B.C. 747	1260 lunar years.	A.D. 476
B.C. 587	1260 lunar years.	A.D. 637

Now what were *the events* of these two years? Were they critical and important in character in connexion with the history of "the times of the Gentiles"? or were they nothing remarkable? Let us note well the reply.

The year A.D. 476 *was the date of the fall of Romulus Augustulus, the last of the long line of the Cæsars, the last of the western Roman emperors. His fall marks the end of the four great pagan empires of antiquity.*

Think of the long, complex, wonderful story that

[1] In this and similar calculations it should be remembered that 1260 lunar years are only 1222½ solar.

terminated in this year; think of the magnitude, variety, and multiplicity of the events constituting the rise, course, decline, and fall of these four universal empires; think of the careers of Nebuchadnezzar and Belshazzar, of Cyrus and Darius, of Xerxes and Alexander the Great, of the Maccabees and the Seleucidæ and the Ptolemies, of Pompey and Julius and Augustus,—above all, of the sublime and ever-memorable events of the career of "Messiah the Prince"; think of the Herods and of Pilate, of Titus and of Hadrian, and of the fall of Jerusalem and destruction of the Jewish nation; think of the long line of the Cæsars, their conquests and their crimes, their glories and their shames, their world-wide dominion and unparalleled power; think of the pagan persecutions of the early Church, and of the first division of the noble army of martyrs; think of the conversion of Constantine, and the establishment of Christianity in the Roman world; think of the division of the empire, and of the removal of the seat of government to Constantinople; think of the dreadful inroads of northern barbarism, and of the long continued decline of the old Roman civilisation; let the mind run slowly over the events of these twelve or thirteen centuries of human history; let the magnificence and the might of Nineveh, Babylon, Jerusalem, Antioch, Alexandria, Rome, Constantinople, and a hundred other great cities, pass like a panorama before the mental eye, and melt away like dissolving views into the contrasted spectacle of their wreck and ruin, their struggles and sufferings, in siege and sack and overthrow; let the myriad episodes of their history recorded by the Jewish prophets and Josephus, by Herodotus and Thucydides, by Eusebius and Gibbon in his *Decline and Fall* be recalled: and let us then measure, if we can, the marvel of omniscience and foreknowledge that is involved in the fact, that, not only the occurrence, the order, and the sequence of this almost interminable series of events was foreseen in detail and foretold in outline from the beginning, but that *the time required for their conjoint occurrence was appointed and arranged, and that even to a day*!

The entire history of the four great empires up to the point of the fall of the fourth in its first or empire form (as distinguished from its last or ten-kingdom phase) occupied precisely "time, times, and a half" on the lunar scale, not only to a year, but *to a day*, for the exact accuracy of the period is perfectly wonderful. From the accession of Nabonassar, Feb. 26th, B.C. 747, to the fall of Augustulus, Aug. 22nd, A.D. 476, there are 1222½ solar years, or 446,503 days; while 1260 *lunar* years (or 15,120 lunations) contain 446,502½ days: so that the difference, if any, is merely one of hours.

Can any candid mind regard this *fact* (which no one can deny or even question) as a mere *chance coincidence*? From the initial date of the rise of Babylon, the beginning of the Jewish Captivity era, to the deposition of Romulus Augustulus, and the end of the western empire of Rome, exactly three and a half "times," or 1260 years, elapsed; not in the open solar form, that might have challenged premature attention, but in that same veiled lunar form in which the "seventy weeks" to Messiah the Prince were measured, announced, and fulfilled.

Nor should we let the mind go *back* merely from this great dividing date; it should be allowed also to glance forward. If A.D. 476 was the terminus of the old world —of the old Roman empire—it was, as we have seen, equally the starting-point of the new.

This **year** was that of the removal of the hindrance to the rise of the *Papal Apostasy*.[1] It marks the "deadly wound" under which it seemed for a time as if the rule of Rome must expire. The old imperial head was wounded to death; and in its place there rose after a time another head—the final, and most evil and anti-Christian form of Roman rule, the Papacy; that line of tiara-crowned monarchs, who, for more than twelve centuries, governed Papal Europe from the seven-hilled city, and ranked, not only as high priests, but as *temporal sovereigns*, uniting under their sway the kingdoms of western Christendom.

Think of the great Apostasy of the Christian Church, brought about in due time by the self-exaltation of the bishops of Rome, when they became Papal pontiffs! Recall the deluge of false doctrines and wicked practices which flooded Europe for twelve centuries, from the river of Papal power which rose as a little bubbling rivulet among the ruins of ancient Rome! Consider the myriads of martyrs who suffered under Papal tyranny in later years when the bishops of Rome had become just as much of "wild beasts" as the old pagan emperors! Consider the more than imperial authority which these Papal pontiffs wielded for long ages over Europe! Consider too the appalling fact that this influence was always used to repress truth and to persecute the saints, to oppose God, to exalt self, to increase sin, to bury in Latin the Bible, to oppress mankind, to ruin souls! Surely if A.D. 476 is a great year because of what it brought to an end, it is an even more momentous crisis on account of what it inaugurated—the long and evil reign of the "man of sin" and "son of perdition"— the "dark ages" of the Papal antichrist.

[1] 2 Thess. ii. 6.

Whatever importance attaches to the history of the Papacy attaches to its initial date; just as the birth of a great man derives its prominence from his subsequent career, he reflecting back on it his own importance, so this year A.D. 476 derives its character from its relation to one of the most momentous movements in history, regarded from the stand of the well-being of the Christian Church.

"Time, times, and a half" from the *first* date of the Captivity era lead us then to the date of the fall of the *western* empire of Rome, which is also the initial date of the rise of the Papacy. The same period measured from the *last date* of the Captivity era, on the contrary, leads us to the *eastern* empire, and to a date connected with the rise of that Mohammedan power before which Constantinople (or new Rome) ultimately fell.

It leads us to A.D. 637. This was, as we have seen, the year of the capture of Jerusalem by the Saracens, under the Caliph Omar. Between the fall of Jerusalem before the hosts of Babylon, in the days of Zedekiah, and its capture by this great conqueror, 1260 lunar years, the fated "time, times, and a half," also elapsed.

Now it is quite true that the *great* destruction of Jerusalem, the one predicted in Daniel ix., was not this one under the Saracen Omar, but that under the Roman Titus, which took place over five centuries previously in A.D. 70. Nevertheless this fall had also its importance, and is well worthy of the chronological position which it occupies in the bisection era.

It is the initial date of the long oppression and desolation of the Holy City under the Mohammedan power, Saracenic and Ottoman, which still exists, and which will probably exist until Jerusalem ceases to be trodden down of the Gentiles, "the times of the Gentiles" having been fulfilled. It is the initial date of *the final desolater of the land of Israel*, and of the last oppressor in the city of the great king, the Mohammedan power. During by far the longer part of the eighteen centuries of the utter desolation of Palestine, Jerusalem has been trodden down by *this* power. Hence the date of its first establishment in the Holy City cannot be an unimportant one. The chronological measures of its occupation of Jerusalem are given in Scripture, and they have nearly run out, as we shall see presently.

The date occurs in that central Bisection era in which, as Luther used to say, "the Pope and the Turk came up together." The seventh century was the one in which the Papal power was fully developed, in which *spiritual* "abomination that maketh desolate" was established in the *spiritual* temple, or the Christian Church, while a literal "abomination of desolation" was established in the literal sanctuary, by the erection of the Mosque of Omar on the site of the temple in Jerusalem, where it continues to this day. Thus:

1. From the rise of the *Babylonian* to the fall of the *Roman* empire was three and a half lunar "times."

2. From Nebuchadnezzar's destruction of Jerusalem and burning of the temple, in the reign of Zedekiah, to the Saracenic conquest of Palestine and capture of Jerusalem was also three and a half lunar "times."

As there are 160 years between the two first events, so are there between the two last; and the double occurrence of the remarkable 1260 years' prophetic measure in this lunar form is a seal of its importance.

The Bisection era to which we are led by these

measures, A.D. 476–637, is well marked in its limits by events of unquestionably terminal character, and it includes all the principal stages of the rise of the Papal and Mohammedan Powers. We shall consider next the

LUNAR MEASURES OF THE WHOLE "SEVEN TIMES"

The full period of "the times of the Gentiles" is not three and a half times, but seven times; we must thus extend the measuring line as far again, if we would reach the commencement of "the time of the end." And what ought we to expect at the close of this period ? We must remember that we are measuring from the *earliest* dates on the *shortest* scale, and are therefore likely to arrive at initial *termini* only. We must also remember that the era of the "time of the end" is in the nature of the case *longer* than either the Captivity era or the Bisection era. As the period runs out on two astronomical scales, differing to the extent of seventy-five years, this margin must be added to the 160 years, and the "time of the end," up to its farthest and *final* close, would thus appear to be 235 years in duration instead of 160. Hence its initial dates will be *farther removed* from its closing dates, and the initial events are likely to be *proportionately incipient in character*. We must expect then, in measuring by the lunar scale from the *earliest* date of the Nabonassar Era to reach events about 235 years prior to the full and final end of the age, and consequently indicating only the beginning of its closing movements. In other words, we are likely to reach very early stages only in the decline and fall of the Papal and Mohammedan Powers: nothing complete, nothing final, but events

12

which, regarded in the light of all that had gone before, of all that has since happened, are clearly the *first links* of a chain, which ends in the predicted overthrow of these last forms of Gentile Power.

This is exactly what we *do* reach! The year 1699, or the close of the seventeenth century, was unquestionably a most remarkable period in the history of two great and long continued struggles: first, that beween Popery and Protestantism in the West; and secondly, that between Mohammedanism and the Christian nations of Europe in the East. Two great treaties of pacification were signed at this period: the PEACE OF RYSWICK in the West, and that of CARLOWITZ in the East. We have before pointed out the nature and effect of these, and historians will at once recognise each as marking the turn of the tide, the incipient beginning of downfall and decay, the first in connexion with the Papacy, and the second in connexion with Mohammedanism.

It was not so much that either began actually to retrograde very perceptibly so early as this; but just as the Nabonassar era—the starting-point which leads us to this date—marked the rise only of that Babylonian empire which was *later on* to overthrow Israel and Judah, so this corresponding *terminus* marks the accession to superior power of the Protestant nations in the West, and of non-Moslem nations in the East. The results of the events which took place at this crisis were then dim in the future, but have since changed the condition of the world. The movements *inaugurated* at that period have never ceased but are still progressing, and now visibly nearing their close.

"The Peace of Carlowitz forms a memorable era in the history of Europe. Austria secured Hungary and

Sclavonia, which for two hundred years had been occupied by the Turks, and made the important acquisition of Transylvania. At the same time the sultans lost nearly half their possessions in Europe; and from this diminution of territorial sovereignty, the Ottoman Power, which once threatened universal subjugation, *ceased to be formidable to Europe.*" [1]

In the West, as we have seen, this period was equally critical. It saw confirmed the " glorious Revolution " and the Protestant succession in England, which put the power of Britain into the hands of the great champion of the Reformed faith, William of Orange. This Christian hero overthrew the reactionary schemes of Louis XIV., whose despotism and persecuting cruelty had roused all Europe against him. The Treaty of Ryswick, marking *the full political establishment of the Protestant religion,* was signed in 1697. Innocent XII., the Pope regnant at this date, had lost much of the old supremacy, and was indeed a mere servant to Louis XIV.; his life abounds with proofs of the fast-increasing degradation of the Papacy. France and other Papal States at this period claimed the absolute control over their own ecclesiastical affairs, and emancipated themselves from all interference by Rome. No historian will for a moment question the critical importance of the end of the seventeenth century, in connexion with Protestant ascendancy, on the one hand, and Ottoman decline, on the other.

We must next inquire, Where does the same period, "seven times" lunar, run out as measured from the *latest* date of the Captivity era, the fall of Zedekiah, B.C. 587 ? The reply is even more striking.

In A.D. 1860,—the year which, as we have seen,

[1] Coxe, *House of Austria,* vol. ii. p. 459.

witnessed the formation of the UNIVERSAL ISRAELITE ALLIANCE, as well as the first inroad on and limitation of Mohammedan power in SYRIA—the placing of the Lebanon under a Christian governor and British protectorate: events which must be regarded as marked stages of that Jewish renaissance which is as characteristic of "the time of the end" as is the fall of "Babylon the Great."

The character of this crisis was very remarkable; it was an evident *beginning* of that unification of the long scattered Jewish people predicted in Ezekiel's vision of the restoration, under the figure of bone coming to his bone. In 1860 an incipient commencement of *national reorganisation* of the Jewish *people* took place, on the one hand, and an incipient "cleansing of the sanctuary," or Holy Land, from Moslem domination, on the other.

Prophecy does not lead to the expectation that Moslem power in Turkey would cease at the end of 1260 years, for Daniel xii. 11 distinctly assigns to it a duration *thirty years longer*: "From the time that the daily sacrifice shall be taken away, *and the abomination that maketh desolate set up,* there shall be *a thousand two hundred and ninety days.*" This period ran out, *on the lunar scale,* in 1889.

The above events were not only significant as stages in Jewish renaissance, but they were also a distinct stage in the *fall of the Ottoman Power,* which was forced by Christian influence to act utterly against its Moslem principles, against the Koran, and against all precedent, in agreeing to appoint a *Christian* governor of the Lebanon province; and still more in permitting England and France to have a veto on the appointment—an admission of its own loss of *independence.* It was one of the many stages of the fall of Islam which we shall have to pass in review, but it was a marked one, and one especially connected with the land of Israel.

This year was also a decidedly critical one, as we have seen, in Italy—the great year of Garibaldi THE LIBERATOR, in which Italy was reconstituted as a kingdom under Victor Emmanuel.

This year, 1860, was not only, be it remembered, "seven times" lunar from the complete overthrow of Judah,—from the burning of the temple in Nebuchadnezzar's capture of Jerusalem,—but it was also three and a half "times" from the Omar capture of the city. In other words, the "seven times" is bisected by the *Moslem capture of Jerusalem*, and the establishment of the Mosque of Omar, which is, in a certain sense, the setting up of the "abomination that maketh desolate" in the holy place.

B.C. 747	A.D. 476	A.D. 1699
B.C. 587	A.D. 637	A.D. 1860

We see then that the "seven times," measured to the inner lunar limits, bring us unquestionably to incipient stages in the decay of the Papacy and the Porte; and that in each case the period is *bisected* by remarkable and closely related events. The bisections are even more strikingly *critical* than the termini, which are too early to bear any character of finality.

The year A.D. 476 is, beyond all question, the end of one great stage of human history; the end of the four great pagan empires of antiquity, and the beginning of another—the Papal empire of Rome, with its dark story of corruption and bloodshed; and the year A.D. 637 is equally critical as that of the fall of Jerusalem and of all Syria under Mohammedan rule, which still dominates and desolates the Holy Land and city. It is evident also that the corresponding terminal years bring to both these "Little Horns" the beginning, though only the beginning, of the end!

CHAPTER X

Solar Measures of the Seven Times

IF now, from the same two limits of the Captivity era, we measure "seven times" on the full solar scale,

B.C. 747	"seven times" solar	A.D. 1774

B.C. 587	"seven times" solar	A.D. 1934

we are led to the year A.D. 1774, and to the yet future year, A.D. 1934. That future date is the year in which the seven times will terminate on the *longest* scale, from the *latest* starting-point, and it is therefore likely to bear to the other critical years of the "time of the end" about the same proportionate importance as the last stage of the fall of Judah, under Zedekiah, bore to the earlier stages. That last stage was *not* the *crisis*, but an after-wave of the Babylonian overthrow, the great crisis of which had come eleven years previously. But of this we will speak more particularly in a subsequent section, as, avoiding final stages and future dates, we are here dealing only with preliminary stages and past dates; that is, with matter of absolute historic certainty, not with anything in the slightest degree speculative or uncertain. We are planting our feet at every step on the *terra firma* of unquestionable *fact*.

For the present then we consider only the first of these two terminal dates, A.D. 1774, a date removed by

2520 *full solar years* from the era of Nabonassar, B.C. 747.

To what crisis did this first full termination of the " seven times " lead ?

To the great crisis which is, by the common consent of all historians, regarded as the beginning of a new era in the history of European Christendom,—to the commencement of the era of retribution on the great Roman Apostasy and its head, the Papacy—to the era of THE FRENCH REVOLUTION—to the year 1774, which was that of the accession of Louis XVI. and Marie Antoinette. The French Revolution had three stages: the *preparatory* stage, in which deistical and infidel doctrines were made the basis of widespread attacks on religious faith and existing political institutions ; the *actual Revolution*, which overthrew Church and State, society and religion, royalty, nobility, clergy, laws, customs, institutions,—everything that had previously existed in France ; and lastly, *the Napoleonic stage*, which, after a series of *aggressive wars*, which upset every kingdom in Europe, dethroned the Pope and five other monarchs, created eight new ones, carried captive two Roman pontiffs, incorporated Rome in the French empire, and ended by subjecting France to a tyranny more complete than that from which it had liberated the country in the beginning. The *whole* movement may be said to have extended from Voltaire to Waterloo ; but the accession of Louis XVI. (A.D. 1774), the accession of the monarch who lost his crown and life in the crisis of the Revolution, may be regarded as the initial date of the central part of the movement. Just as, in the Captivity era, the accession of Nabonassar, the first king of Babylon, and not that of Nebuchadnezzar, the king under whom Babylon reached the climax of its glory and the height of its power, is the starting-point, so here; not the climax of the Revolution which was to overthrow the Papal Babylon, but the accession of the monarch in whose reign it took place, is the *first* point to which we are led. Alison begins his history of the French Revolution with this year 1774.

IN THE EAST this same year brought another well-marked stage in the fall of Turkey: a disastrous Russian war, closed by the fatal and humiliating TREATY OF KAINARDJE, of which we have spoken elsewhere.

Thus in the West "seven times" *solar* lead to the *French*, as "seven times" *lunar* led to the *English* Revolution,—both stages of Papal overthrow, though of widely different character; while in the East "seven times" solar lead to Kainardje, as "seven times" lunar led to Carlowitz—names which sound like death-knells in the ears of Turkish statesmen.

We may add that the previous year, 1773, witnessed the abolition of the order of the Jesuits by Pope Clement XIV., who was forced to issue a bull for the purpose, though well aware it would cost him his life, and endanger the stability of the Papal throne, of which the order had long been a mainstay. The French Revolution and the Treaty of Kainardje mark the full solar commencement of "the time of the end."

To the "seven times" prophecy adds *its own epact*, seventy-five years, or the difference between 2520 lunar years and the same number of solar years. This it adds *in two portions*, thirty years, and forty-five years.[1] It does not distinctly intimate the nature of the terminal event of these added seventy-five years, further

[1] Dan. xii. 11, 12.

than that they will bring the time of full blessedness.
This supplementary period seems to have a special
connexion with Palestine and the Jews, Daniel's people,
and is chiefly to be dated from a later point.   But just
as the oft-repeated 1260 years, or three and a half
" times," measure, as a matter of fact, other series of
events than those to which they are in Scripture
especially *applied*, so these seventy-five years can be
traced from this 1774 terminus as leading to further
stages of Papal decline and fall.   Thus " seven times "
from the earliest Nabonassar date, *plus* its own epact,
which is seventy-five years—divided as the prophecy
divides it, into two sections, the first of thirty, and the
second of forty-five years, reach down to the critical
years A.D. 1804 and 1848–9.   Thus :

1774	30 years	1804	45 years	1849

What were these years ?   A.D. 1804 was that of the
coronation of Napoleon as emperor; and this acme of
the glory of the military hero of the Revolution was
also a stage of *the deepest degradation to the Pope of
Rome.*   The emperor commanded Pius VII. to attend
the ceremony, obliging the old man to cross the Alps in
mid-winter, not to confer a crown, but merely to adorn
a ceremony.   Napoleon himself placed the crown on his
own head, and *the Pope*, who used to claim that by him
kings ruled and princes decreed judgment, *stood by, a
purposely slighted and insulted witness.*   Later on
Napoleon forced this same Pope at Fontainebleau, where
he had kept him for some time captive, to sign a
concordat, by which he renounced his temporal authority
and *all claim to Rome for ever*, and agreed to reside
in France in future, as a salaried servant of the em-

peror! This agreement did not, of course, stand after the fall of Napoleon, but it was a fatal precedent for the Papacy.

In 1849 again the Pope had to flee from Rome; driven away this time, not by foreign enemies, but by his own subjects, who could endure no longer the terrible maladministration of the priestly government, which had so long eaten like a cancer into the vitals of Rome and the States of the Church. Pius IX. was deposed, his prime minister was killed, and an Italian Republic proclaimed, under Mazzini. The violent revolutions which shook nearly *every throne in Europe* during this year 1848 seemed like the result of some *tremendous anti-Papal earthquake.* A mere catalogue of its events sufficiently attests the curiously critical character of the year, which is often called the year of European revolutions.[1]

[1] The year 1848 witnessed the French Revolution, which culminated in the abdication of Louis Philippe on February 24th. A Republic was proclaimed from the steps of the Hôtel de Ville on February 26th, and on May 26th the perpetual banishment of Louis Philippe was decreed. In June, Louis Napoleon was elected to the National Assembly, and in the same month occurred the rise of the red Republicans, the war with the troops, the 300 barricades; Paris also was in a state of siege. The national losses were 30,000,000 francs, 16,000 persons killed and wounded, and 8000 prisoners taken. Louis Napoleon was proclaimed president of the French Republic in December of the same year. The revolution broke out in Paris on February 23rd, and before March 5th every country lying between the Atlantic and the Vistula had, in a greater or less degree, been revolutionised. A little more than a fortnight after the fall of Louis Philippe a revolution took place in Rome, leading to the expulsion of the Jesuits, the assassination of the prime minister and Cardinal Palma; a constitution was proclaimed, and in November the Pope fled to Gaeta, where an asylum had been provided for him by the king of Naples; in February of the following year the Pope was

But, it will be objected, none of these events, even though reaching to the close of the added seventy-five years, are terminal; the Papacy was restored again even after 1848. True; and this is precisely what should be expected; we are measuring still only from the very *earliest* date of the Captivity era. If we want to reach the *terminus* of "the time of the end," the full and final fall of Babylon, we must calculate from the *latest* date, or at any rate from the date of the culmination of Babylonian power in the days of Nebuchadnezzar.

This we will do farther on; but in the meantime we

formally deposed from his temporal authority, and a Republic was proclaimed.

This year 1848 also witnessed a revolt in Palermo and in the eastern provinces of Lombardy, a revolution in the two Sicilies leading to the proclamation of a constitution; a similar change in Sardinia and in Tuscany; the overthrow of the Duchy of Parma; a revolution in Venice; another at Milan; the annexation of Lombardy to Piedmont; the revolt of the peasantry in Cephalonia; tumults in Vienna, involving the flight of Metternich, and the granting of a constitution by the Emperor Ferdinand, and subsequently his resignation of the crown to his nephew Francis Joseph; the king of Bavaria abdicated in favour of his son Maximilian; an insurrection at Prague on June 12th, and at Berlin on the 14th; riots and revolution in Hungary, leading to the investment of Kossuth with dictatorial powers. Schleswig-Holstein threw off the yoke and declared its own independence; the king of Holland had to revise the constitution; Cabrera was in arms in Spain; and in our country Chartist riots were an unsuccessful attempt at insurrection; while the state of things in Ireland was such that the Habeas Corpus Act had to be suspended, and numbers of men tried for high treason. Thus during the course of this one year the whole of Europe was, in a way which is unique in history, shaken by the repeated throes of a great political earthquake, which crumbled into dust the old despotic monarchies, ntroducing in their stead constitutional governments.

must measure the "seven times" from the *intermediate* dates of the Captivity era, the conquests of Shalmaneser, Sennacherib, and Esarhaddon.

The SECOND commencing date is that of the first overthrow of the ten tribes, B.C. 723, the year which witnessed the siege of Samaria by Shalmaneser.

B.C. 723	"seven times" solar	A.D. 1798

This terminus, if our system is well founded, ought to lead to a more marked *stage* of the overthrow of the Papacy, in connexion with the French Revolution. It is only needful to turn to Alison, or any other historian of the period, to see that it did so.

"The object of the French directory (in 1798) was the destruction of the pontifical government, as the irreconcilable enemy of the Republic. They urged their general to drive the Pope and cardinals out of Rome. Buonaparte proposed to give the Eternal City to the king of Spain, on condition of his recognising the French Republic. Failing in this, he resorted to a system of pillage, which exhausted its resources, and finally a democratic demonstration was got up at Rome in the accustomed manner, in which one of the French envoys was killed by the fire of the pontifical troops. This misfortune afforded the desired pretext. The French army, pouring in under Berthier, planted the tricolor on the Capitol, while their Roman confederates, displaying the famous insignia, S.P.Q.R., shouted for liberty. The aged Pope was summoned to surrender the temporal government; on his refusal he was *dragged from the altar, and the soldiers plundered the Vatican in the presence of its owner.* They stripped his own chamber; when he asked to be left to die in peace, he was brutally answered that any place would serve to die in. His rings were torn from off his fingers, and finally, *after declaring the temporal power abolished,* the victors carried the Pope prisoner into Tuscany, whence he never returned.

"The Papal States, converted into the *Roman Republic,* were declared to be in perpetual alliance with France; but the French general was the real master at Rome. The citizens groaned under his terrible exactions. Churches, convents, palaces, were stripped to the bare walls. The works of art were nearly all carried off. The territorial possessions of the clergy and monks were declared national property, and the former owners cast into prison. *The Papacy was extinct* ; not a vestige of its existence remained ; and among all the Roman Catholic powers not a finger was stirred in its defence. The Eternal City had no longer prince or pontiff ; its bishop was a dying captive in foreign lands ; and the decree was already announced that no successor would be allowed in his place."

From the year when these scenes of judgment were enacted in Rome "seven times" carry us back to the year of the invasion and ravages of Shalmaneser, the proud monarch of Assyria. Is this accident or design ?

The THIRD critical date of the Captivity era was, as we have seen, that of the invasion of Sennacherib. This was a question of four or five years, as his ravages of the land of Israel, and subsequently of that of Judah, were extended over several campaigns, from B.C. 713 to B.C. 708.

If now from these four or five years of the military ravages of Sennacherib we measure "seven times," to what corresponding events in the time of the end are we led ?

| B.C. 713–8 | "seven times" solar | A.D. 1808–12 |

To the campaigns of the European prototype of Sennacherib, the modern scourge and destroyer of nations, Napoleon Buonaparte, employed by the hand of Providence as leader of the infidel host of revolutionary France against the Papal nations,—to the years in which he carried rapine and slaughter into all the kingdoms of Europe.

This is surely a most remarkable coincidence! The awful devastating and destructive wars of Napoleon, between 1808 and 1812, terminated in a catastrophe not unlike the one which befell the host of Sennacherib, by the loss of an army twice as numerous among the snows of Russia. Out of nearly half a million of men whom he took over the Niemen, only about three thousand returned to recross that stream! In the course of the years from 1804-1814 no less than ten millions of men—a number absolutely inconceivable by the mind—fell on both sides in these wars, the money cost of which was besides incalculable, and the effects of which have never been recovered by France.

Both Sennacherib and Napoleon were in the zenith of their power and glory when they started on these campaigns which ended so fatally. Sennacherib's ravages formed a marked stage in the *fall* of Judah, which, though spared at the time, never recovered the shock; and Napoleon's campaigns were a *most* marked stage in that course of events which is bringing about the *restoration* of Judah and Israel in these days. It was under the strain produced by these wars that the naval power and vast colonial empire of Protestant England, and the enormous military power and Asiatic empire of Russia, were developed to their present marvellous expansion, while the Latin nations lost ground in proportion. The effect on the Jews we have already noted. The interval between the principal campaigns of these two great conquerors is precisely the great week, or "seven times"—2520 years on the full solar scale.

The FOURTH critical date of the Captivity era is the completion of the deportation of the ten tribes under

Esarhaddon, B.C. 676. " Seven times " solar from this date
lead to A.D. 1844, while " seven times " lunar from B.C. 602
(Nebuchadnezzar) terminate in the same date A.D. 1844,
and are bisected by the date of the Hegira, A.D. 622.

B.C. 676	"seven times" solar			A.D. 1844
B.C. 602	3¼ times lunar	A.D. 622	3¼ times lunar	1844

In this case both the central and terminal dates are
critical in connexion with that Mohammedan power
which has for more than twelve centuries trodden
down Jerusalem.   The central one is that of the
HEGIRA ERA itself, the date from which the entire
Moslem world reckons to this day, as we do from
Anno Domini; and the terminal date is that of the
Hatti Hamayoun, or decree of religious toleration
wrung by the Christian Powers of Europe from the
Ottoman Government.   In 1844 the Porte was compelled, under threat of European interference, to issue
this edict abolishing for ever its characteristic and
sanguinary practice of execution for the adoption of
Christianity.   This compulsory sheathing of its persecuting sword was a patent proof that its independence
was gone, and a marked era in its overthrow.   As the
Mohammedans employ a strictly *lunar* year, A.D. 1844
is the 1260th in their calendar.

THE FIRST AND THE EIGHTH YEARS OF NEBUCHAD-
NEZZAR are the remaining intermediate starting-points
in the Captivity era.   In both these years he besieged
and took Jerusalem, and in both he led large numbers
of Jews captive to Babylon.   The Jehoiakim stage took
place in B.C. 606–5, and the more serious Jehoiachin

stage in B.C. 598. This latter is probably the *principal* crisis in the whole captivity era, as we have before shown. Both years witnessed complete overthrows of Jewish power by Nebuchadnezzar, that singularly typical, self-exalting monarch, who stands as the express image of the Papal dynasty of these latter days. There were other monarchs of Babylon, but HE was the great and typical one. There were other destroyers of Jerusalem, but HE was the fated and final one. Sennacherib and Shalmaneser exalted themselves against God, and persecuted His people; but Nebuchadnezzar exceeded. He is represented as the *great* incarnation of human power and pride. It was he who made a great image of himself, and commanded the world to worship it, and heated the burning fiery furnace of persecution "seven times hotter than it was wont to be heated," for the torture and destruction of those who would not bow down to the idol he had made, or worship the image which he had set up. It was he who boasted in his pride, "Is not this great Babylon, that I have built for the house of the kingdom by the might of my power, and for the honour of my majesty?" It is he who was predicted as the destroyer of the city and temple of God, and against whose city of Babylon such tremendous judgments were denounced. In a word, it is he who is the great *type* of the terrible Papal Antichrist of prophecy and history.

His campaigns consequently against Judah and Jerusalem are the specially important ones; and after the lapse of "seven times" from *them*, we are likely to reach the centre and crisis of Jewish restoration. From the date of his overthrow of the nation, and desolation of the land, we may expect "Seven Times" to lead to an important stage in the restoration of the people of Judah to their land; and from the date of his overthrow of the *throne* of Judah, we may expect "Seven Times" to lead to a like stage in the restoration of that throne; while from his burning of the temple and breaking down of the wall of Jerusalem, we may expect "Seven Times" to lead, it may be, to the restoration of temple and city.

Nebuchadnezzar's three campaigns against Judah took place in the first, the eighth, and the nineteenth years of his reign, extending over a period of nineteen years. The dates of these campaigns were:

B.C.

606–5.   Conquest of Jehoiakim.   Loss of Jewish independence.

598.   Overthrow of Jehoiachin.   Fall of the throne of Judah.

587.   Burning of the temple and complete destruction of Jerusalem in the days of Zedekiah.

From these three dates "seven times" run out on the solar, calendar, and lunar scales as follows:

B.C. 606	Lunar	A.D. 1840
	Calendar	1878–9
	Solar	
		1915

B.C. 598	Lunar	A.D. 1848
	Calendar	1887
	Solar	
		1923

B.C. 587	Lunar	A.D. 1859–60
	Calendar	1898
	Solar	
		1934

It will be observed that the full solar termini from all these three dates do not run out until the early part of the twentieth century. All of the three calendar ran out last century. We postpone any remark on the still future dates to a closing section of this work.

As to those already past, "seven times" calendar from the *first* starting-point brought the year 1878, the year of the Berlin Conference, which, with the war that preceded it, was beyond all question *a very marked stage* in the downfall of the Ottoman Power,—a stage in that dismemberment of Turkey which is to end in the liberation of Palestine from its present oppressor.

By the Treaty of San Stefano a large portion of Armenia (Turkey in Asia) was ceded to Russia, the Dobrudcha was lost to Turkey, the complete independence of Roumania was recognised, the limits of Servia and Montenegro were extended, and Bulgaria was erected into an autonomous Christian principality. The provisions of this treaty were subsequently modified at the Berlin Conference, which divided the province of Bulgaria, refusing independence to that portion of it south of the Balkans; an arrangement which was overthrown in 1885. The signature of the Treaty of Berlin was preceded by the Anglo-Turkish Convention, under which, in return for *the cession of Cyprus to England* — a further step in the dismemberment of Turkey—this country undertook to defend the Turkish possessions in Asia, including the Holy Land, against Russian aggression, the Porte promising necessary reforms, subject to British approval. These reforms have, of course, never been effected.

The year 1878 was also that of the death of Pius IX., the last Pope wielding temporal power.

It is also noteworthy that "seven times" calendar

measured from B.C. 606, the first of Nebuchadnezzar, is,
like the "seven times" lunar from B.C. 587, his last
overthrow of Judah, bisected by the Omar capture of
Jerusalem.

	"seven times" calendar	
B.C. 606	A.D. 637	A.D. 1878–9

	"seven times" lunar	
B.C. 587	A.D. 637	A.D. 1859–60

Thus these two periods, though starting from different
dates—the beginning and end of the nineteen years of
Nebuchadnezzar's overthrow of Jerusalem,—and reaching different termini by different scales, meet in this
central date of the Omar capture of Jerusalem.

As to the briefer and earlier lunar *termini* of the
"seven times" from the Nebuchadnezzar starting-
points, they are all past, 1840, 1848, and 1859–60; and
each of these years unquestionably witnessed stages of
decay and fall either of the Papal or Mohammedan
Power, or of both.

In A.D. 1840 *Egypt* was virtually lost to the Porte.
Mehemet Ali, the wise, despotic, powerful, and warlike
viceroy of the country, had been in rebellion against the
Sultan since 1831, when his forces invaded Syria, and he
defeated the Turks in the decisive battle of Konieh
(1832). He had been remarkably successful in his
career, and with the help of his son Ibrahim had conquered Syria, Arabia, Candia, and a considerable part of
Asia Minor. The Turkish fleet, which had been sent
against him, was by treachery surrendered to him at
Alexandria in 1839, and the empire of the Osmanlis
seemed menaced with dismemberment, if not ruin.
Under these circumstances, the Powers of Europe intervened, and the British fleet took Sidon, Beyrout, and
St. Jean d'Acre. Mehemet Ali had to submit to their

dictation, and surrender some of his conquests; but he obtained from the Sultan *the hereditary possession of Egypt* and the life governorship of Syria as far as the north of the Lake of Tiberias. The treaty was signed in the month of *July* 1840, and was a great stage in the dismemberment of Turkey, Egypt and Syria being two of her finest and most important provinces.

The second lunar terminus is the year 1848, of which we have already spoken in another connexion; its importance in the movement we are considering, the fall of Papal and despotic power, is conspicuous. Such a year of revolution was probably never known in Europe before or since. So strange and unaccountable was the revolutionary fever which broke out in Christendom that it attracted everywhere a marvelling attention. One nation caught it from another; the infection spread very rapidly, and produced a kind of political delirium; constitutional freedom was everywhere demanded, and everywhere granted. In many of these revolutionary movements emancipated Jews took a leading part; as, for instance, Fould, Crémieux, and Goudchaux in France, Pincherle in Vienna, Jacobi in Berlin, Riesser in Frankfort, Fischhof in Austria, and Freund in Hungary.

That this year was a great prophetic crisis may be gathered from the fact that four distinct periods terminate in it:

1. "Seven times" solar from the era of Nabonassar, with the added seventy-five years (Dan. xii. 11).

2. "Seven times" lunar from the Jehoiachin date.

3. "Time, times, and a half," or 1260 solar years, from the bisection date of Gregory the Great.

4. The same period *calendar* from the bisection date of the Pope-exalting decree of the Emperor Phocas.

We may add also that, dated from this critical year,

Diagram of the Periods of "Seven Times" and "Three and a Half Times," terminating in A.D. 1848-9.

30 years.   45 years.

A.D. 1774.   1804.   1848-9.

Nabonassar,
B.C. 747

2520 years solar+75 years.

1849

Jehoiachin
B.C. 598

2520 years lunar

1849

Gregory I.,
A.D. 590

1260 years solar

1849

Phocas,
A.D. 607

1260 years calendar

1849

seventy-five years more bring us to 1923, the full solar close from the principal date of the Captivity era, that of Jehoiachin—the great Ezekiel starting-point.

Of the year 1860 we have already spoken fully, so need not here repeat its events.

The three final Nebuchadnezzar dates of the Captivity era give rise in the terminal era of the "time of the end" to nine years of crisis: three at the *lunar*, three at the *calendar*, and three at the *full solar* close of "seven times" from the three starting-points. Of these nine those we have now considered, being only imperfect lunar and calendar closes of the great period, the crises in the fall of Babylon the Great and Islam, to which they conduct us, have *no character of finality about them*. That is natural, and must be so, if the system we seek to unfold be the true one. The end is not yet; we must for it await the full solar close of "seven times" from these dates.

CHAPTER XI

MEASURES OF THE SECOND HALF OF THE SEVEN TIMES

WE must next note a number of deeply interesting facts connected with the measures of the SECOND HALF of this great dispensational week of "seven times"—facts which seem to indicate that the oft-repeated "time, times, and a half" is adjusted, like the whole period, to run out on the three astronomical scales, and to lead, in a similar way, to successive stages of the predicted historical movements.

The bisection dates of the rise of the Papacy are, as we have shown, especially the following :—

A.D. 533. Justinian's Pope-exalting decree.
   „ 590. Accession of Gregory the Great.
   „ 607. Decree of Phocas (see p. 80).
   „ 663. Vitalian's Latinising decree.

Now from these dates, *as starting-points*, measure on the three astronomic scales the "time, times, and a half" of the predicted duration of the Papacy.

The result is three groups of dates, the two first of which are all connected with Papal overthrow in the most definite and unquestionable manner.

The first group consists of, first, Voltaire's literary incendiarism; secondly, the accession of Louis XVI. and Marie Antoinette; and thirdly, the reign of terror.

A. D. 533	Lunar	1755
	Calendar	1774–5
	Solar	
		1793

A.D. 607	Lunar	1830
	Calendar	1848–9
	Solar	
		1867–70

A.D. 663	Lunar	1885
	Calendar	1905
	Solar	
		1923

The second group gives the dates of the anti-Papal revolutions, which caused—

1. The abdication of Charles X., after the three days' war of the barricades in Paris and the victory of the people. Belgium became independent this same year; Saxony, Hesse Cassel, Mannheim, Weimar, Hanau, and Jena all obtained from their rulers constitutional government; and the Papal chair was for two months vacant.

2. The remarkable set of anti-Papal revolutions eighteen years later, 1848, the year of the great revolutionary earthquake before alluded to.

3. The year 1870—the final fall of the temporal power. The four years 1866–70 witnessed the *final* stage in the overthrow of the long-falling temporal power of the Papacy. The first Napoleon had dealt it heavy blows, blows of such stunning force that it seemed almost dead. But it still possessed some vitality, and revived for a time. The injuries received had nevertheless been fatal, and the recovery was more in appearance than reality.

The powerful reactionary policy of the allies, and the fears of the generation which had witnessed the French Revolution, and of the succeeding one, threw back the cause of liberty and the progress of nations for a time. The former tyrannies were reinstated, and maintained with a vigilance born of fear; and just as France had to submit to the old Bourbon despotism, so Rome had for a time to submit again to the Popes. The submission, however, was an unwilling and restless one during the whole period from the peace of 1815 to the overthrow of 1870. Italian aspirations for national unity and for political liberty—kindled by the French Revolution, and quickened by subsequent ones and by the examples of other nations—formed a powerful factor in the question. The Popes adopted a line of conduct which could not have been better chosen had they desired to secure their own overthrow. They had learned no lesson from the adversity they had suffered.

Pius IX., who became Pope in 1846, attempted at first some liberal reforms, and had he continued this policy he might have staved off the evil day. But it was not to be; the long impending downfall was to reach its close during his pontificate, and, all unwittingly to himself, he consistently acted as if he wished to hasten it. The adversities of his predecessor, and his own, had taught him no wisdom. Even after the revolution of 1848, which made him for two years an exile, he pursued the same tyrannical course. When in 1850 he returned to Rome, under the protection of French soldiery, his policy became only more suicidal than ever. He re-established the Jesuits, reopened the dungeons of the Inquisition, and deliberately set himself to re-organise the European commonwealth on the model of the darkest days of the dark ages. On his own sole

authority, without the concurrence even of a council—
a thing that no Pope had ever done before—he added a
new dogma to the faith of the universal Church, the
doctrine of the "Immaculate Conception," which all men
were required, on pain of damnation, to receive. He
reorganised a Roman Catholic hierarchy for Protestant
England, and busied himself in canonising saints and
gathering around him in Rome numerous and imposing
bodies of bishops and dignitaries from every part of the
world. He enforced in Rome a law prohibiting Protestant worship, save at the embassies; persecuted those
who dared to read the Scriptures in the social circle;
and at last compiled and published his famous *Syllabus*;
gathered his great Œcumenical Council of the Vatican;
so managed it that the assembled archbishops, princes,
cardinals, patriarchs, bishops, abbots, generals of orders,
etc., had no liberty even to discuss the great question
brought before them, but were fraudulently forced to
pronounce in favour of the monstrous dogma of Papal
infallibility. This new canon of the Roman Catholic
Church was decreed July 1870.

The blindness of the Roman pontiff and his hierarchy
to the truth, to the temper of the times, to the state of
Europe, and to the doom immediately impending over
them, was complete. A strange, judicial insanity seemed
to have befallen them. Men marvelled at their madness,
and Bible students recalled the solemn statement of the
apostle about this Romish Apostasy—that because they
would not receive the truth of the gospel in the love of
it, therefore God would send them, in judgment, strong
delusion, so that they would believe a lie, to their own
condemnation and ruin.

Very speedily was the blasphemy of this infallibility
decree rebuked by the Most High! The same day that

it was published, there was dispatched from Paris to Berlin the declaration of war which sealed the fate of the second French empire, and *with it that of the temporal power of the Papacy.* On July 18th, 1870, the day on which the Pope read, amid the thunder and lightning of an awful storm, the decree which marked the climax of Papal pretension, the announcement of his own infallibility, Napoleon III. dispatched his challenge to Germany. We know what followed: how Protestant Prussia humbled herself before God by a day of special prayer on the 27th, and besought His blessing on her quickly gathering armies; how the emperor of Roman Catholic France, accompanied by his unfortunate boy, assumed the next day the command of the wretchedly organised French troops; how the Germans defeated the French, both at Weissembourg and at Geisburg, on August 4th, and on the 6th at Wörth and Forbach; how they bombarded Strasburg and defeated Bazaine, and drove him back into Metz, gained another great victory at Gravelotte, and forced the emperor and the entire army into SEDAN, where, on September 2nd, they had to surrender, and were all taken prisoners; how 300,000 men marched on Paris, and establishing their headquarters at Versailles, besieged it in September; how other German armies overran all France; how Bazaine had to surrender Metz and 173,000 men in October; and how, before the end of the year, France lay bleeding and prostrate at the feet of her Protestant foes, without an army in the field or an ally in Europe. And we know also how, long before this crisis arrived in France—Rome having been evacuated by the French troops, which were sorely needed at home—the pontifical government fell, to rise no more. The king of Italy forewarned the Pope of his intention to occupy

Rome on September 8th, and did so in the following
month. Rome decided, by an overwhelming vote, for
union with Italy, and was, with its surrounding territories, incorporated by royal decree with the Italian
kingdom in October 1870.

*This was the full and final fall of the temporal
power of the Papacy.* It was on the day of the last
meeting of the council which had deified a man by
declaring him possessed of the Divine attribute of
infallibility that Victor Emmanuel's announcement
reached Rome; it was on the day that the German
armies closed round Paris that the Italian general
Cadorna invested Rome. The struggle lasted but a
few hours; the Pope understood that further resistance
would be mere wanton waste of life, for his Zouaves
numbered but 8000, and 50,000 Italians were arrayed
against him. As soon as a breach had been made
in the walls of Rome, the word to surrender was
given.

"There, yea, there, on the proud dome of St. Peter's, being
raised, and beginning to flutter, was the white flag; and there,
unwinding itself, did it float out upon the September breeze, and
waved in the forenoon sun—waved over pontiff and cardinal, over
the circus of Nero and the inquisition of the popes. Was it real?
Eyes would be wiped to see if they did not deceive. Eyes—ay,
the eyes of soldiers—would be wiped from thick, hot tears. Could
it be—could it ever be? Come at last! The hour for which ages
had impatiently waited, for which myriads of Italians had died.
Italy one! Her arms, outstretched from Etna and Monte Rosa,
clasping at last every one of her children; and even availing, by
their returning strength, to lift up her poor old Rome from under
the load of the priest and the stranger.

"He who two brief months before had, amid deep darkness at
noon-day, read out by artificial light the decree of his own un-
limited power and irreformable law, lay down that night amid
a rude and intrusive glare streaming from across the Tiber into

the multitudinous windows of the Vatican. It came from the lights of Rome, all ablaze with illuminations for the fall of the temporal power." [1]

Even so Romanist an authority as Cardinal Manning admits that *this* fall is unlike any of the previous preliminary temporary falls. He says: "There is one point in which the present crisis of the Holy See and of the Christian Church differs from all that has gone before it. Always in the ages past, when one or more of the European Powers were in conflict with the Holy See, one or more of the other powers were friendly and gave it protection. Now not one stands in its defence; they have all with one accord hid their faces from the vicar of our Lord; they are all consenting to the deed. The princes and rulers of Christendom have forsaken their Master, and their silence in the hour of danger is right. Never till now have all the nations of Europe consented in the deed of the nations who have usurped Rome. Never till now has the public law of Europe been changed to sanction the usurpation. For the first time the HEAD OF CHRISTENDOM is excluded from the senate of Christian sovereigns, though the temporal sovereignty of the supreme pontiff is of Divine institution." [2]

Chronologically the four last years of the temporal power of the Papacy were removed from the four last years of the Emperor Phocas, whose decree appointed the Pope to the headship of all the Christian Churches, by

"TIME, TIMES, AND A HALF,"

or, 1260 full solar years. The decree of Phocas,

[1] Rev. W. Arthur, M.A., *The Pope, the Kings, and the People.*
[2] Manning, *Temporal Power*, Preface, p. xiii, Third Edition.

memorialised by a pillar still standing in Rome, was given in A.D. 607, and the emperor died in A.D. 610.

A.D. 606-10.	1260 years, solar	1866-70

The whole course of these four years was filled with events singularly fatal to the Papacy, including overthrows of Catholic Austria, Spain, France, and the Papal States of Italy. The decisive battle of Sadowa, in 1866, between Protestant Prussia and Papal Austria, settled the question of ascendancy in Central Europe in favour of Prussia and Protestantism, and that for the first time in history. The conspicuous loss of power in all Papal countries was crowned at last, when the prophetic period had fully run out, by the final overthrow of the secular power of the Popes in Rome itself. The year 1866 was the 1260th solar year from the *decree*, and 1870 the 1260th from the *death*, of Phocas.

Can any one suppose that these things happen by accident? Consider what a combination is here! Far back, at the beginning of the dark ages, a wicked usurper and murderer, thinking perhaps to atone for his crimes, presumes to bestow a prerogative which pertains to Christ alone—the headship of all the Christian Churches East and West—on the bishop of the ancient seat of the empire, ROME; and the ambitious and worldly-minded bishop dares to accept the gift, and seat himself in the temple of God, as if he *were* God. Divine prophecy had foretold, more than a thousand years before, the uprising of this power at this period, and had foretold also that it should endure in the Roman world for 1260 years. We pass on through the centuries, and note how this same power grows greater and greater, till it wields an authority mightier than that of the Caesars at the pinnacle of their glory, for it rules

over two hundred millions of mankind, and, according to
its own account, rules not in earth only, but in heaven
and in hell. We note how the saints are given into its
hand, and perish by millions at its instigation. We
note how all the monarchs of the Roman world give it
their voluntary submission for centuries, and how at last
they rebel against it, and seek to overthrow it; how
they succeed in doing this time after time, though not
fully or finally, till, when eleven centuries have been
left behind us, we see this Power declining and failing.
Twelve pass away; it is weaker still! Will it last out
to a thirteenth? No; its duration is fixed at 1260
years. We scan its condition more closely. Fall succeeds fall; yet it rises again, or rather, is helped up
again. The last four years are come; it still stands
trembling. The fateful year is ushered in. Its first
six months pass, and there is no sign of a crash; mid-
summer comes, and, lo! the storm breaks, and before
winter appears all is over—as a reigning dynasty in
Europe it has fallen, to rise no more! Is not this the
finger of God?

Another fact should also be noted here. From this
notable date of the fall of the most idolatrous, corrupt,
and persecuting Power which the world has ever seen,
the Power which, in the ancient prediction of Daniel vii.
is represented as the cause of the destruction of the
Roman world,—from the fall of the temporal power of
the Papacy, we go back "seven times"; and where do
we land in the remote Captivity era of Israel and Judah?
In the reign of *Manasseh*, whose sins are especially
assigned as the provoking cause of the Babylonian overthrow. Of him it is said, in 2 Kings xxi.—

1. That he went to the greatest lengths in idolatry,
introducing carved images into the very temple of God,

14

restoring the altars and groves which his father Hezekiah had destroyed, making his son pass through the fire, and worshipping and serving all the host of heaven.

2. That he imitated and even exceeded the wickedness of the heathen round about him in their ways, and seduced his subjects to follow his example, until they were more corrupt and abominable than the Canaanites whom the Lord had cast out before Israel.

3. That he filled Jerusalem from one end to the other with innocent blood.

It is scarcely needful to point out that in all these points, idolatry, corruption, and bloodshed, as well as in his being the cause of the ruin of Judah, this Manasseh was a most striking type of the Papal antichrist, who filled the Church with image and saint worship and mariolatry, with indulgences and corruptions, and with persecution and bloodshed.

B.C. 650	A.D. 610	A.D. 1870

EASTERN BISECTION DATES

If we take now the two bisection dates which have to do with the rise of the Mohammedan Power and the Eastern Question, instead of with the rise of the Roman Papacy in the West, we shall find that three and a half "times," both from the Hegira era and the Omar capture of Jerusalem lead down to years which witnessed stages of overthrow of the Ottoman Power. The Mohammedan calendar is, as we have said, strictly lunar, and dates from the Hegira era, as our calendar, which is solar, dates from *Anno Domini*. Measuring 1260 years from the Hegira, we reach on the lunar scale 1844, and on the solar 1882.

A.D. 622	1260 Lunar Years	1844
	1260 Solar Years	
		1882

It will be remembered that the first of these years, 1844, was that of the Turkish Hatti Hamayoun, or enforced decree of religious toleration—a decree, the granting of which was a proof of the complete loss of independence of the Porte; and 1882 was the year which witnessed the bombardment of Alexandria, the notable victory of Tel-el-Kebir, and the occupation of Cairo, the total defeat of the Mohammedan rebellion, and the virtual establishment of an English protectorate in Egypt—a movement, the whole of which was a heavy blow to the Porte, as her authority was through it, virtually though not nominally, brought to an end in Egypt.

From the second bisection date, the Omar capture of Jerusalem, A.D. 637, three and a half "times" have already run out on all three scales, lunar, calendar, and solar.

A.D. 637	Lunar	1860
	Calendar	
		1877–8
	Solar	
		1897

The first of these years was, as we have already shown, a most critical one in the history of the Porte and in the history of the Jews. It was the first stage in the liberation of the Holy Land from direct Turkish rule,—an early stage in the cleansing of the sanctuary from the power of the desolater; and it was also the year of the formation of the "Universal Israelite Alliance," an initial step towards Jewish national re-organisation. The action of England and France in

Syria on this occasion must be considered a marked stage in the decline of the Ottoman Power, as each such interference with its governmental action is an additional demonstration to the world of its loss of independence.

Though having mainly to do with the East, this year was, as we have seen, a critical one in the West also. It was the year of Garibaldi's victories in Italy, and of the proclamation of the first Italian king who reigned over that long-divided and priest-ridden land since the days of the old Roman empire. The calendar termination from this Omar date is the year 1878, the year of the Berlin Conference, with its wholesale dismemberment of Turkey. The remaining solar termination was the year in which Crete was lost to Turkey.

CHAPTER XII

THE SANCTUARY CYCLE

A SECOND long period of time, "2300 days," or years, is, in the third vision of Daniel (chap. viii.) announced by the "wonderful numberer" who makes the revelation. It was given in reply to a question with regard to the duration of that taking away of the restored daily sacrifice, and that casting down of the restored sanctuary which had just been foretold as destined to take place, and to continue until "the time of the end," or "the last end of the indignation"; that is, until the period of Divine wrath against the Jewish people should terminate, until the close of the present Gentile age. The question and answer are recorded as follows :—

"How long shall be the vision concerning the daily sacrifice, and the transgression of desolation, to give both the sanctuary and the host to be trodden under foot ?

"And he said unto me, Unto two thousand and three hundred days ; then shall the sanctuary be cleansed. . . . Understand, O son of man : for at *the time of the end* shall be the vision. . . . And he said, Behold, I will make thee know what shall be in *the last end of the indignation : for at the time appointed the end shall be* " (Dan. viii. 13–19).

In order to the clearer comprehension of the nature of this predicted period, its position in the Book of Daniel must be borne in mind. It is one of the *later* and not one of the earlier group of visions ; one belonging to the days of the Persians, not to those of the Babylonians; to the Restoration era, not to the Captivity era.

It is a remarkable fact that the Book of Daniel is written in two different languages. It opens in Hebrew ; but from chapter ii. 4 to the end of chapter vii. is Aramaic in the original, the remainder of the book reverting to the Hebrew. Thus the prophecies of the "times of the Gentiles" are given in Gentile Aramaic, and the employment of Hebrew in the remaining predictions seems to indicate that the events foretold in them are viewed from a more Jewish standpoint, and that the revelation has a more direct reference to the Jewish people and the Holy Land. On examination such is found to be the case. The "times of the Gentiles" have, of course, a certain relation to the Jews, as they measure the twenty-five centuries of their subjection to Gentile power; but their details are given from a distinctly Gentile point of view. They start with the literal, and end with the spiritual Babylon, and have to do mainly with the four great Gentile monarchies, and in the fourth, with the western and not the eastern empire of Rome. The kingdom of God in which they terminate embraces, of course, both Jews and Gentiles, each in their separate sphere, as we learn from other Scriptures.

But with the three last prophecies of Daniel the case is somewhat different. The second—the celebrated prophecy of the Seventy Weeks in chapter ix.—foretells the events of history from a decidedly Jewish point of view. The Redeemer of mankind at large was recognised and anticipated by the Jews principally as their Messiah. He was to be the Consolation of Israel, the Lion of the tribe of Judah, the Prince of the house of

David; and in this prophecy He is mentioned harmoniously as "Messiah the Prince." The destruction of Jerusalem by Titus, and the long desolation of Judæa, are predicted at the close of the prophecy; the establishment of the new covenant, or new testament, with many is also foretold; but there is no intimation of the fact that it was to be established with Gentiles as well as with Jews, for the calling of the Gentiles was to be a mystery until the days of Paul (Eph. iii.).

The other two of the later visions of Daniel, in the former of which occurs the period we are now considering, are similarly sketched from Jewish, and not Gentile, standpoints. The western empire of Rome is scarcely alluded to. Eastern history and the Eastern Apostasy are the subject-matter of the predictions. Gentile action is, of course, abundantly described: the conquests of Medo-Persia, the wars of Xerxes and Alexander the Great, the cruelties of Antiochus, the struggles of the Seleucidæ and the Ptolemies. *Eastern* rather than western events are foretold in detail, but all in their relation to the Jewish people and their sanctuary, the Holy Land and city and temple of Jerusalem. The people of God contemplated are mainly the Jews, in their dispersion and in their restoration; and the eastern empire of Rome and the Moslem Power replace in these visions the Papal Power, which figures so largely in the "times of the Gentiles."

We may not pause here to justify these statements, though it were an easy task to do so, as we are not writing an exposition of the Book of Daniel, but have limited ourselves in these pages to an elucidation of the *chronological* rather than of the historical portion of the prophecy, the portion which it is especially stated ' the wise shall understand " in these last days. But it is

needful to premise thus much, as regards the scope of
these later visions, in order to introduce in its place this
most important period, connected with the still future
restoration of Israel, when the sanctuary shall be
cleansed.

Careful students of Scripture, who have reflected at
all on these topics, must have observed that in the Book
of Revelation there is comparatively little about the
Jews and their restoration, that subject having been
fully treated in the Old Testament. The Saracenic
invasion and the Turkish overthrow are indeed predicted in Revelation, for the Fifth and Sixth Trumpets
are universally recognised as prefiguring the sore " woes "
which were inflicted on the apostate Christian Church
of the East by these desolating Powers. But the
Mohammedan conquests are there viewed in connexion
with the Christian Churches of the East, and not in
connexion with Syria and the Jews. Yet they stand in
a most important relation to Israel also, and in *this*
connexion they are presented in Daniel viii. It is as
the desolater of *Jerusalem,* and the ruler of *Judœa* for
twelve centuries, that this Moslem Power principally
affects Israel; it occupies the Holy Land and treads
down Jerusalem, and has done so ever since A.D. 637,
when the Caliph Omar first brought the country under
subjection to Mohammedan despotism.

Now just as the Papacy could not be developed while
the emperors were ruling at Rome, so the Jews cannot
be restored while the Turks are masters in Jerusalem;
the one Power must needs fall before the other can rise.
The promised land must be freed from Moslem occupation before it can revert to its lawful heirs, the seed of
Abraham. Hence the Mohammedan Power has a double
relation: it has been, and is, the cruel foe of Christians;

it has been, and is, the obstacle in the way of Israel's restoration. Its removal, under Divine judgment, must therefore figure prominently in prophecies of Jewish restoration in the last times; just as largely as the removal of the Papal Apostasy, under similar judgments, in the predictions of the deliverance of the Gentile Church, prior to the establishment of the kingdom of God on earth.

The Moslem Power has merited judgment as much as the Roman Apostasy. Its cruelties, its corruptions, its massacres and its oppressions, its opposition to the truth, its persecutions, its wide dominion and long duration make it a marvellously suitable companion to the Papacy. But its sphere is the East, and not the West; its city is Constantinople, and not Rome; and its destruction bears a closer relation to Jewish questions than to Christian ones.

It should be noted further that both in Daniel and in Revelation this foe is represented as destroyed, not by the brightness of Christ's coming, not suddenly in an hour like "Babylon the Great," but as perishing by inherent decay—"he shall be broken without hand"; "he shall come to his end, and none shall help him"; and under the symbol of the Euphrates, "the waters thereof were dried up." This, as is well known, is, and has been, the characteristic fate of the Ottoman empire. Europe would fain have arrested its decay if she could; she would not suffer any enemy wantonly to attack Turkey; she would not permit it to be roughly overthrown in selfish aggression. From motives of policy she would fain have upheld it in its position, but found it impossible. Corruption and death are working in the body politic; vitality is failing at the centre; and Ottoman dominion must,

in spite of every effort, soon cease to exist. It is like
a patient already drawing his last breath; it has
still a name to live politically, but it is virtually
dead. One by one its own provinces are dropping
off, and it is becoming evident to all politicians
that nothing can arrest its ultimate extinction. The
historian Lamartine long since perceived this, and
wrote:

"I wish that Turkey may not perish, that an extensive empire
may not be trampled down to nothing, or driven into the deserts
of Asia. But what is the state of the case? Plains without
ploughs, seas without vessels, rivers without bridges, lands without possessors, villages built with mud and clay, a capital of
wood, ruins of desolation on all sides, are what constitute the
Ottoman empire. In the midst of this ruin and desolation which
they have made, and make daily, some thousands of the Turks
in each province—all concentrated in the towns, drowsy, dis-
couraged, never working, living miserably upon the spoils of
Christian and laborious races—constitute the inhabitants and
masters of the empire; and that empire is alone worth the whole
of Europe. Its sky is finer, its earth more fertile, its ports more
extensive and more safe, its productions more precious and more
varied, than those of any other country; it contains 60,000 square
leagues. You see by this rapid sketch that the Ottoman empire
is no empire at all; that it is a misshapen agglomeration of
different races, without cohesion between them, without mutual
interests, without a language, without laws, without religion, and
without unity or stability of power. You see that the breath of
life which animated it—religious fanaticism—is extinct; you see
that its fatal and blind administration has devoured the very race
of conquerors, and that TURKEY IS PERISHING FOR WANT OF
TURKS!"

There is a difference in the chronological as well as
in the linguistic and historic features of the two portions
of Daniel. The characteristic measure of the "times
of the Gentiles," "seven times," does not appear in this
prediction of the cleansing of the sanctuary in the

eighth chapter; we find instead this other period of 2300 years,—a period 220 years *shorter* than the duration of the "times of the Gentiles," but one which nevertheless expires at or very near the same point as the earlier, the establishment of the kingdom of God on earth. How is this? These twenty-three centuries begin later. They measure the history of events in the last three empires only. They start, *not* from the beginning of the kingdom of Babylon, but from the earlier years of Medo-Persia; they commence, not with the era of Nabonassar, nor with the Captivity era, but with the

RESTORATION ERA OF EZRA AND NEHEMIAH

In this vision of the Ram and the He-goat (Dan. vii. 3), the first action described—the starting-point of the prophecy—is the pushing of the Ram Westward, Northward, and Southward. Not the lion-like Babylon, but the massive, heavy, ram-like Medo-Persia, is the first empire here; and it was at the point where this latter empire succeeded the Babylonian that Jewish restoration commenced.

The predicted 2300 years must consequently date from *some point in the restored national existence and ritual worship of the Jews*, and they include, not only the whole of *that* period—the whole of the "seventy weeks," or 490 years to Messiah—but also the whole duration of the present second dispersion, accompanied by a second desolation and defilement of the sanctuary. This second dispersion commenced with the fall of Jerusalem under Titus, and was completed by Hadrian, at the close of the Jewish war, A.D. 135. The whole period has lasted therefore, not only through nearly five centuries before Christ, but through all the nineteen centuries since.

The intended *terminus a quo* is not very distinctly assigned, but as both the 2300 years of chapter viii. and the "seventy weeks" of chapter ix. start from the Persian period of Jewish history, in other words, as they both date from the RESTORATION ERA which followed the Babylonian captivity, their starting-points must be either identical or closely related, chronologically. Now there is, and can be, no question that the two years, B.C. 457 and B.C. 444, the dates of the two restoration decrees of Artaxerxes, are the starting-points of the 490 years to Messiah the Prince, because *the fulfilment of that prophecy has demonstrated the fact.* We may therefore safely take them as two of the starting-points of the longer period also. But one earlier and two later dates are also indicated by the vision. Its *opening* events are, not the restoration decrees of Artaxerxes, but the wars and victories, the pushing westward and northward and southward of the Persian ram. What point in this career of conquest is the most marked and critical? Unquestionably the celebrated invasion of Greece by Xerxes with an army, according to Herodotus, of five millions of men—the greatest of his military exploits, and at first a victorious one. It is true that in its results it brought about the ultimate ruin of his empire, but its beginning must nevertheless be regarded as the climax of his career; when he captured Athens he reached the farthest point of his advance into Europe, and the height of his glory. Napoleon's Russian campaign similarly brought about his ruin; but historians agree that the climax of his greatness was just before he started on that ill-fated expedition. " Earthly state had never reached a prouder pinnacle," says Dr. Arnold, "than when Napoleon, in 1812, gathered his army at Dresden, that mighty host unequalled in all time, and there received the homage of subject kings." [1] Xerxes' invasion of Greece took place in the year B.C. 480, and this date may be taken consequently as the *first* commencement of the Sanctuary Cycle, or period of 2300 years, to intervene before the full and final cleansing of the sanctuary. The first stage of Jewish restoration under Cyrus had already taken place at this time.

On the other hand, the edict given in the twentieth year of Artaxerxes did not *conclude* the Restoration era, for it was not until the thirty-second year of that king's reign that Nehemiah accomplished the work of reformation described in chapter xiii. 6 of his book; while the first "seven weeks," which are distinguished by the angel from the rest of the "Seventy," [2] as the Restoration era—at the time of the reconstruction of the Jewish city and polity—did not terminate in their earliest form till the reign of Darius Nothus, called "Darius the Persian" (Neh. xii. 20). Forty-nine years, or "seven weeks," from B.C. 457, the decree of the seventh of Artaxerxes, expired B.C. 408; and the same period, reckoned from B.C. 444—the Nehemiah edict of the twentieth of Artaxerxes—expired thirteen years later, in the time of Artaxerxes Mnemon, in B.C. 395. These two dates may consequently be taken as marking the two latest termini of the Persian Restoration era of Ezra and Nehemiah.

The Restoration era, from which these twenty-three centuries date, is consequently that lying between Xerxes' invasion of Greece, B.C. 480, and the completion

---

[1] *Lectures on Modern History*, p. 177.
[2] In chap. ix. 25.

of Nehemiah's cleansing of the sanctuary, B.C. 395. It includes the following dates:—

B.C.

480. Grecian expedition of Xerxes.

457. The Ezra decree in the 7th of Artaxerxes.

444. The Nehemiah commission in the 20th of Artaxerxes.

432. Nehemiah's second commission, in the 32nd of
Artaxerxes.

408. End of the "seven weeks" from the Ezra decree.

395. End of "seven weeks" from Nehemiah's commission.

This last date may be considered to mark the end of Old Testament history, and the closing incidents recorded are all, it will be observed, of the nature of a cleansing of the sanctuary (Neh. xiii.).

At a distance of twenty-three centuries from the *earlier* of these six dates of the Restoration era we may expect to meet incipient and then fuller stages of the final and everlasting "cleansing of the sanctuary," and at the same distance from the *latest* of these dates we may look to see the full accomplishment of the process.

The restoration of Israel and the cleansing of the sanctuary, accomplished during this era under the patronage of the Persian monarchs, were *imperfect and temporary*. Antiochus Epiphanes, the Seleucidæ, and the Romans, one after another defiled the sanctuary again, even during the course of the "Seventy Weeks" to Messiah the Prince; and forty-one years after His cutting off, the Roman armies under Titus overthrew Jerusalem, burned the temple, and took away both the place and nation of the Jews, inaugurating thus the present long dispersion of the people and desolation of their sanctuary.   The subsequent Jewish war under Hadrian completed the exile of the remnant of the Jews in A.D. 135, after which it was made illegal for any Jew even to set foot on the soil of Palestine.

That imperfect and temporary cleansing of the sanctuary in the days of Darius was, however, *typical* of the true and everlasting restoration yet to come, and now close at hand; and this chronological prophecy of twenty-three centuries was given to measure the interval to this latter — the great *antitypical* reality.

Now, first, let it be noticed that this period of 2300 years is *a most exact and beautiful cycle*, as was discovered by a Swiss astronomer, M. de Cheseaux, about the middle of the eighteenth century; a very wonderful cycle, and of a kind that had long been unsuccessfully sought for by astronomers; a cycle thirty times longer than the celebrated cycle of Calippus, and having an error which is only the seventeenth part of the error of that ancient cycle.   It is a period as distinctly marked off as a unit of time, as is a month or a year.   Yet in the days of Daniel this fact cannot, of course, by any possibility have been known, as there were no instruments in existence capable of measuring solar revolutions with sufficient accuracy to reveal its cyclical character.

The selection and employment of *this* period consequently in this place is an unanswerable proof of the inspiration of the Book of Daniel, and was felt to be such by M. de Cheseaux when he discovered the astronomic nature of this period.   It would be a million chances to one that such a cycle could have been employed by accident.   If selected intentionally as a cycle, it must have been by Him who timed the movements of the sun and moon in their orbits.

The question now arises, Where does this long period run out? and to what events does its termination lead? We may reply, first, generally.

It runs out like the " Seven Times," both on the lunar and solar *scales*, and its various termini fall within "the time of the end"; that is, in the period that has already elapsed since the middle of the eighteenth century. It leads to several of the dates we have already considered as stages in the downfall of the Mohammedan Power, as well as to others which have not yet come before us. One of the measurements is exactly bisected, just as one of the measurements of the seven times was, by the Saracenic capture of Jerusalem. In fact, this period may, in a certain sense, be considered as simply a briefer form of "the times of the Gentiles"; it covers the same period chronologically, *omitting the first of the four empires*. Starting as it does, not from the Babylonian Captivity era, but from the Persian Restoration era, it includes the last twenty-three only of the twenty-five centuries of the great Gentile dispensation.

Its lunar measurements run out in the years A.D. 1753, 1776, 1789, 1808, 1825, and 1838; while its solar termini extend to the years 1821, 1844, 1857, 1876, 1893, and 1906. The frontispiece diagram will show the relation of these dates, all included in "the time of the end" to their respective *termini a quibus*, the Persian Restoration era.

And what were the events of these different terminal years? From the nature of the period we are considering we should expect them to be critical, especially in connexion with the modern Jewish emancipation movement, and the fall of Mohammedan power. But as the French Revolution was also a principal factor in the liberation of the Jews, we need not be surprised to find it also indicated.

THE FIRST CLOSE, the middle of the eighteenth century, is recognised as a marked turning-point in Jewish history by its own distinguished historian, Prof. Grätz.

"So clearly and indubitably does the middle of the eighteenth century mark a turning point in this respect in the history of the Jews, that the eminent Jewish historian, Prof. Grätz, in his great work on *The History of the Jews*, dates the beginning of the fourth and last of the periods into which he divides Jewish history from A.D. 1750, and introduces that part of his work with the following words—words which, in the light of the present argument, are very suggestive :

"'Can a nation be born in a day? or can a nation be born again? . . . Yet in one nation a new birth appears, a resurrection out of a state of death and apparent corruption ; and that in a race which is long past the vigour of youth, whose history numbers thousands of years. Such a miracle deserves the closest attention of every man who does not overlook all wonderful phenomena. Mendelssohn has said at the beginning of this period, "My nation is kept at such a distance from all culture that one might well doubt the possibility of any improvement." And yet she arose with such marvellous quickness out of her abasement, as if she had heard a prophet calling unto her, Arise! arise! Shake off the dust. Loose the bonds of thy chains, O captive daughter of Zion.'"[1]

The year 1753 witnessed the first Jewish emancipation Act in England, an Act which, although it was repealed the following year, yet indicates the beginning of a movement which has never since been arrested. This was the period of the rise of the distinguished Jewish writer MOSES MENDELSSOHN, who prepared the way for the great change that was so soon to pass over

[1] Dr. Kellogg, *The Jews*, p. 144.

15

his people. Of the influence of Mendelssohn, Dr. Kellogg writes:

"Mendelssohn prepared the way for the great change that was so soon to pass on Israel, both by his influence on his own people, and by the effect of his life and work upon the sentiments and prejudices of the Gentile peoples of Europe. Till his day the Jews, in a proud isolation, had held themselves in a great measure aloof from the thought, and even from the language, of their merciless oppressors. . . . It was Mendelssohn, first of any among the German Jews, who ventured to enter the profane precincts of Gentile literature. While none the less familiar with his native Hebrew, he became a master of the classic German; and so by his writings brought the German Jews for the first time into contact with the Gentile life and thought of which the German language was the channel. . . . Thus after an isolation of centuries, they began to feel the full force of the influence of German thought and culture, and so were gradually brought into a position to exert in turn a mighty influence on the Gentiles. Besides this, Mendelssohn, by his notes upon and translation of the Pentateuch, and also by his constant protest against the authority of the synagogue to interfere with the right of individual opinion in religious matters, initiated a great movement against the old rabbinical Judaism, which had for so long a time stood as an impassable barrier between Jews and Gentiles. Thus quite without intention of his own he became the immediate author of all that deadly rationalistic tendency which has now so great prevalence and power among the Jews. As Mendelssohn did so much to bring his people in various ways nearer in sympathy to the Gentiles, so, on the other hand, he did scarcely less to enlist Gentile sympathy for the Jews. His rare intellectual endowments, together with the singular attractiveness of his personal character, did very much among the influential circles of Europe to diminish that indiscriminating prejudice of ages, which could believe no good thing of a Jew. How much he influenced Gentile thought and action we can apppreciate, when we recall his intimate relations with such men as Lessing, Goethe, Chancellor Dohm, and Mirabeau; and *the active influence of Mendelssohn dates from the same decade which saw the initial act of Jewish emancipation in England.*"

This, it will also be remembered, was the decade

of the commencement of Voltaire's anti-Christian influence in Europe, which provoked the French Revolution.

THE SECOND LUNAR CLOSE is the year A.D. 1776, the date of the American declaration of independence which was indirectly one of the causes of the French Revolution; and the other two lunar closes are, as will be recognised at a glance, leading crises of that great Revolution itself.

But what has the French Revolution to do with Jewish emancipation, or the cleansing of the sanctuary?

Much every way. Louis XVI. sent his French troops under Lafayette to assist the United States in their struggle for freedom and independence. When that struggle was crowned with success, these French officers and troops returned to France, carrying with them seed-germs of republican ideas, which, while they developed beneficently and gloriously in the virgin soil of a new and unpeopled continent, produced, on the contrary, in the exhausted soil and amid the old world institutions of Catholic Christendom a poisonous and destructive harvest. The force engendered a few years later on by these revolutionary notions induced the destructive volcanic action which shook into ruins the governments and institutions of Europe, and desolated all its countries with sanguinary and long continued wars. In the midst of the great upheaving and dislocation of society which resulted, *Israel obtained her emancipation.* The fetters fell everywhere from the limbs of the long oppressed and long suffering Jew, and before the revolutionary earthquake subsided he was no longer the slave of the Gentile, but a free man among his fellows. The newborn United States were the first nation to embody the principle of Jewish equality before the law in the fundamental statutes of their new constitution of 1776.

Nor was this all. The fearful judgments which in these years crushed all the Catholic nations of Christendom, had two other unlooked for and most important results. They established the military and maritime supremacy and the vast colonial empire of Great Britain, which went into the revolutionary wars a dwarf and emerged from them a giant; and they established also a new power in Europe, the mighty military empire of Russia, which now rules a non-Catholic empire extending from the walls of China to the Baltic Sea, and from the Arctic Ocean to the Himalayan Mountains. This is *the* power to which has been allotted the task of overthrowing Mohammedan rule in Europe and Asia; its greatness has ever since grown exceedingly year by year, and it has yet a most momentous part to play in the near future. Russia is the great foe of Islam, and Britain is the great friend of the Jews, because the great protector of the oppressed; both are strongly anti-Catholic, and Russia is in addition strongly anti-Mohammedan. The French Revolution movement, which unintentionally placed these two nations in the forefront of the family of European peoples, must needs be regarded therefore as *an all-important one* in connexion with the fall of the Papal and Mohammedan Apostasies, and in the cotemporaneous liberation of the Jews and cleansing of their sanctuary. Though called the French Revolution, because it happened to originate in France, that great movement really ran on into a European one, the duration of which was not limited between the convocation of the States-general and the entry of the Allies into Paris, but reaches back to the middle of the eighteenth century for its commencement, and continues as to its consequences to this day.

THE THIRD LUNAR CLOSE, A.D. 1789, which terminated twenty-three centuries from the Nehemiah starting-point, was in the West the year of the destruction of the Bastile in Paris, marking the actual outbreak of the French Revolution; and in the East that of a most disastrous war between Turkey and the Empress Catherine of Russia in alliance with Joseph of Austria, —a war which resulted in a decided advance in the downfall of the Porte.

THE FOURTH LUNAR CLOSE, A.D. 1808, witnessed the foundation of the first society for the evangelisation of the Jews. And the FIFTH, 1825, fell in the midst of the Greek War of Independence, and coincides with the point at which the Porte, "tired and terrified with a struggle in which its armies had been swallowed up during three successive years without any result,"[1] was driven to call in the aid of Egypt, a step which afterwards led to its loss of that country also.

THE SIXTH AND LAST LUNAR CLOSE, 1838, was marked by the outbreak of the Egyptian insurrection of Mehemet Ali, which led to the independence of Egypt.

THE SIX SOLAR CLOSES of the period of twenty-three centuries from the six starting-points of the Restoration era are the years A.D. 1821, 1844, 1857, 1876, 1893, and 1906. All the first four, as we have previously shown, brought most marked crises in the fall of Turkey, and ought consequently to be regarded as so many stages in the cleansing of the sanctuary.

A.D. 1821 was the year of that insurrection in Greece which ended in its total liberation a little later on

---

[1] *Turkey, Old and New*, p. 362. Menzies.

Greece had always been regarded by the Porte as one of its most important and valuable provinces, and vehemently did it strive to avert Greek independence.

At the news of the outbreak in the Morea the ferocity and fanaticism of the Ottomans were aroused, and the Greeks in Constantinople were mercilessly massacred, the churches pillaged, the patriarch hanged at the door of his own palace, while three archbishops, eighty bishops, and numbers of other members of the synod shared the same fate. In Thrace, Macedonia, Thessaly, and all parts of the empire, peaceable and defenceless Greeks were pillaged and slain, and the cruelties and enormities perpetrated roused all their fellow countrymen at home to desperation. One wealthy man alone contributed five millions towards the cost of the war.[1] The insurrection made progress; the Turks were beaten; and in their fierce indignation they committed a suicidal act in commanding the massacre of the male population of the island of Scio. Ten thousand Asiatic Moslems landed on its shores, and in a brief time out of one hundred thousand inhabitants, only nine hundred remained! This action raised a cry of horror throughout Europe, and the maddened Greeks took a startling vengeance. They set fire to the Turkish fleet, half of which was destroyed, beat enormous armies of Turkish soldiers, and continued to struggle till they gained their complete liberation from the Turkish yoke.

Of the year 1844 we have before spoken, as it is indicated by other periods than the one we are now considering. This year brought no military defeat, but one of a far more important character, both as marking the loss of the independence of the Porte, and the liberation

[1] *Turkey, Old and New*, p. 359. Menzies.

of its Jewish and Christian subjects. It was the year in which the united Powers of Europe obliged the Turkish Government to cease the practice of execution for apostasy; in other words, to cease persecuting on religious grounds. This, being contrary to the fundamental principles of Mohammedanism, would never have been conceded until all power of resistance had failed.

The grand vizier, in a correspondence with the English Government on this subject, says: " The laws of the Koran are inexorable as regards any Mussulman who is convicted of having renounced his faith. No consideration can produce a commutation of the capital punishment to which the law condemns him without mercy." The only reply was: " Her Majesty's Government *require* the Porte to abandon once for all so revolting a principle. If the Porte has any regard for the friendship of England, it must renounce absolutely and without equivocation the barbarous practice which has called forth the remonstrance now addressed to it." Russia wrote with similar distinctness, " We positively expect no longer to witness executions which excite the indignation of all Christendom." Even after similar appeals from all the great Powers the Porte would have put them off with the statement that " the law did not admit of any change," but the ambassadors would not receive it. At last a concession was obtained with the greatest difficulty, and only by the firmest resolution, and the following official declaration was published: " The Sublime Porte engages to take effectual measures to prevent henceforward the execution and putting to death of the Christian who is an apostate. Henceforward neither shall Christianity be insulted in my dominions, nor shall Christians be in any way persecuted for their religion."

This decree was published in the 1260th year of the
Hegira. It is dated March 21st, 1844. This date is the
first of Nisan in the Jewish year, and is exactly to a day
twenty-three centuries from the first of Nisan, B.C. 457,
the day on which Ezra states that he left Babylon in
compliance with the decree given in the seventh year of
the reign of Artaxerxes.

Of the year 1856–7 we have spoken fully elsewhere ;
it marked the close of the Crimean War, and the adoption of the EUROPEAN CONCERT ON THE EASTERN
QUESTION, by which the five great Powers undertook
conjointly to regulate the dissolution of the Ottoman
empire—the date of the Treaty of Paris.

And lastly, the year 1876 witnessed, as we know, the
commencement of the Russo-Turkish War, the result of
which would have been the total overthrow of the
Ottoman empire but for the action of England. By the
Conference of Berlin the larger part of the remaining
portion of the Turkish dominions in Europe was
rendered independent of the Porte, and England established a protectorate over the Asiatic dominions of the
Sultan. Of the last two solar closes, A.D. 1893 and 1906,
we will speak later on.

It is evident that the 2300 years of the sanctuary
cycle indicate, not so much a closing year as a closing
era, not so much a point of time as a process. The
expression, "unto 2300 years, then shall the sanctuary
be cleansed," seems to mean, then shall the cleansing
process begin, not then shall it come to an end. Jewish
restoration is going on gradually and by stages, as
Jewish decline and fall did 2520 years ago, and as the
former Persian restoration did 2300 years ago. The
process is naturally a slow one. The once mighty
Ottoman empire could not be overthrown in a year, nor

in a decade, nor in a century.   Empires that spring up gourd-like in a night may perish in a night, as did the empire of Napoleon III.; but in the case of mighty and extended ones, consolidated by powerful bonds and ages of duration, decay is as slow as growth.   The oak, that is a century in attaining maturity, and lives for many centuries, takes centuries also to perish.

The terminal years of this great period, if we include its lunar measures, take us back to the middle of the eighteenth century; and if we confine our attention to its principal solar closes, to the time that has elapsed since 1821, covering thus the events in Jewish, Mohammedan, and Syrian history which have occurred during the last sixty-five years.   They have not brought the cleansing of the sanctuary.   They have brought many stages leading to that great result; they have brought it perceptibly nearer; they have shown the means by which it is likely to be at last accomplished — the gradual rise of the Jews, and the gradual decadence of the Ottomans; they have led us to a point at which the climax of the liberation of Syria and the restoration of Israel may be said to have come within the range of practical politics: but they have not brought the end. We are still some few years distant from the close of the period when, according to prophecy, that end is to come.

It is useless to speculate as to the detail of future events, even when the occurrence of the events themselves is distinctly predicted, and is near at hand.   We may know that certain things will happen, because the Scriptures distinctly predict them, and we may know when they will happen, because the time of their occurrence has been revealed; but we may yet be entirely ignorant as to how they will be brought about, because the *mode* has *not* been revealed. That the sanctuary will be cleansed, or Syria freed from Moslem domination, at the close of this cycle of twenty-three centuries, there seems little room to doubt; but how the deliverance will be effected, or with what immediate results, it is not for us or for any one to say: time will declare. The ultimate result is clear: the rapid restoration of a considerable number of the Jewish people to the land of their fathers, where they will repent and be converted, led to say, "Blessed is He that cometh in the name of the Lord!" and be thus prepared to welcome their long rejected King, Messiah.

What the interval between the cleansing of the sanctuary and the final and glorious crisis is likely to be, we must learn from the chronology of the times of the Gentiles. This cycle of twenty-three centuries from the Persian Restoration era leads no further than the deliverance of the Holy Land from Gentile rule.

CHAPTER XIII

The Connexion between the Sanctuary Cycle and the "Seventy Weeks," or 490 Years, Extending from the Persian Restoration Era to the Era of "Messiah the Prince"

BEFORE passing from the consideration of this Sanctuary Cycle, we must indicate some links of connexion between it and the celebrated prophecy of Seventy Weeks, which have, we believe, never before been pointed out. They possess, however, the highest interest, both as confirming the view that chronological prophecy deals with eras rather than with years, and as showing that there is a fulness and an exactitude of chronological prediction in this prophecy of the "Seventy Weeks" which is not generally recognised, making its inspiration more evident than ever. The facts to which we are about to call attention confirm also, if confirmation be needed, the importance of the six dates which we have indicated as starting-points of the Sanctuary Cycle.

We mentioned above that two of the starting-points of the twenty-three centuries of the Sanctuary Cycle (Dan. viii.) are the same as those of the seventy weeks (Dan. ix.). The following diagram shows that the chronological correspondence between the two prophecies is more full and exact than this. The prophecy of the Sanctuary Cycle indicates, as we have seen, four

other starting-points in addition to the decrees of Artaxerxes; and we have considered the various years of
close as measured from all six.

If now we take all these six dates as starting-points
for the Seventy Weeks to "Messiah the Prince," what
do we find? That not only do the dates of the two
decrees of Artaxerxes lead up, as is generally recognised,
to the ministry and death of Christ, but that the analogy
extends farther and is even more complete, affording a
fresh proof that there is more in these sacred predictions
than lies on the surface, more than is actually stated,
and that they are adapted to history and to astronomy
in a way that is marvellous in its delicate complexity,
and Divine in its absolute accuracy.

The prophecy of the Seventy Weeks was given at the
close of the Babylonish captivity of seventy years. It
announced that a week of such captivity periods, or
seventy weeks of years, that is 490 years, would elapse
to "Messiah the Prince." It foretold besides certain
events which would follow the cutting off of Messiah,
the fall of Jerusalem and the desolation of Judæa; but
to these latter events it did not attach any chronological
statement, it did not seem to intimate when they would
take place, further than that they would follow the
cutting off of Messiah. Moreover, the prophecy did not
indicate any date for the birth of Messiah, but only for
that of His "cutting off," or death; that supreme event,
which was to make reconciliation for iniquity and bring
in everlasting righteousness, is distinctly assigned to the
middle of the last week; and, as we have shown,[1] it
actually occurred exactly 69½ weeks of years, or 486½
lunar years, from the Nehemiah date, B.C. 444.

The six different commencing dates to which we have

[1] P 66.

been led by the study of the Sanctuary Cycle extend, it will be observed, over an interval of eighty-five years in the fifth century before Christ. Now the following diagram shows that the corresponding terminal period after the lapse of seventy weeks, or 490 years, included, not only the death of "Messiah the Prince," doubly indicated both by lunar and solar measures, but also the date of His birth,[1] and that of the Jewish war which led to the siege of Jerusalem and the desolation of the land, and that of the close of the Messianic and apostolic era, and of the canon of Scripture.

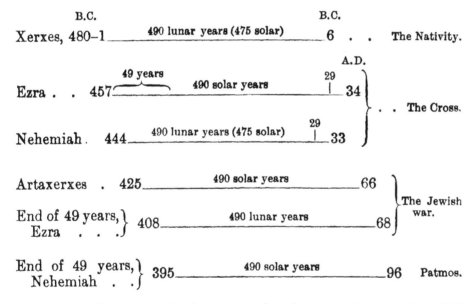

Hence this wonderful period of seventy weeks did actually measure, from the different *termini a quibus* in the Persian Restoration era, the interval—

1. To the birth of the Babe of Bethlehem.

2. To the very day when Christ our Passover was sacrificed for us.

[1] We have elsewhere demonstrated that the most probable date of the nativity is B.C. 6, and not, as commonly supposed, B.C. 4. See *Approaching End of the Age*, p. 519.

3. To that terrible Roman war, which fulfilled the predictions of the judgment which should fall on the Jews in consequence of their rejection of Messiah. "The people of the prince that shall come"—that is, the Roman soldiery of Titus—"shall destroy the city and the sanctuary; and the end thereof shall be with a flood, and unto the end of the war desolations are determined. . . . Even until the consummation, and that determined shall be poured upon the desolate." The Jewish war began in May, A.D. 66, and it terminated in A.D. 70, with the fall of Jerusalem and the burning of the temple.

4. To the close of the reign of the Roman emperor Domitian, which was also the close of the Messianic era—the date of the last appearance of Christ in glory to one of His apostles, the date of the giving of the Apocalyptic visions to the last of the apostles, and thus of the close of the New Testament and of the entire canon of Scripture.

That the year A.D. 95–6 is the true date of these events is capable of most satisfactory proof. Domitian reigned from A.D. 81 to A.D. 96. It was in the year previous to his death that his severe persecution of the Christians took place, in the course of which he banished the Apostle John to Patmos. This fact is expressly asserted by almost contemporary testimony; for Irenæus, the disciple of Polycarp, who was himself the disciple of John, writing shortly after this date, says that the visions of the Apocalypse "were seen no very long time ago, but almost in our age, towards the end of the reign of Domitian."

"The varied historical evidence which has been inquired into all concurs to confirm *the date originally and expressly assigned by*

Irenæus to the Apocalypse, as seen and written at the close of the reign of Domitian; that is, near the end of the year 95 or beginning of 96. Accordingly, the great majority of the most approved ecclesiastical historians and Biblical critics, alike Roman Catholic and Protestant, French, German, and English,—writers who have had no bias on the point in question, one way or the other, from any particular cherished theory of apocalyptic interpretation ; for example, Dupin, Bossuet, Tillemont, Le Clerc, Turretin, Spanheim, Basnage, Lampe, Mosheim, Mill, Whitby, Lardner, Milner, Tomline, Burton, etc., etc.,—have alike adopted it ; to whom I am happy to add the living names of the German ecclesiastical historian Gieseler, and of our own learned chronologist, Mr. Clinton. We may, I am persuaded, depend on its correctness with an unhesitating and implicit confidence as on the truth of almost any of the lesser facts recorded in history. And I must say it seems to me most surprising that respectable and learned commentators should have spent their time and labour in building up apocalyptic expositions that rest wholly and only on the sandy foundation of an earlier Neronic date."— Elliott, *Horæ Apocalypticæ*, vol. i. pp. 45, 46.

Thus not only was the cutting off of Messiah the Prince separated by 490 years to a day from the Nehemiah decree "to restore and to build Jerusalem," but the *whole* Messianic era—from the birth of Christ, B.C. 6, to His last appearance to John in Patmos in A.D. 95 — was similarly separated from the *whole* Persian Restoration era. The different years of crisis which form starting-points in this latter are answered by events of supreme importance in the Messianic era ; and the close of the Old Testament history is separated by " seventy weeks " from the close of the New.

This hidden yet exact analogy is all the more interesting because the clue to it is found, not in the prophecy of the Seventy Weeks, but in that of the cleansing of the sanctuary.

Now when we remember that the former prediction

was given in the first year of Darius, that is to say, 600 years before the closing event which it indicates, the destruction of Jerusalem by Titus; when we note that it does not profess to give its chronological point at all,—its exactitude and comprehensiveness are surely a new and eloquent testimony to the Divine inspiration of the Book of Daniel, and a fresh encouragement closely to scan and deeply to ponder the sacred chronological predictions of Scripture.

CHAPTER XIV

The Future Dates of this Series

UP to this point of our investigation we have been dealing exclusively with past events and past dates; that is, with fulfilled prophecy. This should be distinctly observed. *We have been studying facts, not theories.* In our investigation of the dates of the "seven times" and of the Sanctuary Cycle, we reserved for consideration in a separate group all those which are still future. The two last dates we considered were 1882 and 1885. The dates we have now to consider are the few last of the long series, numbering many score, and extending back over eighteen centuries, which we have studied in the foregoing pages. All the previous dates in this series have brought about stages in certain definite historical movements, and the events which prophecy attaches to these future dates are mainly final stages of the same movements. The analogy of the past, from which we may judge of the future, is therefore a broad and strong one, as regards the nearer dates; and the word of prophecy throws a flood of light upon the closing events of this dispensation, which would seem to be indicated by the more remote ones.

The detailed and exact order of those events is to some extent doubtful, but their nature is indisputable. When the "times of the Gentiles" close, the millennial age begins, and at the junction of these two great ages

16

lies the glad fruition of our "blessed hope," the second coming of our Lord and Saviour Jesus Christ. Daniel's grand prophetic outline of the future places this beyond dispute; the second advent of Christ in glory is there connected again and again with the termination of the fourth, or Roman empire, in its divided, ten-horned, Papal form. The stone cut out without hands falls upon the feet of the Image, breaking them and the whole Image to pieces, before it becomes a mountain and fills the whole earth. The Son of man comes with the clouds of heaven, and receives dominion and glory and a kingdom, that all people, nations, and languages should serve Him. At the advent of the Ancient of Days, the dominion of the persecuting Horn is taken away, and "the kingdom and dominion, and the greatness of the kingdom under the whole heaven, shall be given to the people of the saints of the Most High, whose kingdom is an everlasting kingdom, and all dominions shall serve and obey Him." Numerous prophecies, both in the Old and the New Testaments, treat of this solemn and glorious crisis, and of that which succeeds it. The 2520 years of the "times of the Gentiles" extend from the fall of Judah's independence *up to this crisis*, from which dates a *new* chronological period — the thousand years of the millennial age.

Now, not only have by far the greater number of the events foretold by Daniel and the prophets, and by our Lord and His apostles, as destined to intervene before His return, already taken place, but by very far the longer portion of the "times of the Gentiles" has, as we have seen, already elapsed. Measured on the lunar scale, and from the *earliest* date, the period expired 218 years ago, at the beginning of this era of the "time of the end "; and measured on the full solar scale, from the *latest* date in the Captivity era, we are now within seventeen years of its final close. There is not, therefore, chronological room for any large number of future events of a critical character, nor are there many such on the scroll of prophecy. The complete fall of " Babylon the Great," the entire removal of the Mohammedan power from Syria, and the restoration to a larger extent, and in a more corporate and national sense, of the Jews to their own land,—these seem to be the principal remaining events predicted in prophecy as destined to occur before the end of the " times of the Gentiles," the end of the indignation against Israel, and the advent of the manifest kingdom of God on earth.

Hence the future, prior to the second advent, is a question, not of new and different historic events, but simply of fresh stages in existing and progressing movements. How many more stages are there likely to be in the fall of Babylon ? How many more in the fall of Islam ? How many more in the restoration of Israel ? This it is not for us to say ; but we may point out that *only a few more dates are indicated* by the chronological prophecies we are considering ; so that if the system we have sought to unfold be true and scriptural, the remaining crises cannot be numerous.

Five of the closing dates are the full *solar* termini of the respective prophetic periods as measured from their *latest* starting-points in the Captivity, Restoration, and Bisection eras. They extend to the *end* of the " time of the end "—to the *full* close of this closing era, to the *last* events of this Gentile age. Grouping them according to their astronomic and historic nature and connexion, they are as follows :—

I. Two of the calendar termini from the two last

Nebuchadnezzar starting-points of the Captivity era—the years 1887 and 1898.

II. The three full solar termini from all the three Nebuchadnezzar starting-points (that is, from the falls of Jehoiakim, Jehoiachin, and Zedekiah), the years 1917, 1923, and 1934.

III. The two solar termini from the two latest starting-points of the Sanctuary Cycle, the years 1893 and 1906.

IV. The lunar closes of the *supplementary* periods of Daniel xii., the added thirty and forty-five years—which, measured on the lunar scale from the Omar capture of Jerusalem, run out respectively in the years 1889 and 1933.

Arranged in chronological order, the dates we have named lie thus, 1887, 1889, 1893, 1898, 1906, 1915, 1917, 1923, and 1933–4.

We are not about to attempt any prediction of the specific events which may be expected to occur in these years of crisis in the near future, but we may point out, that analogy seems to warrant the assumption that the dates which remain will bring events harmonious in character with those which have been brought by *previous dates of the same series*. The series, for instance, which starts with the Zedekiah destruction of Jerusalem and the burning of the temple, and which led us in the Bisection era to the Saracenic capture of the city and conquest of the land, and in this "time of the end" to the "Universal Israelite Alliance" and the European protectorate of Northern Syria in 1860, ran out in its extended form of 1290 lunar years in the year 1889. That year witnessed, not a Papal crisis in *western* Europe, but the loss of Crete to Turkey. The dates

1893 and 1906 are both of them termini of the Sanctuary Cycle, and have to do with Palestine, not Rome.

On the other hand, the four years of the series which, starting from the Babylonian overthrow of Judah, have led us to so many stages, first in the *rise* and subsequently in the *fall* of Rome Papal, seem likely to bring fresh crises *of a similar character*, or further stages in that fall of Babylon the Great, whose final judgment is to be the immediate precursor of the Marriage of the Lamb. Especially *the three full solar termini* from the three latest Nebuchadnezzar starting-points of the Captivity era, are likely to prove years of solemn and terrible crisis to "Babylon the Great," and of blessed liberation and uplifting to the people of Israel, and to the true Church of God. The solar termini from earlier stages of the Captivity era have already brought most momentous events, though only of the nature of preliminary stages. The solar terminus of the period of "Seven Times" from *Shalmaneser* brought the Papal overthrow connected with the French Revolution. The solar terminus of the same period from *Sennacherib* brought Napoleon's awful wars, including the retreat from Moscow, in which an army of half a million of men perished almost as tragically as did the hosts of the Assyrian monarch of old when the angel of death passed over them. The solar terminus of "Seven Times" from the captivity of *Manasseh* brought the final fall of the temporal power of the Papacy; but from only two of the *Nebuchadnezzar* starting-points has the period yet run out on the full solar scale. The years in which it will yet do so are *the two closing ones of the series given above*—1923 and 1934.

The question as to what events are likely to be brought by these future dates is a deeply interesting one, which no reader who has intelligently followed us thus far can avoid pondering, as we have pondered it, but which no one who realises as strongly as we do the utter folly of speculation will venture to answer dogmatically. When we glance back over the many stages of fulfilment which we have indicated in the past, we feel little difficulty in anticipating the nature of the crises which may be brought by the *nearer intervening dates*, though they afford but slender help when we attempt to conceive the close. We need to remember that the symbolic language of some prophecies, and the poetical imagery of others, are too often permitted to create expectations for which, in reality, they give no ground. The final fall of the anti-Christian Roman Apostasy is predicted, as we before stated, to occur in two contrasted ways: the first, a gradual consuming; the second, a sudden destruction. The latter is to take place at Christ's coming, the former prior to that coming. The instrument of the latter is to be the brightness of His epiphany, the power and glory of His advent. The instruments of the previous consumption are twofold: first, a *spiritual* movement; and, secondly, a *political* one. The spirit of God's mouth, or truth of Scripture, has been the one agency, and the hatred of the " ten horns " the other.

We have seen both these agencies at work. In the Reformation movement, and in all subsequent Protestant evangelistic movements, in the circulation of the Scripture and religious literature, we have seen the first, the spirit of God's mouth, undermining and destroying the vitality and power of the Papacy; and in the atheistic revolution born of the revulsion from degrading superstition and of hatred to the lying pretensions of the Papacy, we have seen the second—the kingdoms of modern Europe hating and destroying the Romish Church and Papal Power, and liberating themselves through vehement revolutions and bloody wars from its yoke. These opposite agencies are probably destined to continue, each in its own way, the predicted consumption of the anti-Christian Apostasy, until the last stage of the great prophetic drama arrives, the supreme crisis for which apostles and prophets and martyrs have waited, and for which the Church has watched through many a century,—until the cry is heard, "Behold, the Bridegroom cometh: go ye out to meet Him." We ought to expect then at the earlier of these future dates only such events as have fallen out at the previous closes of the prophetic periods; nothing supernatural, nothing unprecedented, nothing that cannot be perfectly well accounted for by second causes, nothing that will irresistibly fix the attention of the world, or even of the Church—events of a certain definite character that cannot be overlooked or misinterpreted by those who understand the counsels of God, but which will no more disturb the wicked or arouse men from their fatal dreams of peace and safety, than did the fall of the temporal power of the Papacy in 1870.

That further and notable crises in the movements, already so far advanced, are likely to occur at the still future dates of this series, there seems little room to doubt. The light of analogy is here full and perfect; whoso is wise, and will observe the providential acts of God in the past, will understand the moral character of the events which may be anticipated between these days and the close. Their precise political nature is a matter of very secondary importance. If, for instance, in the past the idolatry and corruption of Catholic Christendom were at a certain point of time to be judged and punished by a fearful democratic revolution; if a modern Sennacherib was to be raised up to afflict the Papal nations of Europe with the scourge of war, it was comparatively unimportant that the revolution began in France, and the conqueror's name was Napoleon; the number and dates of his battles, and the details of his career are *little*, the episode as a whole is *much*.

So, if now we know that worldly ecclesiastical systems, the baptized heathenism of modern Europe, the idolatrous and corrupt Papal system and all Church systems which in their essential features resemble it,—if we know that all these are destined to decay and decrease in power, we do not need to discern beforehand the precise geographical or national features of the process, though it will be profoundly interesting to watch the playing out of the last acts of the great Papal drama, and to see again, as we have already seen so often in the past, the predictions of prophecy transforming themselves into the facts of history. If we know that Mohammedanism is to decay with increasing rapidity until the Ottoman empire falls to pieces, and its place in Europe and in Syria knows it no more, it little matters by what exact means the change is to be brought about. The wise will note each stage of the process and its date with exceeding interest, and will greet each one as it arrives as one greets an expected guest. Prophetic students can possess their souls in patience, and calmly watch the unfoldings of Divine providence; they know beforehand what the end will be, and they know that God has never lacked means to accomplish His own purposes. Without pretending to predict a single stage in the process or a single incident in the drama, they foresee the character of the events to be expected, and can accurately anticipate the close, which must come in its due season.

We cannot love Christ's appearing, or long for the promised times of the restitution of all things, the glorious millennial Sabbath, without inquiring, "When shall these things be?" Nor can we, after the careful study of chronological prophecy in the light of history and astronomy, avoid the question, Which of the closing dates of this series is likely to bring the promised consummation? In considering this subject we must bear in mind the connexion in which these dates are given. They do not occur in the Gospel of St. John, nor in the epistles of St. Paul, but in the prophecies of Daniel. Their object is to measure the duration of Gentile sovereignty in the earth up to the time of the restoration of Judah's throne—up to the time of the accession of the Son and Lord of David to the empire of the earth as God's King on His holy hill of Zion—up to the time when the heathen shall be given Him for His inheritance, and the uttermost parts of the earth for His possession; when He shall reign in righteousness, and rule in judgment, and have dominion from sea to sea, and from the river to the ends of the earth; when all kings shall fall down before Him, and all nations serve Him; when men shall be truly blessed in Him, and all generations call Him blessed. Up to this great public crisis of world-wide importance the "times of the Gentiles" extend. They have not primarily to do with the hope of the Church—with the coming of the Bridegroom to take to Himself His long-loved and blood-bought bride; but the second advent has to do with both, and in whatever connexion we view it, that advent is one and the same event.

We are not of the number of those who make a

chronological distinction between Christ's coming *for* His people and His coming *with* them, who teach that there will be a secret rapture of the Church first, and a public epiphany afterwards; we see no Scripture warrant for any such chronological distinction, though the moral distinction between the two aspects of the second advent is exceeding broad. Prophecy announces two advents only, *not three*. All along it has announced a first advent to suffer and to die, and a second to rule and reign; but of a third it makes no mention. Our Lord Himself says that as the lightning cometh out of the east, and shineth even unto the west, so shall also the coming of the Son of man be; and He could hardly have used a stronger figure to imply suddenness and universality of recognition. The passage which describes the rapture of the Church speaks of a shout, and the voice of the archangel, and the trump of God; while another passage distinctly states that the event will take place in a moment, in the twinkling of an eye.

While therefore we see no authority for making chronological distinctions between separate stages of the one *advent*, we see, on the other hand, abundant reason in Scripture to believe that the millennial *reign* of Christ will not be fully established in a day or in a year. It must be remembered that He comes, not peacefully to ascend a vacant and waiting throne, welcomed by a willing people, but to dispossess a mighty usurper and to overthrow a great rebellion, to right the accumulated wrongs of ages, to introduce moral order and righteous government into the moral chaos created by the long domination of the prince of darkness, the god of this world, the deceiver and destroyer of men.

The second coming of Christ is associated with the work, the strange, sad work, of judgment—of the judgment of apostate Christendom, as well as with the rapture of His Church and the restoration of His ancient people Israel. Like the cloud of old, bright to the Jews and dark to the Egyptians, His advent in glory has a different aspect to the Church and to the world. There can be no stages or differing dates for an instantaneous advent, but there may be, and probably must be, many stages in the work of bringing into order a rebel and ruined world. Just as an interval elapses between the accession and coronation of an earthly monarch, so it may prove to be in this case.

The first nineteen or twenty years of Nebuchadnezzar, which witnessed all the stages of the fall of Judah before Babylon, were the main and terminal years of the Captivity era. All that had gone before was only preparatory. The fall of the ten tribes before the Assyrian conquerors, and even the brief captivity of Manasseh, did not permanently shake the throne of Judah, or compromise the independent sovereignty of the house of David. The penumbra of the eclipse had indeed fallen on the moon, but not as yet the dark shadow. All through these years Babylon was steadily rising, and with the accession of Nebuchadnezzar, and his first campaign against Judah, reached its climax. In the eighth year of Nebuchadnezzar the throne of David fell, and the independent national existence of Judah ceased until the "times of the Gentiles" should be fulfilled. Hence those nineteen years especially form the important critical era; the rubicon of history was crossed at one or other of the crises in its course. It extended from B.C. 605 to B.C. 587, and the principal crisis in it was the fall of Jehoiachin in the eighth year of Nebuchadnezzar, B.C. 598. The corresponding terminal years after the lapse of "Seven Times" in full solar measure, extend from A.D. 1915 to A.D. 1934. During these years then we may expect to see the full and final fall of the antitypical "Babylon the Great"; and if that event is to answer chronologically to the culminating point of the ancient Babylon, it seems probable that it will occur at one of the central dates, A.D. 1917 or 1923. This Gentile age closes, as we have seen, with an era, and not with a date.

One date, A.D. 1923, has a distinct historical pre-eminence as corresponding chronologically to the Jehoiachin overthrow of B.C. 598. Of the four campaigns of Nebuchadnezzar against Judah this was by far the most fatal; indeed, we may say it was not *an* over-throw, but *the* overthrow of the kingdom of Judah; it was emphatically the breaking up of the nation and the fall of the independent sovereignty. It was, moreover, the date of the captivity of the prophet Ezekiel, the date from which he uniformly reckons the visions of the remarkable series that were granted to him in Babylon and by the river of Chebar, visions of the departing and returning glory; and the question naturally occurs, Is its answering year in this "time of the end" destined to witness the return of the glory and the re-establishment of the throne of Judah?

On the other hand, the astronomical features of this measurement of the "Seven Times" are not as remark-able as are those of two other measurements; that from the first of Nebuchadnezzar, and that from his final overthrow of Zedekiah. It was in the year B.C. 606 that Nebuchadnezzar first came against Judah, and carried Daniel and the Hebrew children among others captive. At this time he was acting on behalf of his father, and it was not until nearly two years later, B.C. 604, that he himself acceded to the throne. That

year is consequently, properly speaking, the first of
Nebuchadnezzar; and it was probably also the year in
which he saw the vision of the Great Image, in connexion with which it was said to him, "Thou art this
head of gold." This year has therefore some special
claims to be considered as a very principal starting-point
of the "times of the Gentiles." Measured from it the
period runs out in A.D. 1917, and it is a very notable
fact that a second most remarkable period does the
same. The 1335 years of Daniel xii. 12, the *ne plus
ultra* of prophetic chronology, which is evidently
eastern in character, and consequently lunar in scale,
measured back from this year 1917, lead up to the great
Hegira era of Mohammedanism, the starting-point of
the Mohammedan calendar, the birthday of the Power
which has for more than twelve centuries desolated
Palestine and trodden down Jerusalem.

B.C. 604	2520 solar years	A.D. 1917
	A.D. 622 1335	A.D. 1917

The year 1917 is consequently doubly indicated as a
final crisis date, in which the "Seven Times" run out,
as measured from two opening events, both of which
are clearly most critical in connexion with Israel, and
whose dates are both absolutely certain and unquestionable. In 1335 years' measure is, as we before pointed
out, the half week, or 1260 years, *plus* the additional
seventy-five, which in the prophecy is added in two
sections of thirty and forty-five years. The passage in
which these periods are announced gives no distinct
indication of the events to which they lead, nor does it
state whether lunar or solar years are intended. Prophecy indeed never does this; but the astronomic

features of this period seem to indicate distinctly that lunar years are intended, for seventy-five years is exactly the difference between seven times lunar and seven times solar, and hence the addition of seventy-five years to the lunar measurement of the period makes it equal to the solar measurement. We have before stated that both Jewish and Mohammedan chronology are strictly lunar, and that chronological periods connected with eastern events seem to be always calculated on this scale, while those connected with western or Papal events are measured by the solar year.

The coincidence of the close of these two periods seems to answer a question which will occur to every reflective mind, the question, Are the supplementary seventy-five years of the last verses of Daniel to be added to the latest solar terminus of the seven times? The answer is, They may be; it is possible: but it seems extremely unlikely, because of the astronomic fact just indicated.

The year in which these two periods—the one of over twenty-five centuries, and the other of over thirteen centuries—run out together is astronomically a notable one. We have before met, in the course of our investigation, years such as 1848, in which several prophetic periods meet; but they were only those from more incipient starting-points, and minus the seventy-five terminal years. Here, on the contrary, we have a main starting-point, the first of Nebuchadnezzar, as our terminus *a quo* for the one period, and the acknowledged commencing date of the great eastern Apostasy, Mohammedanism, as that of the other; and we see that the latter in its extended form meets the former, and expires with it in the year A.D. 1917.

Thoughtful readers will weigh the facts and draw their own conclusions, asking themselves, in the light of all the chronological facts mentioned in this work, *if* the year B.C. 604 witnessed the rise of the typical Babylon, the supremacy over the typical Israel, what event is the corresponding year in this time of the end likely to witness? There can be no question that those who live to see this year 1917 will have reached one of the most important, perhaps *the* most momentous, of these terminal years of crisis.

Yet we must also call attention to a further interesting fact connected with the last possible measure of this comprehensive and wonderful "Seven Times," that starting from the capture of Zedekiah and the burning of the temple in the nineteenth year of Nebuchadnezzar, and terminating in A.D. 1934. The termination of the "times of the Gentiles" meets at this point the 1335 lunar years, dated from the Omar capture of Jerusalem, an event more momentous in its effects on Palestine and Jerusalem than the Hegira era of the commencement of Mohammedanism. No chronologic prophecy of Scripture indicates any date whatever beyond this year, as astronomic considerations forbid the thought that the supplementary seventy-five is to be added to these solar measures.

Here then we reach the close of this long chronological section of our endeavour, like Daniel, to understand by books the number of the years whereof the Lord hath spoken; and here, like that holy prophet, when he was convinced that the end was close at hand, may we set our faces to the Lord our God, to seek by prayer and supplication with confession that He will fulfil His own word, and cause His face to shine once more upon His sanctuary, which has so long lain desolate, and on His people, who have so long been a reproach; that He will do as He has said, and speedily send Jesus Christ, whom the heaven must receive until the times of the restitution of all things, which God hath spoken by the mouth of His holy prophets since the world began—that the times of refreshing may come from the presence of the Lord!

What is the result of our investigation? Is it not a strong confirmation of our blessed hope? Is it not a conviction that we may well lift up our heads, because our redemption draweth nigh? Slowly and cautiously we have descended the long stream of time, with its turnings and windings, and confluences with many tributaries. It has flowed through broad Assyrian and Babylonian channels, through Persian plains and Grecian islands and Roman provinces; it has rushed in revolutionary rapids, and broadened in lacustrine empires; it has divided itself into a tenfold delta, and is moving on to mingle its waters with those of the ocean. We have carefully noted each chronological waymark as we passed it by, and compared its position with that assigned to it in the chart of sacred prophecy. Already we have verified nine-tenths of such waymarks; the few remaining ones lie close together on the chart, and close ahead: can we question that they will do so in the facts of history? Can we doubt that the "times of the Gentiles" are all but over?

We have not been in this investigation following cunningly devised fables, nor elaborating fantastic and baseless theories; we have been studying the mutua. relations of three sets of unquestionable facts: the occurrences of history and their dates, the astronomic measures of periods of time, and the sacred prophecies of the Word of God. We have been studying facts written large in the book of providence, the book of nature, and the book of revelation. No sciences lend themselves less readily to the service of mere imagination or of foolish speculation than chronology, astronomy, and arithmetic ; yet these are just the three that have led to these profoundly interesting and important results. History is, of course, less rigid, and there is room for some diversity of opinion as to the character and importance of the events it records.

But will any one question the critical character of the conquests of the Assyrian and Babylonian monarchs, or of the Persian restoration decrees, in the history of the Jews? Will any one question that the fall of the western empire of old Rome, or the Hegira of Mohammedanism are great dividing lines on the page of history? Will any one question that the English or French revolutions had a momentous bearing on the fall of the Papal power in Europe, or that Carlowitz and Kainardje and the treaties of Paris and Berlin mark stages in the decay of the Ottoman empire? Is it a mere matter of opinion that the condition of the Jews has undergone a startling and marvellous change within the last century, or that the evangelisation of the world has received within the same period an unprecedented impulse? Is there any uncertainty about the dates of these events, or any difficulty in calculating their chronological distance from the events of the Captivity era?

None of these things are obscure or doubtful, they are evident and acknowledged facts ; their relation to the predictions of Scripture has long been seen and acknowledged by the most cautious and reverent students of the prophetic word ; never demonstrated before, they are sufficient of themselves to prove the true scale of prophetic chronology, for the chances are,

17

of course, a million to one that so many accurate correspondences as we have here indicated are not fortuitous. Not a few of these facts have been noted and explained by other observers, and placed on record even centuries ago; but as far as we know they have never before been grouped together as we have here grouped them, and their united testimony, which is strictly cumulative, seems to us to raise probable proof to the rank of demonstration and moral certainty.

CHAPTER XV

SIGNS OF OUR TIMES

TO sum up the conclusions we have reached so far. Divine wisdom has seen fit to order human history according to a chronological plan, measured, not only by days and weeks and months, but by solar, lunar, and calendar years; by cycles which harmonise solar and lunar movements; and by periods which are days and weeks and months and years of larger cycles, created by the revolution, not of the sun and moon themselves, but of their orbits.

The lapse of six thousand years of history, and the science arising from four thousand years of astronomical observation, as well as the light afforded by the fulfilment of nine-tenths of the predictions of Scripture as to historical events, enable " the wise," or the godly students of the works and Word of God, to understand in these days His revealed purposes as regards the times and seasons of the redemption of our race, as earlier students could not do.

To encourage us to such studies we have the definite promise that " the wise shall understand " in the time of the end much that was, for kind and wise purposes, hidden from earlier generations. This promise is in its context especially connected with *chronologic* prophecy; but a comprehension of the true scale and scope of this, an understanding of the times and seasons of sacred predictions, determines to a very large and important extent their true historic meaning and application.

The chronological prophecies of Daniel are all included within a period of "Seven Times," or 2520, years, and the greater part of them relate to its second half; one prediction, however, and that the most important in the book, measures the interval from the restoration of the Jews after their captivity in Babylon to the first advent of Christ. This last prediction of 'Seventy Weeks" was fulfilled on the scale of a year to a day; and led up to the advent and death of Messiah, and the subsequent destruction of Jerusalem as foretold, running out, as regards the central event, the Crucifixion, *to a day*, when measured on the lunar scale from its Nehemiah starting-point.

This accurately fulfilled chronological prediction determines the scale on which all such predictions are to be understood in Daniel and in similarly symbolic prophecies—a day is to be regarded as meaning a year. It also determines the fact that lunar as well as solar years are employed in these predictions—a fact which can be otherwise proved also.

The great week of "the times of the Gentiles" is the lifetime of the fourfold Image, and of the Four Wild-beast empires of Daniel—Babylon, Persia, Greece, and Rome; the last in its two stages, first pagan, and secondly Papal. The four pagan empires did actually, as a matter of fact, last half "seven times" (lunar), *i.e.* 1260 lunar years; and the second half of the great week has been occupied by the rise, culmination, and decay of the Papal empire of Rome.

The great chronologic prophecies of Daniel are not to be measured from one special *year* to *another*, but from one *era* to another, because the rise and fall of nations

—the great movements of history—must in the nature of the case occupy more or less extended *eras*. An *event* like the Crucifixion might be and was predicted to a day. Historical movements, like the birth and death of nations, cover many years, or decades, or centuries, in proportion to their greatness and duration. The fall of Israel and Judah covered a period of 160 years, and their restoration and recovery is likely to extend over an equally prolonged period, at least.

The Captivity era of Israel and Judah marks the beginning of the "times of the Gentiles," and the present era of their elevation and emancipation indicates the close of that dispensation.

This great week was bisected by a third era, signalised by the rise of the two anti-Christian Powers, the Papacy and Mohammedanism; and the present Restoration era of the Jews is marked by the gradual decay and fall, under Divine judgments, of both these iniquitous systems.

The chronology of these events confirms most wonderfully this general view, and evidences most marvellously the hand of God in history, and the inspiration of Bible prophecy.

On both lunar and solar scales, the opening and closing eras are separated from each other by "seven times," or 2520 years; and their years of crisis also correspond. Both are consequently separated from the Bisection era by half that interval, the oft-predicted "time, times, and a half," or 1260 years.

The era of the "time of the end" is longer than the earlier eras, because the 2520 years and its half run out on both lunar and solar scales. It seems to cover 235 years, of which 218 are already expired. It dates back to the establishment of Protestantism in Europe, and includes all the stages of modern Jewish emancipation, of the great anti-Papal democratic French Revolution, as well as of all subsequent anti-Papal and anti-Moslem revolutions and changes. The system indicates several dates in the early part of this century, as terminal in character.

Concurrent with the fall of the Apostasies and the renaissance of the Jewish people, there has taken place within the last hundred and fifty years a most notable revival of true faith and practical godliness among the *reformed* Churches everywhere, so that there is now an immensely larger number of truly converted and renewed men and women in the world than ever before. There has been a revival of the spiritual Israel even more marked than that of the natural Israel; and this has been accompanied by an influential and widely spread evangelisation of the heathen, and by a marvellous circulation of the Scriptures, missionary and Bible societies having all sprung into existence during this "time of the end."

An entirely unprecedented progress has also been made in the elucidation and comprehension of the prophetic Scriptures, so that a large and annually increasing number of Christians are looking for "that blessed hope, and the glorious appearing of the great God and our Saviour Jesus Christ."

Our blessed Master, when reproving the Jews for not recognising Him as their Messiah, blamed them for *not understanding the signs of the times.* They wished Him to give them a sign from heaven, something wonderful, something supernatural, something miraculous. He refused and said: "O ye hypocrites, ye can discern the face of the sky; but can ye not discern the signs of the times? A wicked and adulterous generation seeketh after a sign; and there shall no sign be given unto it but the sign of the prophet Jonas. And He left them, and departed."

Did He object to their wishing for signs? No; for He gave such in abundance to His disciples and to the multitude, and He appealed to the witness borne by these signs to His Messiahship. He objected to *their refusal to discern the signs that abounded on every hand* in the shape of fulfilled prophecy, chronologic and otherwise, gracious miracle, and moral and spiritual revelations. He objected to their craving for the supernatural, the sensational, instead of taking to heart the abounding signs that were actually present.

He subsequently gave signs of His second advent in glory to His disciples, and charged them, saying, " When ye see these things begin to come to pass lift up your heads; for your redemption draweth nigh." After His resurrection He upbraided the two disciples on the road to Emmaus for not believing *all* that the prophets had spoken of the Christ—His sufferings as well as His glory. It is evident therefore that He wishes His people to study and comprehend prophecy, and to be alive to every true sign of the times.

Remarks on this subject are too often made, which betray a want of intelligent comprehension of the *nature* of the signs that are, according to Scripture, to indicate "the time of the end." A careless reading of our Lord's prophetic discourse on the Mount of Olives seems to be the cause of much of this misapprehension. His prediction of wars and rumours of wars, famines, pestilences, and earthquakes, are quoted as if *they* and such like things were to be the signs of the end of the age. A little accurate attention to the order of His statements would at once show that, so far from this being the case, He mentions these as the characteristic and common events of *the entire interval prior to* His coming. Wars and calamities, persecution and apostasy, martyrdom, treachery, abounding iniquity, gospel preaching, the fall of Jerusalem, the great tribulation of Israel, which has, as we know, extended over eighteen hundred years, — all these things were to *fill the interval*, not to be signs of the immediate proximity of the second advent. How *could* things of common, constant occurrence be in themselves signs of any uncommon and unique crisis ? What commoner all through the ages than wars and rumours of wars, famines, pestilences, and earthquakes ? These, as marking the *course* of the age, can never indicate its *close*, to do which something distinctive is evidently requisite.

Many who perceive the folly of thus looking at every great natural calamity as a sign, go to an opposite extreme, and expect wonderful, unprecedented, supernatural, and impossible signs, basing their expectations on a literal interpretation of the symbolic hieroglyphs of the Apocalypse. Such signs would be so grotesque and absurd in character, that it is an insult to human intelligence, not to say to Divine revelation, to assert that they are to be expected. There is one simple and all-sufficient answer to this childish conception of the signs of the last days. Our Lord and His apostles alike furnish the reply. Our Lord says :

" As it was in the days of Noe, so shall it be also in the days of the Son of man. They did eat, they drank, they married wives, they were given in marriage, *until the day* that Noe entered into the ark, and the flood came, and destroyed them all. Likewise also as it was in the days of Lot ; they did eat, they drank, they bought, they sold, they planted, they builded ; but the same day that Lot went out of Sodom it rained fire and brimstone from heaven, and destroyed them all. Even thus shall it be in the day when the Son of man is revealed." [1]

And the Apostle Paul confirms this:

"For yourselves know perfectly that the day of the Lord so cometh as a thief in the night. For when they shall say, Peace and safety ; then sudden destruction cometh upon them, as travail upon a woman with child ; and they shall not escape." [2]

If such signs as are imagined by some *were* to precede the advent, the state of society predicted in these passages could not by any possibility exist.   If monstrous, unheard of, supernatural, portentous events were to transpire, would they not be telegraphed the same day all over a startled world, and produce such a sense of alarm and expectation that buying and selling, and planting, and building, and marrying and giving in marriage, would all be arrested together, and "peace and safety" would be far from any one's lips or thoughts ? And if *one* of the Apocalyptic prodigies is to be thus fulfilled, *all*, of course, must be so. Conceive a succession of such supernatural prodigies, and a world asleep in fancied security, and overtaken by sudden destruction ! No; there was nothing special to alarm the antediluvians before the day that Noah entered into the ark; nothing special to startle the men of Sodom ere the fire from heaven fell: and *like as it was in those days*, so will it be in *these*. All going on just as usual, no stupendous sign to attract the world's attention. "None of the wicked shall understand" the true state of affairs, only the "wise," enlightened by the word of prophecy.

It will be objected, perhaps, But if the signs of the

---

[1] Luke xvii. 26–30.   [2] 1 Thess. v. 2, 3.

times which we are expected to recognise are neither ordinary natural events, nor extraordinary unnatural ones, what are they? Scripture abundantly answers this inquiry. *They are special but perfectly natural events, occurring in a predicted order, and at a predicted time*, and of various and widely differing events occurring in combination. They are not sudden, startling, supernatural phenomena, but *definite stages in long progressing natural movements*, whose history was written twenty-five centuries ago by Daniel.

In the evidence which compels us to conclude that we are on the eve of the great and long predicted change, there is nothing supernatural, nor will there be, nothing extraordinary, nor will there be, until the epiphany of the Son of man in glory startles a sleeping world as a thief in the night. Each of the signs taken separately and singly, or occurring in any other connexion, or at any other time, might argue nothing remarkable; but occurring as they do, as links in a predicted series, as the closing stages in a long movement, and at the precise periods indicated twenty-five centuries ago, they become to "the wise" clear signs that the end of the present state of things is at hand. To the world they *seem*, as they *are* in themselves perfectly natural and ordinary events, easily to be accounted for by second causes, and having about them no special providential character or evidential value as signs of the approaching end; but to the understanding eye they portend the near approach of "that sudden destruction" which impends over a guilty and Christ-rejecting world, and over a corrupt and apostate Church, as well as the glorious deliverance speedily to arise to the true people of God, though there is nothing in them to interrupt the world's dream of "peace and safety," or to disturb the scoffer's conviction that " all things continue as they were."

We have six separate and distinct *sets of signs,* each sufficient by and of itself alone to indicate that we are on the verge of the establishment on earth of the eternal kingdom of the Son of man—that blessed reign of righteousness and peace, of which the millennial Sabbath is only the portal and introduction. We have :

    I. Political signs.

    II. Ecclesiastical signs.

    III. Jewish signs.

    IV. Mohammedan signs.

    V. General social signs.

    VI. Chronological signs.

I. The POLITICAL SIGNS lie in the wonderful fulfilment of the *broad outline* of Gentile history given by Daniel twenty-five centuries ago, in the succession, order, and events of the four great empires. There neither is nor can be the slightest doubt in the mind of any educated man, that in that part of the world in which the people of God, natural and spiritual, have existed, and the redemption of mankind been wrought, four great universal empires have succeeded each other since Daniel's day, nor that the fourth has been in every sense the greatest of them all.

ROME, the city which gives its name to the fourth, was in Daniel's day a mere cluster of huts, surrounded by a wall of mud, and inhabited by a handful of discontented and turbulent outlaws. Its existence was unnoticed and unknown beyond the limited sphere of the barbarous tribes of its own neighbours in Italy. Yet its matchless might and dominion, its iron power, its universal and long-lived empire, are foreseen and foretold as the fourth in succession from that founded by Nebuchadnezzar. The ruins of Babylon, the monumental writings of Medo-Persia, the statues and temples and literature of Greece, are with us to this day, and we are ourselves a fraction of the empire of Rome. We ride over ROMAN roads, we visit ROMAN baths, we use the Latin tongue of ROME; ROMAN law is the basis of our jurisprudence, we are a witness to ourselves of ROMAN dominion to the ends of the earth; while the Church to which most of the continental nations still belong is the Church of ROME, and the professedly infallible teacher to whose doctrine they bow is the Pope of ROME, who claims supreme dominion to-day over two hundred millions of mankind.

Unlike the ancient oracles of an idolatrous priesthood, obscure, enigmatical, and having reference only to petty present or proximate matters, these simple, sublime, far-reaching oracles of God stretch over empires and ages, arching in under one vast, unbroken vault the infinitely numerous and ever-varying changes among nations and peoples, and kindreds and tongues, from Daniel's day to our own and to still future days, comprehending the whole in this marvellously clear and simple outline, with its fourfold division.

The fourth or Roman section of the history is represented in this prophecy as divided into two parts; the first a united empire, and the second a tenfold commonwealth of kingdoms under Roman sway.

Now it is clear that the Babylonian empire passed away even in Daniel's own lifetime; that the Medo-Persian fell under Alexander the Great, more than three centuries before the first advent of Christ; that Greece in its turn passed under the all-embracing, all-crushing power of Rome; that the first stage, or *empire* of Rome ceased with Romulus Augustulus in the fifth century; and that the commonwealth of ten Gothic nations which then arose, and has ever since existed in the sphere of the old empire of Rome, owning for ages a voluntary subjection to the Roman pontiff, has already been in existence for between twelve and thirteen centuries. In a word, the first half of the Roman dominion ended in the fifth century, and the second, extending to the present day, has already lasted as long as the four pagan empires put together. Judging then from these broad outlines alone, whereabouts are we in the lifetime of the image of Gentile monarchy? How much of the prophetic programme remains unfulfilled? May we not feel absolutely certain that since all the foretold events, *stretching over twenty-five centuries* of history, have been accomplished in their time and in their order, the minute fraction that remains will be the same? How near then must be the great change? Whereabouts are we? The reply of this first witness is clearly—*on the very verge of the establishment of the kingdom of God* on earth, at the second coming of Christ.

It should be noted that the first coming of Christ is not glanced at in the prophecies of the succession of Gentile monarchies. That coming made no change in their history at the time of its occurrence; pagan Rome was in the plentitude of its power when that event took place, and it continued to be so for centuries afterwards. The first advent did not crush, grind to powder, and extinguish for ever Gentile monarchy, as is evident from the fact that it continues until this day. Christ Himself was put to death by Roman authority, the object of His first advent having been to save, and not to govern the world. That first advent is described in the prophecy of Daniel ix., but is not mentioned in the visions of chapters ii. and vii. It resulted in the establishment of the present spiritual kingdom of God in the hearts of men; but what are to be the results of the second advent, which it is predicted will follow on the close of this Gentile age?

"In the days of these kings shall the God of heaven set up a kingdom, which shall never be destroyed: and the kingdom shall not be left to other people, but it shall break in pieces and consume all these kingdoms, and it shall stand for ever."

Now if no other line of evidence existed, if this grand outline of prophecy which has now become so largely fulfilled history stood alone, if we had nothing in Scripture to guide us but this one broad political outline, ought not every believer in inspiration to feel satisfied that we are living in the very end of this age? Heaven and earth shall pass away, but God's word shall not pass away. Four empires, *and four only*, fill the interval from the fall to the restoration of the throne of Judah in the person of David's Son and David's Lord; four great universal empires, *and four only*, are to be governed by Gentile rulers, who resemble wild beasts in their cruel ferocity and in their ignorance of God. Four such empires, *and four only*, precede the coming in glory of the Son of man, and the setting up on earth of the kingdom of the God of heaven, the kingdom which is to replace all others and stand for ever. We live not only at the close of the fourth, but at the close of its last form, the Roman Papacy. Already that Power has ceased to exist as a secular government. What is to come next? Scripture says, the glorious kingdom of God. But there are plenty of confirmatory signs, and we will consider next the

II. ECCLESIASTICAL SIGNS. The professing Christian Church is, and has been for sixteen hundred years, that is, since the days of Constantine, a great and important institution and organisation in the sphere of the old Roman empire. Germs of corruption were apparent even in the days of the apostles; inspiration foretold that they would develop, till the professing Church, on the removal of the old Roman empire, would, while retaining the name of Christ, become a mighty anti-Christian system—a system energised and utilised by Satan for his own diabolical purposes. It was foretold that this apostasy would be headed and governed by *a specially evil and wicked ruling dynasty, which would succeed the Cæsars at Rome.* The apostles Paul and John present different but harmonious prophetic portraits of this evil power, both distinctly associating it with Rome. Daniel, in his much earlier vision relating to the succession of Gentile monarchies, also introduces (chapter vii.) this very same Power as ruling throughout the whole period of the tenfold state of Rome, over its commonwealth of nations, and as *causing* the destruction of the whole Roman earth, by its boastings and blasphemies, at the second advent of Christ. The other Christian apostles confirm this account of the time of the destruction of the Apostasy, presenting it, as Daniel does, as *the terminal event of this age,*—an event, as regards the Roman Catholic Church, closely preceding the marriage of the Lamb. The destruction of the Papacy comes later.

History tells us that gross corruption, worldly ambition, and carnal strife rapidly developed in the Church after imperial Christianity was introduced by Constantine, and that a ruling ecclesiastical system *did* arise at Rome on the fall of the old Roman empire in the fifth and sixth centuries; that this Power, the Papal dynasty, did become a supremely wicked one, and has fulfilled with marvellous exactitude every feature of the prediction; that like the ivy, from lowly beginnings on the ground, it climbed, by means of the very obstacles that thwarted its progress, ever higher and higher, till in the course of centuries it overtopped all the branches of the great tree of the European commonwealth, and the humble Christian bishop became, in the Roman pontiff of the Middle Ages, king of kings and lord of lords in Latin Christianity. It tells of the centuries during which this great Papal Apostasy continued to corrupt the gospel, oppose the truth, and persecute the saints, as predicted; and it tells us that for three hundred years since the Reformation this ecclesiastical system and its head have been rapidly losing power and influence, until some 150 millions of Protestants now exist in the world free from its domination, while an immense number of infidels have in Latin Christendom equally thrown off its yoke. After listening to and pondering the testimony of this ecclesiastical witness, we ask ourselves, If this great predicted apostasy has thus arisen, culminated, and been, moreover, for upwards of three centuries sinking, falling, and decaying, what remains? The reply is inevitable: One more stage, and only one; its destruction as predicted, by the brightness of Christ's coming. The Apostasy of the Christian Church has run its course. The final act of the long drama is due.[1]

Further. If, instead of looking at the *ruler* of this great ecclesiastical apostasy, we look at *the Church he so long ruled*, the result is the same. That Church is represented as a woman riding the Roman wild beast (Rev. xvii.); *i.e.* an ecclesiastical system identified with

[1] Dan. vii. 2, 26; 2 Thess. i. 9, 10.

the secular power of Rome, influencing and guiding the tenfold commonwealth on the one hand, and upheld by it on the other. In "the time of the end" the mutual relation is changed; the ten kingdoms get tired of their burden, rebel against their would-be guide, throw off her yoke, hate her, spoil her, and consume her. At last a voice from heaven cries, "Come out of her, My people, . . . that ye receive not of her plagues"; and then adds, "Babylon the Great is fallen, is fallen: in one hour is her judgment come, in one hour she is made desolate."

History tells us how the Gothic and Frankish kingdoms that arose in Europe on the fall of old Rome gave voluntarily their support and allegiance to the Romish Church for well-nigh a thousand years; how as the result of her gross corruptions they ultimately came to despise, loathe, and reject her teachings, her government, and her rule; how they have for the last three hundred years thrown off her control, appropriated her revenues, destroyed her priesthood, despoiled her monasteries, refused her claims for support, and forsaken her company. Reviewing carefully the history of this Roman *Church* as foretold by inspiration, we ask, *What then remains unfulfilled?* The answer comes again more clearly than ever—only her final fall under Divine judgment; that final fall of Babylon which precedes the marriage of the Lamb.

We summon next a third witness, who has no connexion with the two previous ones, and who looks at the question from an altogether different standpoint; and we seek to ascertain how his testimony bears on the question of "the signs of the times." He knows little of political or ecclesiastical questions, for he is a Jew; but he boldly says: "These are the last days, and I will undertake to prove it from

18

III. "JEWISH SIGNS. Long ago, six hundred years before the Christian era, my nation lost its independence; it fell under Gentile rulers. But its fall was illumined by hope, for our restoration had been predicted a thousand years previously by the same God who had also foretold our fall. Many particulars were associated with our fall in sacred prophecy, and *they all came true*. Many more were associated with our restoration, and one by one *they have been coming true for the last* 150 *years*. Not a single jot or tittle has failed of the threats of judgment; all came on our people and lasted through ages. And now the promises are coming upon us; one by one they have been fulfilled, and there remain unfulfilled but one or two, and even of these we are already receiving the first instalments—the conversion of our people and their restoration to the land of promise. *We* cannot from *our* experience doubt that the day is near at hand when the throne of Judah will again be established on earth, and when Messiah, Son of David, will be King over the whole world.

"You need not take my word for it; judge for yourself! Compare the condition of the Jews in Europe and the wide world to-day, with what it was only two centuries ago! *Then* our portion was, and for ages had been, homeless exile, perpetually renewed banishment, cruel and constant massacre, ruthless spoliation, social contempt and degradation, destruction by torture and fire and sword; we were despised until we became despicable, oppressed until we became wicked, crushed down until we lost the power to rise, deprived of all chance of culture till we sank into almost brutal ignorance; we were enslaved and ill-treated till we hardly remembered we were *men*: and this for long, long centuries! *Now* all is changed, and our portion in most lands is as good a one as that of the Gentiles themselves. In some few countries we are still reminded of olden times occasionally, when our people by their financial dealings excite popular prejudice; but this is the exception, not the rule. Everywhere we are now emancipated, possessed of civil, social, and religious liberty, and of citizenship in all lands; we take our places in every class, even among the legislators and judges of the Gentiles; we teach their youth, we conduct their Press; we enjoy honour and power, rank and wealth, and perfect equality with our Gentile neighbours. Further, we have once more AN INTERNATIONAL BOND OF UNION, and are one of the most rapidly rising, fast multiplying, vigorous, and advancing nations on earth. We can compete with Gentiles in the mart, in the study, in the senate, whenever we get fair play; and *we are getting it everywhere now.* Our restoration to our own land is but a question of time, and probably of a short time. If *our* revival, uplifting, and restoration mark the terminus of *your* Gentile age, then you may be very sure its years are few!"

So speaks the Jewish witness, and every fact he indicates is a true sign of the times.

And there is further confirmation still in connexion with *the land* of the Jews, as well as with their people. For eighteen centuries it has lain desolate and forsaken of its sons, occupied and oppressed by strangers, and its condition was indicated by our Lord Himself as *especially* a sign of the times. "Jerusalem shall be trodden down of the Gentiles, until the times of the Gentiles be fulfilled." The condition of Palestine, be it observed, is a wholly independent question to that of the state of the Jews. Since the close of the Jewish war 1800 years ago, the Jews have had no more to do with it practically than the Chinese. It has passed under the power of one Gentile nation after another, and no improvement in the condition of the Jews has as yet had any direct influence on the fate of Palestine. For the last twelve centuries it has lain desolate under Mohammedan despotism, and for 400 years it has been wasted by Turkish tyranny. But the cruel grasp that has held it so long is fast relaxing; paralysis has smitten away its strength; the slightest effort would remove the weak and unwelcome constraint; yea, it would have failed long since had not outsiders upheld the arm and steadied the hand. It must evidently, as all admit, resign its hold ere long.

But perchance some other *Gentile* Power may succeed the Turk? It does not follow that Jerusalem must cease to be trodden down by Gentiles because it ceases to be trodden down by the Turk.

True; but this decay of Turkish power is represented elsewhere under the figure of the drying up of the Euphrates, and that figure points back to Cyrus' capture of Babylon, when the river Euphrates was actually dried up, that Israel's liberator might enter Babylon and set the captive people free. Of this Cyrus it was said, " He shall build My city; he shall let go My captives." He is a type of Christ, who is now by His providence drying up the anti-typical Euphrates, *i.e.* the Turkish Power, that He may effect a greater deliverance.

Furthermore, facts indicate that it would be impossible permanently to replace the Turks in Jerusalem by any nation except a Jewish one. The Powers of Europe would not suffer any one of themselves to possess it; when the Eastern Question comes to its solution, the probability is that the best course, even from a merely political standpoint, will be seen to be *a Jewish occupation*, under European guarantee as in the case of

Belgium. In any case, the condition of Jerusalem, and of the Eastern Question generally, seems to agree with all the rest in indicating that we have nearly reached the close of the "times of the Gentiles."

IV. MOHAMMEDAN SIGNS. This set of signs, though closely connected with the previous one, is yet to a certain extent independent, and may be regarded apart. The testimony of the Moslem witness to the chronological character of our days harmonises with that of the other witnesses, but has distinctive and confirmatory features of its own. Not only must it be considered in connexion with the land of Israel, as above indicated, but independently as a vast anti-Christian system, parallel with the Papacy in some respects, though contrasted with it in others, having opposed the truth, and persecuted the saints, and being doomed to be "broken without hand," and to come to its end, with none to help it (Dan. viii., xi.).

When we remember what the Mohammedan Power is and has done in the world; when we remember that the Apocalypse—which reveals, not only, like Daniel, the outward and visible action of the potentates and powers that influence the destiny of myriads of mankind for many generations, but goes further and shows their *origin*, whether from above or beneath—distinctly declares that *this* system, like the Papal system, originated with SATAN, and issued from the bottomless pit; when we remember that its sway at one time extended from the walls of China to the Atlantic, and from the Danube to the Nile; when we remember that it well-nigh extinguished Christianity throughout the whole of northern Africa, and cruelly persecuted it in all the rest of its dominions; when we remember that one hundred and fifty millions of men are still believers in its Christ-rejecting creed, and that millions more of nominal Christians are still the victims of its oppressions and cruelties: its present and rapidly progressing *decay*, and the consequent gradual liberation of its Jewish and Christian victims, and the near prospect of its total extinction in Europe, become "a sign of the times," gigantic in its importance, and carrying a weight which a thousand brief and passing signs could never do. Every fresh stage in its fall is a confirmatory sign, as is every fresh manifestation of the decay of the Papal nations, and of the increasing spread and ascendancy of the Protestant Powers.

V. GENERAL AND SOCIAL SIGNS. But confirming all these great and principal signs, derived from the history of nations and the course of ages, we have also more specific ones of a different nature: such as the moral character both of the Church and of the world in the days in which we live; the prevalent philosophy of this time of the end; the inventions and arts of the nineteenth and twentieth centuries, with their habits and customs;—foretold, some of them nineteen and some of them twenty-five centuries ago. As these are more frequently recognised as signs of the time than the others to which we have alluded, we do not dwell on them at any length here, though to reflecting minds their testimony is clear and conclusive.

In 1 Timothy iv. 1–3 we have a prophecy of Paul's of "the latter times," an expression which may refer to any part of the second half of the times of the Gentiles, though it is never used with regard to the first half. Paul in this passage describes the characteristic features of the Papal Apostasy, which deluged Europe with superstition during the Middle Ages.

"Now the Spirit speaketh expressly, that in the latter times some shall depart from the faith, giving heed to seducing spirits and doctrines of devils; speaking lies in hypocrisy; having their conscience seared with a hot iron; forbidding to marry, and commanding to abstain from meats."

In 2 Timothy Paul predicts later events still, the perilous times of "the last days," an expression markedly distinct from the previous "latter times."

"This know also, that in the *last days* perilous times shall come. For men shall be lovers of their own selves, covetous, boasters, proud, blasphemers, disobedient to parents, unthankful, unholy, without natural affection, trucebreakers, false accusers, incontinent, fierce, despisers of those that are good, traitors, heady, high-minded, lovers of pleasures more than lovers of God; having a form of godliness, but denying the power thereof: from such turn away."

Now while certain of the features here enumerated are evidently not peculiar nor distinctive of any one special period of history, yet a high state of civilisation has a tendency to produce, not exaggerated individual cases, but a *general prevalence* of selfishness, pride, luxury, and corruption. The old Roman civilisation, with which Paul was acquainted in the city of the Cæsars, was not certainly lacking in individual instances of these things, though it had also features of a very different character. But there were to intervene between those early days and "the last times" long ages of semi-barbarism, during which all that old civilisation would cease to be—ages which would be distinguished by other crimes, and especially by superstition and by a Christianised idolatry. But "the last days" were to witness the revival of the crimes incident to high civilisation, with certain special classes of sins super-added. Boasters, blasphemers, disobedient to parents despisers of those that are good, lovers of pleasure more than lovers of God, and especially "having a form of godliness, but denying the power thereof," "ever learning, and *never able to come to a knowledge of the truth.*"

That these features are all singularly characteristic of our days none can question. The most popular philosophy is agnosticism,—a confession that after all the vast and far-reaching discoveries, after all the profound researches, men are unable to reach any knowledge of the truth on the highest of all subjects. Agnosticism is simply know-nothingism. It is more: it is not only an assertion that nothing is known, but that nothing can be known; it puts an extinguisher on even the attempt to know Him, whom to know is life eternal. Our age has a form of godliness, a Christian Church is established in most of the States of Latin Christendom, and is sustained by the different Powers of Europe; but where is the power to maintain purity in the Churches, or righteousness in the laws of Christendom? Where is the power to arrest war and bloodshed, rapine and slaughter? Where is the power to subject the counsels of nations to the law and will of God, to produce in society any sort of resemblance to the kingdom of God? The religion of these last days has well been called a baptized heathenism; Christian in creed, heathen in practice.

Another feature of the philosophy of these last days is given by Peter, and is singularly characteristic of our times. "Knowing this first, that there shall come in the last days scoffers, walking after their own lusts, and saying, Where is the promise of His coming? for since the fathers fell asleep, all things continue as they were from the beginning of the creation." Or as Darwin, the apostle of the nineteenth century, put it: "All things continue as they were since the beginning of the creation; there is no need for miraculous intervention, no room for supernatural action. We live under a reign of law; as it was in the beginning, so it is now, and so it ever shall be as regards the succession of physical phenomena. One form of life is evolved out of another in endless succession; in physical, mental, moral, and religious spheres, all things continue as they were," or rather, change so slowly and gradually that no sudden catastrophe need ever be apprehended; on the contrary, "we may count on an assured future of great length."

Such is the fashionable creed, such the universal doctrine. But its teachers are, as the apostle states "willingly ignorant" that all things have *not* continued in one long, uninterrupted succession. They are willingly ignorant of the all-important fact that a flood once broke in on ungodly men, and "took them all away." They are willingly ignorant that the invariable law of death has been conquered by the glorious fact of resurrection. If the combined voices of the most universal and ancient traditions and of the most authentic and well-attested history demand credence for any fact, they demand credence for these two; and these two facts once admitted, Divine intervention—the control of the law by the Lawgiver—is demonstrated, and the occurrence of such a crisis as is predicted in Scripture is not only possible, but in the light of analogy likely. If what is called the course of nature has been interfered with in the past, it may be interfered with in the future, and in the near future.

Daniel's prophecies also, though dealing principally with the course of nations and the lapse of ages, give us two or three general social signs of the state of things at the close of this age, and it cannot be denied that these apply to our day as to no previous one. He does not say the power of steam will be applied to locomotion, and the art of travel will be revolutionised, and aviation will be introduced; but, looking at the result rather than the cause, he mentions in half a dozen simple words a most characteristic feature— "many shall run to and fro." Now to an eye that could embrace in one glance the civilised world, all its seas and all its shores, all its roads and all its rivers, all its towns and its cities, what would be the first and strongest impression produced on considering the scene? Surely that of ceaseless motion; many running to and fro, like ants around an anthill. No previous age of the world's history could have presented this spectacle; it is unique, it is becoming ever more marked, as year by year hundreds of miles of fresh railroads open up new districts, as motors by hundreds of thousands rush about, and as population and emigration increase, and as commerce spreads. There is no mistaking this sign of the time of the end; it is distinctive, and so conspicuous and unprecedented as to be a subject of constant comment. How few, as they point to it with pride and pleasure, remember it is a Divine mark of the time of the end, and associated with the second coming of Christ and the resurrection of the dead!

Nor is the second prediction less remarkable and distinctive, "Knowledge shall be increased." Education in most of the countries of Christendom is now *compulsory*, and the result is that every child can read, on the one hand, while literature floods every home, on the other. All that is going on all the world over is known by the masses of the people as well as by their rulers day by day. The knowledge of these days is real knowledge, an acquaintance with the facts and forces of nature, a rediscovery of the records of the past, and, above all, an immensely widespread acquaintance on the part of mankind with "the volume of the Book," containing that Divine revelation which imparts the highest of all knowledge, the knowledge of God and of His Son Jesus Christ our Lord.

If this expression, "knowledge shall be increased," be taken as referring especially to a knowledge of the meaning of the prophetic Scriptures, a signification which its context quite justifies, then also it is characteristic of these days, and of these alone. The Early Fathers understood the predictions about the second coming of Christ, but they were inevitably in the dark, as indeed they were intended to be, as to the meaning of the prophecies about Antichrist, and the events of the second half of the times of the Gentiles. Light dawned gradually after history began to fulfil the predictions; each stage of accomplishment has made the meaning of the prophecies clearer, and since the Reformation progress in a true knowledge of their meaning has been solid and rapid. Now, in the close of this time of the end, the clouds of obscurity have completely rolled away; the whole plan and order of events, the succession of empires, the limits of chronology, the scales of measurement, the nature of fulfilments, all have become, in the combined light of facts and of analogies, so clear, that he who runs may read; and the fulfilment of ancient Messianic predictions in the first advent of Christ is scarcely more clear than the fulfilment of the predictions of Antichrist in the history of the Papacy, and those of the incipient restoration of Israel in current events.

VI. CHRONOLOGICAL SIGNS. Sacred prophecy presents us with only three main periods, extending into days still future; all these three, starting from different and widely severed dates in the past, *converge in our days*, indicating thus that they are the last days of this age. The three periods are:

1. The twenty-five centuries of the "times of the Gentiles."

2. The twenty-three centuries of the Sanctuary Cycle.

3. The twelve and a half centuries of the duration of the apostasies.

The initial eras of these periods are perfectly clear. The first dates from the Babylonian Captivity era; the second, from the Persian Restoration era; the third, from what we may call the Gothic era of the breaking up of the old Roman empire. No one will question that the days of Nebuchadnezzar are removed by twenty-five centuries from the present time, nor that the days of Xerxes and Artaxerxes are similarly removed by twenty-three centuries. No one can question that the Papal and Mohammedan Powers rose at the end of the sixth century, which is twelve and a half centuries distant from our days; nor that the Reformation took place in the beginning of the sixteenth century, while we are living in the twentieth. Without descending therefore to any detail at all, it is plain to the most superficial observer, that all the three main periods of chronologic prophecy converge in our days and expire within a comparatively few years.

CHAPTER XVI

ANSWERS TO OBJECTIONS

WE believe that the system of chronologic prophecy which we have in the foregoing pages to some extent expounded is a strictly Biblical one, though in no one passage or book of Scripture is it plainly set forth as a whole. Its various parts are found in the Bible embodied in Levitical ordinances, involved in Old Testament histories and simple gospel records, or revealed in prophetic visions. It lies latent in the Bible, as all science lies latent in nature, and can only be presented in a systematic form after numerous observations of apparently disconnected phenomena have been combined into wide generalisations. So this system, though not as a whole set forth anywhere in Scripture, has its basis laid deep in the inspired writings, and results from a careful comparison of Bible statements with each other, with the facts of nature, and with the actual providence of God in history. We do not assume that we have expounded or even discerned with perfect accuracy *all* the features of this system, but believe, on the contrary, that passing years will clear up many of its remaining obscurities, and reveal more clearly the exactness of its adjustments As the late Rev. T. R. Birks wrote of our former work on this subject, so we feel as to this one, though it is more exact and more thorough on this point than its

predecessor; it is probably a penultimate and not an
ultimate arrangement of the times of sacred prophecy.
We believe it to be in advance of any previous exposition of the subject both in comprehensiveness and
in accuracy, but we do not claim for it that it is final.
The unfoldings of history within these closing years
will do much to confirm or to shake its credibility; and
we are content that it should be judged in the light of
proximate events.   But we are anxious to secure from
all lovers of truth, of whatever shade of opinion on
these subjects, a candid examination of *the facts* we have
observed and here arranged, and in order to do this must
now remove out of the way certain stumbling-blocks
which might hinder some readers.

I. (1) The first and main objection which will be felt
by many is the apparently strong and well-founded one
that this exposition, and especially our remarks on the
future dates of the series—cautious and interrogative as
they are—come dangerously near an unjustifiable
attempt to fix the time of the Second Advent. It will
be alleged that the clear, unambiguous statements of
Scripture prove that to do this is impossible, and even
to attempt it foolish and reprehensible: for that it is
evidently not the purpose of God that the time of that
supreme event should be known; that Christ and His
apostles founded their exhortations to constant watchfulness on the ground of our *ignorance* of the time of His
return; that He used the most emphatic expressions
on the subject, saying, "Of that day and that hour
knoweth no man, no, not the angels which are in
heaven, neither the Son, but the Father"; and again.
"Take ye heed, watch and pray: for ye know *not* when
the time is."[1]   It will be urged that even after His

---

[1] Mark xiii. 32, 33.

resurrection He said, in reply to the question of His disciples as to the time at which He would restore again the kingdom to Israel, "It is not for you to know the times or the seasons, which the Father hath put in His own power"; and that consequently we must be wrong in attempting to indicate from the prophecies of Daniel the chronologic date of the end of this age.

This objection appears at first sight so weighty and well grounded, that unless we can completely remove it, and even draw from these very passages an argument in defence of our position, we might as well refrain from publishing this book. We could neither expect nor desire these solemn statements to be lost sight of, nor the objection founded on them to be waived. It must be met, and we need hardly add there is no difficulty in its removal. Had it been otherwise this investigation would not have been undertaken. Had it been true, as some assert, that in face of these solemn and emphatic Scripture assertions we ought to be silent on this question of the time of the end; had it been true, as is assumed in this objection, that these statements apply as fully to the last as to the first generation of the Christian Church; had it been true, as the objection also implies, that the God who has given chronologic prophecy in Scripture does not intend the gift ever to become of practical value to His people, by permitting such prophecy to be understood: had these things been true, we should never have undertaken the research of which the results are here presented. That research was commenced and continued under a conviction that the exact reverse is the truth; that so far from fearing to intrude into forbidden regions by such sacred studies, we might look for Divine light in pursuing them, seeing it is promised that in this " time of the end " the saints *shall* understand, as previous generations could not do, the chronologic predictions of Scripture.

We are the more careful to examine and remove this popular objection, because its results are widespread and serious. On the one hand, it disinclines many sober-minded Christians from studying the subject at all, because they conceive light on it to be unattainable; and on the other, it drives not a few to the adoption of the Futurist system of interpretation— a system which we earnestly believe to be seriously injurious to the Church, as depriving her of a much needed bulwark to her own faith, and of an invaluable advantage in the present conflict with infidelity, by robbing her of the cogent and unanswerable argument of daily fulfilling prophecy. Futurism, by insisting on the literality of the symbols of time employed in symbolic prophecies, makes the predicted periods to be only a few years in duration, and thus finds no difficulty in assigning them all to the future, and in asserting that there *are* no chronologic prophecies relative to the Christian dispensation, but that the Church is left in ignorance as to her own present position in the stream of time. This is to rob the " more sure word of prophecy "—that " light that shineth in a dark place "—of some of its brightest rays, and to deprive this incredulous age of a great present miracle, with which, by the true interpretation, it is confronted.

It should be recognised that this objection is, of course, a fundamental one, and lies against all study of chronologic prophecy in the light of history, independent of any specific results arrived at. If we are bound to shrink with a religious horror from definite conclusions, *we say not as to the day or hour, but as to the general period* of the second advent, it were a clear folly to enter on investigations which must needs issue in such conclusions. There can be no question that the great historical predictions of Daniel lead up to the establishment of the kingdom of God on earth, that is, to the end of all *Gentile* monarchy—including that of Antichrist; the cleansing of the sanctuary, or Holy Land, from all Gentile oppressors, the first resurrection and the era of blessedness: in a word, to events which, as we learn from other Scriptures, are *synchronous* with the second advent.

Now these predictions contain *distinct chronologic statements*; so that the more closely we study and the more clearly we understand them, the more nearly we must needs approximate to a knowledge of the position of the second coming of Christ, not only in a series of historical events, but in a definite period of time. Hence if such knowledge be dangerous, such study should be avoided, for moral and mental danger must be shunned as cautiously as physical risk. If the ice be thin, we must refrain from going on it; if the vessel be unseaworthy, we ought not to embark. *But we are not at liberty to refrain from the study of chronological prophecy, any more than from the study of any other part of Scripture.* It is especially commended to us as a subject to which we *do well to take heed,* as one which both saints and angels in other days desired to look into, as one which carries with it peculiar blessing; and it is one in connexion with which there is the special promise that *it shall be understood* in this "time of the end." It cannot therefore be a duty to neglect it lest we *should* receive light, lest we should come to understand with some clearness "what manner of *time*" the

19

Spirit of God has signified as the duration of this present Gentile age. There must be some explanation of this seeming inconsistency!

It should, moreover, be remembered that our Lord Himself made use, not only of the expressions on which the objection we are considering is founded, *but also made use of others which inculcate the opposite duty of observing "the signs of the times," and of drawing from them the legitimate conclusions as to the proximity of His return.* He not only said, "Of that day and that hour knoweth no man," but He also said, "When ye shall see all these things, *know that it is near, even at the doors*"; "When ye see these things come to pass, *know ye* that *the kingdom of God is nigh at hand.*" Our Lord thus inculcated constant watchfulness and hopeful expectation, on two distinct and contrasted grounds: first, on that of His people's *ignorance* of the exact time of His return; and, secondly, on that of their *knowledge*, derived from fulfilled predictions, that it must be close at hand. He said, "Ye know not," and He said, "Know ye." He taught the same double truth in His parables. On the one hand, it was uncertain whether it would be the first, second, or third watch of the night that the Lord of the servants would return to his household; on the other, it was "after a long time" that the master, who had taken his journey into a far country, came and reckoned with his servants. Again there would go forth the midnight cry, "Behold, the Bridegroom cometh!" and then the indefinite waiting of the virgins would give place to immediate expectation.

The real question is, Which of these two attitudes better becomes Christians in the twentieth century? Should ours be merely the watchfulness based on utter ignorance of the times, or the earnest expectation and hope based on knowledge? Each in its season is good and right, for each has been expressly commanded; but for which is *this* the season? It is clear that the two states of mind cannot coexist, they mutually exclude each other. Surely the explanation of the apparent inconsistency is, that the former style of watchfulness was adapted to the first disciples of Christ and to the early Church, and the latter to the Church of these last days. The statements about *not* knowing the times and seasons are applicable to those who as a matter of fact *did* not know them, but expected the return of Christ in their own day; and the statements about *knowing* them, to those who have learned by experience that a period of eighteen hundred years at least was appointed in the councils of eternity to intervene between the departure of Christ and His return in glory.

It is self-evident that in respect of their knowledge of the true length of the Christian dispensation, these two classes, owing to the lapse of time, occupy wholly different ground, and that, but for chronologic prophecy, the Church of these last days would be exposed to fearful disadvantages compared with the early Church. The true length of this age was, of course, from the first known to God, but He did not reveal it to the early Church. He gave them general promises, like, "Behold, I come quickly"; "Yet a little while, and the coming One shall come, and will not tarry"; but He did not specify whether the interval was to be brief, according to human reckoning, or only according to the Divine scale of "one day is with the Lord as a thousand years." Did He therefore deceive them? No; but He allowed them to remain in ignorance of things it was better for them not to know, and that because He loved them, and sought their present comfort and sanctification. Had they been informed beforehand of the predestined twelve centuries of apostasy and persecution, they would have been deprived of the cheering hope that they might be of the number who would be alive and remain at the second advent. What help would it have been to the martyrs under pagan Rome to look down the long, dark vista of ages, and behold the worse martyrdoms under Papal Rome? What present influence could an advent promised at the end of well-nigh two thousand years have had in cheering and strengthening and purifying the early Church? None! The knowledge would have paralysed faith and hope and courage. Their ignorance was best for them, and God, in mercy, did not remove it.

But we of these last days are not ignorant of the facts of the case. The strange and momentous historic drama of which they little dreamed, the great Apostasy of the Christian Church, the long ages of Papal usurpation, corruption, and persecution, all lie open before *our* eyes on the page of history.

" A knowledge of the limits of the great anti-Christian Apostasy would not now deprive us of hope, but the very contrary ; in fact, we need some such revelation to sustain our faith and hope to the end of the long delay ; without the chronological data afforded us by the prophecies of Daniel and John, we should be in a position of fearful temptation to doubt and despair. The early Church was entirely ignorant of the length of the interval which we know to have occurred, and this knowledge absolutely prevents the general promises of the nearness of the second advent from having the same power over us that they had over it. Those statements cannot convey to us, after a lapse of well-nigh two thousand years, the impressions they conveyed to the primitive saints. They seemed to justify them in expecting the coming of Christ in their own day; but each succeeding generation would have less and less ground for such an expectation; and when the promise was already one thousand years old, who could avoid the reflection, 'Since it has included one thousand years, it may include another'? We, after nearly two thousand years, could not, as we read the promise, escape the conviction, that, having already included two thousand years, it was perfectly possible that two thousand more were yet to come. Each century of delay would thus increase the heart-sickness of hope deferred, and the Church of these last days might well hang down her head in the sorrowful but irresistible conviction that her redemption might still be at an immeasurable distance; she could have no well grounded hope that the Lord was, in any strict sense, 'at hand.'

"Now one generation of His saints is as dear to God as another; we may be sure He did not secure the holiness and happiness of the early Church at the expense of ours, nor conceal what might be a blessing to us, because the knowledge might not have been a blessing to them. No; He provided some better thing for us than that we should float uncertainly on the stream of time, not knowing whether we were any nearer to the future than to the past advent of Christ. He revealed, but revealed in a mystery, all the main events of this dispensation, and nearly two-thirds of its duration; He revealed them in just such a way as best to secure a renewal of hope that should give consolation, and revive in these last times a 'patient waiting for Christ.' Since continued ignorance of the true nature and length of this dispensation, as determined beforehand in the counsels of God, would have produced the very opposite effects designed by the permission of temporary ignorance, we have every reason to conclude that God would in due time replace this latter by knowledge, and give a gradually increasing understanding of the inspired predictions." (See *The Approaching End of the Age*, p. 87.)

The change from utter ignorance to *comparatively* full knowledge on the subject of the chronologic measures of this Gentile age has been, and was doubtless intended to be, general and progressive through its entire course. It has been secured by a gradually increasing comprehension of the symbolic prophecies of Daniel and the Apocalypse. These have slowly become clear in the light of history, and their true scale, suspected and vaguely suggested but always wrongly applied by earlier generations of students, has since the Reformation been demonstrated with ever-increasing distinctness. In the focused light of all the facts mentioned in our chronological chapter, *our* position in the time of the end seems indicated with such a measure of exactness, that knowledge ought assuredly to be to us a far mightier motive than ignorance, to patient waiting for Christ. We add on this point the weighty words of another, whose cautious and reverent spirit, combined with clear, intelligent grasp of these subjects, has never been excelled:

"We are often reminded that the secret things belong to the Lord our God; and doubtless, even in searching God's holy prophecies, the spirit of that caution may be transgressed by a vain curiosity and irreverent boldness. But when the words are perverted into an absolute prohibition, the rest of the verse supplies a conclusive answer. The things that are revealed belong to us and to our children. Surely every part of God's Word is a revelation. To number it among the secret things which are best honoured by neglect is really to fling back the Divine gift in the face of Him who bestows it. He solemnly declares that all inspired Scripture is profitable for us, and that whatever is written therein is written for our learning. Who are we that we should pretend to be wiser than God, or profess that some of His revealed sayings would have been more wisely kept back from us? as if our neglect were to remedy the unwise loquacity of the Spirit of God !"

Perhaps the most common objection to the study of chronologic prophecy is based upon our Lord's words, "It is not for you to know the times or the seasons, which the Father hath put in His own power" (Acts i. 7):

"These words, however, when searched narrowly, are a strong warrant for an inquiry into the times and seasons of prophecy, while they suggest a needful caution for its due exercise. The words are not general, as our version seems to imply, but special. 'It is not for you to know the times or the seasons, which the Father hath reserved in His own power.' There is here a direct allusion to a text familiar to the apostles, and which explains the true meaning of the answer. Daniel (chapter xii.) had heard two angels put the inquiry, How long shall it be to the end of these wonders?' The Son of God replies with a solemn oath, that 'it shall be for a season, and seasons, and half a season ; and when He shall have accomplished to scatter the power of the holy people, all these things shall be finished.' The prophet then asks for further light, but receives the answer, 'The words are closed up and sealed till the time of the end.'

"The answer then of our Lord to His apostles on earth is only the echo of His reply to the prophet in the vision. The event spoken of is clearly the same in both, the restoration of the king-dom to Israel, and the end of the scattering of the holy people. The seasons of delay before the event were sealed till the time of the end ; until then the Father, by the lips of the Covenant Angel, had expressly reserved them in His own power. The disciples asked the time of that restoration. Our Lord, as if pointing them to the words of Daniel, introduces the very term employed in the vision, 'It is not for you to know the times or the seasons, which the Father hath put in His own power.' As if He had said, 'The time of which you speak follows certain seasons of predicted delay; and these seasons have been reserved at present from a complete revelation, until the Father Himself, at the time of the end, shall begin to unseal them.'

"We have thus a threefold and fourfold answer to the objection. First, the words are not general as to all times, but refer specially to the three times and a half which were to be sealed and closed until a later period. Secondly, they are not general as to Christians, but relate with a marked emphasis to the apostles themselves, and Christians in their day. 'Such knowledge,' our Lord implies, 'may be hereafter given to others, but it is not for you. Another work is assigned you, to found the Church, and spread the gospel through the world.' It is only when the faith of the Gentiles begins to decay that the Father will unseal the times of that blessed hope which will be as life from the dead to the unbelieving world. And hence, further, they are a secret assurance that there will be other Christians of a later age, to whom these times will be unsealed, as those of Jeremiah were to Daniel himself, shortly before their close.

"The words of Christ, 'Of that day and that hour knoweth no man, no, not the angels which are in heaven, neither the Son, but the Father,' are often viewed as a clear censure on all these inquiries. How far the spirit of this caution extends may require much spiritual wisdom to determine; but conclusions loosely and rashly drawn from it have nothing to sustain them. First, the assertion is strictly true only of the time when our Saviour spoke; for surely with regard to the Son of God, they must have ceased to be true when He was risen and ascended into glory. Our Lord Himself, since they were uttered, has received in His human nature immeasurable wisdom; and we may infer that His Church also, though in measures infinitely short of His own, will receive from age to age a like increase. Again, the words refer to the day and the hour, not to the year, much less to the generation in which that great event will occur. Minute conjectures on the time of the advent may still be forbidden us, and the spirit of the caution may extend itself beyond the strict letter; but still the spirit of the previous verse, 'When ye shall see these things begin to come to pass, *know that it is nigh, even at the doors,*' has a voice not less plain, and speaks with the same authority. The first generation of the Church then is made a precedent for the last, and leads us to expect that Christians, whenever that generation has come, will be able to ascertain it, and may know by clear signs that the Lord is really near at hand." [1]

(2) The second obvious and easy objection which will be alleged against our exposition is *the repeated failures* which will have attended previous attempts to demonstrate the limits of the prophetic periods and to indicate the probable date of the end of this age. A little consideration will show the baseless nature of this objection.

The frankly admitted fact that the study of chronologic prophecy has led to premature anticipations of the end, is no more an objection to its divinely intended use than is the still more conspicuous fact that the general promises of Scripture as to the coming of the Lord have done the same. Not more than twenty generations have elapsed since the study of *chronologic* prophecy began to be pursued; while sixty generations at least have been exposed to erroneous anticipations based on non-chronologic predictions. If we are justified in declining investigation of the revealed "times and seasons," because such investigation has led to some false anticipations, we should also be justified in paying no attention to the general promises of Christ's speedy advent, which have thus led to tenfold more numerous disappointments. The fact is, that such disappointments are no argument against the value of either class of predictions, but are, on the contrary, an intended and inevitable result of both the one and the other.

It is perfectly evident from all the statements of the New Testament on the subject that the Lord desired

[1] Rev. T. R. Birks, *Thoughts on the Times and Seasons of Sacred Prophecy.*

all the generations of His Church to live in *continual expectation of His return*. It is equally certain that in the Divine counsels a period of about nineteen centuries was appointed to elapse before that event should take place. What wonder then that promise and prophecy were so bestowed as to secure the maintenance of watchfulness through all the nineteen Christian centuries? That this is what has been done is evident from the objection that premature and mistaken expectations of the end have always prevailed in the Church. Such is the case, and there *are* instances on record in which these expectations have done temporary harm, by unsettling the minds of the weak and unstable, as in the Thessalonian Church for instance, in very early days, and among the Millerites and others in America in recent times. But such premature anticipations have *as a rule* had, as they were designed to have, a beneficial effect on the different sections of the Church in which they have prevailed. They have tended to cheer and strengthen those who have sincerely entertained them; to encourage separation from the world, study of Scripture, and practical earnestness in the work of evangelisation. These were the effects intended, and history testifies that these have generally been the effects produced.

It must not be rashly and wrongly assumed that God has intentionally deceived His people on this point. He has simply withheld from them, and for a time, light which He might have given, but which it would have been injurious for them to have received too soon. Tender seedling plants cannot bear the blaze of the noonday sun, and a wise husbandman shields them from it until it will be beneficial rather than harmful; in due time it will be the best tonic they can have, and absolutely indispensable to the final ripening of the fruit. So as to this truth of the appointed length of the Christian dispensation. There was a time when the infant Church would have withered and drooped under it ; the fore-view of eighteen hundred years of apostasy and persecution would have destroyed its hope, and have been too severe a test of its faith. To the Church of these last days, on the other hand, light as to the limits of this age of long-suffering with sin is not only good but indispensable. That such light should dawn on the Church, and brighten gradually as needed, was by Divine wisdom arranged for and secured by the use of two sorts of predictions. First, general ones, adapted to earlier ages; and secondly, chronological ones, intended for the last days. That the latter should not be prematurely understood was provided against by the use of symbols for the periods of time, as well as for the events. Church history proves that these arrangements prevented premature discovery, and present experience proves that it has secured the right reading of the mysterious revelation by the light of its own fulfilment in these last days, when its comprehension is a needful aid to faith and hope.

Why should we deem it unlikely that God should on this subject allow the truth to be concealed for a time ? How much scientific truth of immense practical value to mankind did He permit to remain unknown until the nineteenth century ! It was reserved for this " time of the end " for the wise to understand many things. What if early attempts to understand chronologic prophecy were erroneous ? Do we doubt and despise the conclusions of astronomy because the astrologers of other days had erroneous notions ? Do we ridicule the early and clumsy attempts to adapt to each other steam-power and machinery because they did not immediately produce such power-looms and loco-motives as those of our own day? Why then despise the early attempts to read the riddle of prophetic chronology?

As this point is one of considerable importance, we will give a further answer to the objection in the well-chosen words of the author previously quoted:

" These successive anticipations are just what it was reasonable to expect. Only by this gradual approach to a correct view of the times and seasons could the two main purposes have been fulfilled —growing knowledge of the prophecy, with a constant and unbroken expectation of the Lord's coming. The fact, therefore, is so far from refuting the theory, that it might rather be viewed as a direct corollary from its truth. The objection, in reality, assumes that the Church must either be in total ignorance of the times, or vault at once into the possession of exact and perfect knowledge. Either she must entirely renounce the use of the prophetic dates, as having no connexion with her past history, and float in a complete uncertainty concerning her own place in the stream of providence, or else may claim to decide with unerring exactness on the very year in which particular events shall be fulfilled. Now this is a monstrous alternative to propose; neither Scripture nor reason lend it the slightest warrant. . . .

" Let us now suppose that the year-day system is the Divine instrument for conveying to the Church this partial light. Every exposition based on it must then partake of two opposite characters. Compared with the exciting prospect of the instant coming of Christ, as entertained in the Thessalonian Church, it would be a protraction; measured by the event, or by a full and perfect knowledge, it would be an anticipation. It would serve as ballast to those who were shaken in mind and troubled by a false im-pression of the imminent nearness of the judgment; and it would be a wholesome stimulus to the slothful servant who should say in his heart, 'My Lord delayeth His coming.' Now these, *which are the very marks of its practical worth*, form the two counts of the inconsistent indictment which has been laid against it. 'It interferes with the expectation of the advent.' That is to say in reality, it serves from age to age for a partial corrective of false anticipations, like that of the Thessalonians. 'It has repeatedly failed in its predictions, ministered occasion to the scoffers, and thrown discredit on the study of prophecy.' In other words, it has not prematurely revealed the whole interval while the end was still distant, nor given more light to earlier generations of the Church than was profitable for them to receive. It has ministered occasion to the scoffer, and in so doing has fulfilled the prediction that none of the wicked shall understand; while, by the gradual approaches to a just estimate of the times, it has fulfilled the contrasted promise, that knowledge shall be increased and that the wise shall understand. The opposite objections urged against it are the very proof of its adaptation to the wants of the Church. . . .

" The successive failures, as they have been called, are no real failures in a practical sense. They are only waymarks in the progress of the Church from that entire ignorance of the times in which she was purposely left in the apostolic age to the full and certain knowledge that the Bridegroom is at hand, which shall prepare her, like the wise virgins, to enter in with her Lord to the marriage feast."

But we must go further than this, and remind those who object on the ground of false anticipations, that to the system here expounded may be traced many true anticipations of a very remarkable character— anticipations which can hardly be accounted for save on the ground of the truth of the system which led to them. Some of these anticipations were absolutely correct; others correct within a year or two; and it should be remembered that the growth of light is always gradual, and that only within the last few years has astronomy lent its aid to chronological calculations. In the earliest ages of the Church chronologic prophecy was, as it was intended to be, absolutely an enigma; Bible students felt it to be so, and only occasionally hazarded remarks on the subject. Only in the twelfth and thirteenth centuries did any real light begin to dawn. A great step was made when the year-day principle of interpreting the periods was recognised; though for some centuries they were dated from altogether wrong starting-points, and attention was directed exclusively to the second half of the great week, the dates of the Captivity era never being used as starting-points.

The era of the Reformation witnessed a great advance in prophetic interpretation, as it was then that the true character of the Papal Antichrist was first generally recognised. Aritius, an expositor who died in 1574, saw and taught the year-day system, but dated the 1260 years from Constantine's establishment of imperial Christianity, A.D. 312; he consequently expected the period to run out in his own days. David Chrytæus, in 1571, suggested that the period might perhaps be measured from Alaric's destruction, A.D. 412, and so run out in A.D. 1672; he thought it more likely that it was dated from the edict of Phocas, 606, and hence that it would run out in 1866. Pareus, writing in 1608, fixes on the same date, as did also many later expositors; they were justified by the result, for the four years 1866–70 were, as we have shown, critical and terminal in the existence of the temporal power of the Papacy.

Robert Fleming, in his work on *The Rise and Fall of Rome Papal, published in the year 1701,* anticipated the years 1794 and 1848 as great *crises* in the downfall of the Papacy, even as we know they proved to be; and he added, "Yet we are not to imagine these events will totally destroy the Papacy, for we find it is still in being and alive when the next vial is poured out." There were no signs when Fleming wrote, at the very commencement of the eighteenth century, of the awful revolutionary crisis that was to arise ere its close, still less of the events of the revolutionary year 1848. He was led to select them solely by the light of chronologic prophecy; and so were the *numerous* writers who, long before the years 1866–70, foretold that those years would be most critical ones in the downfall of despotic power and Papal usurpation, many predicting definitely the cessation of the temporal power. Similarly the date of the Greek insurrection, and of other stages in the fall of Turkey, have been foreseen and indicated by students of the prophetic world.

(3) One objection likely to be raised against this whole exposition is, that it deals with so large a number of events and of dates, and that some of them do not seem to be of first-rate importance. It will be said that with three scales of measurements, and a variety of points to measure from and to, it is easy to make out anything, and that the very multiplicity of coincidences decreases confidence in the worth of any of them. Now while such an impression may naturally arise from a superficial survey of the subject, yet closer study and more careful examination will turn it from an objection to a powerful corroboration. The best reply is a glance at the diagram (see Frontispiece), which shows

I. That the still unfulfilled chronological periods announced in Scripture, and here considered, are mainly three, and three only.

i. The 2520 years of the "seven times," or great comprehensive week of the prophetic calendar.

ii. Its latter half, the 1260 years, or three and a half times of the Papal and Mohammedan apostasies. And

iii. The shortened form or the 2300 years of the

Eastern Sanctuary Cycle, dating from the Persian Restoration era.

Hence there is no great multiplicity of periods. The other prophecies alluded to, such as the sixty-five years to the fall of Ephraim, the seventy years of Judah's captivity, and the 490 from the Persian Restoration era to the Messianic era at the first advent, are all, of course, fulfilled predictions, and bear on the question of the end of this age mainly as affording lessons as to the style of fulfilment to be expected at the close of the longer periods. It is from them we learn the two great principles: that all the different astronomic measures of the year are employed in chronologic prophecy; and that such predicted periods extend, not merely between specific years, but also between eras of wider extent.

II. A glance at the diagram shows also that the commencing and closing eras of these long periods, the briefest of which extends for more than twelve centuries, are, though actually long, relatively very short. To the periods themselves they bear just such a relation as infancy and old age generally bear to mature life, such a relation as the growth and the decay of an oak tree bear to its whole existence—in other words, a natural relation. The great movements of history are as a rule slow. Vast empires are not consolidated in a year, and world-wide dominion does not suddenly collapse; the movements of history are as gradual as are the processes of nature. It is difficult to decide the year in which the youth stops growing, and "coming of age" has to be fixed at an arbitrary point. So the rise and fall of empires cannot be assigned to exact dates, but must needs occupy eras more or less prolonged.

On the other hand, it is no less certain that in such eras several dates will naturally stand out as critical, some more decidedly so than others; but many will mark *stages* of development and decay. Surely no objection should lie against an exposition because it takes into account facts so harmonious with the laws of nature! If it would be accepted as a proof of Divine inspiration that a predicted period should prove to have elapsed between any *two* given dates, is not the proof strengthened when it is demonstrated that the same period similarly extends between *all* the corresponding crises of the commencing and terminal eras? Not only did the seventy years of the Babylonish captivity elapse between Nebuchadnezzar's first invasion of Judah, B.C. 605, and the decree of Cyrus, B.C. 536, they also elapsed between the final destruction of Jerusalem, B.C. 587, and the fourth year of Darius, B.C. 517. Not only did seventy weeks extend from the edicts of Artaxerxes to the cutting off of "Messiah the Prince," but they also extended between the different crises of the Persian Restoration era and the Messianic era. This principle, *proved by history* to have governed the accomplishments of the *fulfilled* predictions, we have applied to the still partially unfulfilled predictions, and the result proves that it holds good so far, and leads to the anticipation that it will do so to the close.

As to *the three astronomic scales*, they are all employed in human computations and in Divine predictions; and the two fulfilled predictions to which we have just alluded were, for instance, actually measured on both lunar and solar scales; hence we feel warranted in using all three, and the result shows that they are intended to be so applied.

As regards the *character of the events* which we have

20

pointed out in the critical eras, it should be remembered that they are indicated only as *links in a chain*; they must not be considered as isolated events, but as units in a group, members of a series. Standing alone, some of them might seem comparatively unimportant, but collectively they make up historical movements whose critical nature cannot be questioned. Strike out half the dates if you will, you cannot strike out the historical movement as a whole; it is there, prominent in the records of history, conspicuous as a fulfilment of prophecy. Each of these stages derives its importance from its relation to the rest. The abdication, for instance, of Charles X. and of Louis Philippe, and the fall of Napoleon III., may not have been occurrences of the first magnitude; but they were clearly links in the chain of events which overthrew Papal supremacy in Europe, and that overthrow *is* an event of supreme importance to the human race, and of vital connexion with the themes of prophecy. So as to Kainardje, Carlowitz, the Crimean War, and the Treaty of Berlin; looked at as standing alone, they may rank as comparatively unimportant in their influence on the history of the people of God; but looked at as stages of the overthrow of the once mighty and dreaded anti-Christian Turkish empire, as the first fatal blows to a Power which still hinders the restoration of the Jews to Palestine, their important relation to the prophetic programme cannot be questioned.

Each of the events of a series, if taken singly and separately, may lose entirely the character it bears when regarded in all its connexions. A destructive swarm of locusts, for instance, is no unusual occurrence in Egypt, and an objector might well refuse to regard it as any special Divine judgment. But when it occurs as one of the ten plagues, which issue in a predicted result so remarkable as the exodus of Israel from Egypt, who can refuse to recognise its true character? So as to the various stages of the judgments under which the Papacy and Mohammedanism are perishing. They resemble the plagues of Egypt in this respect, that they are distinct and successive inflictions, from no one of which is there any real recovery, whose effects are consequently cumulative, though the end in view, the utter destruction of the adverse Power, is not accomplished exclusively by them, but by direct Divine interference at last.

Moreover, careful examination will show that these events, which fell out at the various closes of the prophetic periods, as measured from their successive starting-points, comprise really *all* the critical stages of the movement in question which have happened so far. Will any one indicate events having a vital connexion with the fall of the Papacy and Mohammedanism, other than those which sacred prophecy has thus indicated? It may be said that we have not alluded to the Reformation, which was the most important of all the causes of the fall of the Papacy. That is true; but the Reformation was a *spiritual*, and not a *political* movement. The periods of Daniel start from and lead to *political changes*. The Reformation changed the hearts of men and the creeds of Churches, and led in the end to political changes also, but not at the commencement. It does not fall within the chronological range of the " time of the end."

4. Some, again, may object to the system here developed, on the ground that it is somewhat complicated, involving research and calculation, and lacking in that notable characteristic of all truth, simplicity.

It will be alleged that it is the glory of both the moral law and the gospel that children can understand and obey them, and that the ignorant and unlearned can appreciate them; while neither of these classes could follow the reasonings or grasp the conclusions of this investigation. The answer to this objection is that Scripture avowedly contains, not only milk for babes, but solid meat for those of mature intelligence; even those who by reason of use have their senses exercised to discern both good and evil.

It is the same with nature; the fundamental and essential laws on which existence depends lie on the surface, and commend themselves to the least developed intelligence. But has Nature no precious secrets which she yields only to patient observation, earnest research, and continued meditation and reflection? And are these long ignored causes and unperceived laws destitute of practical importance? Let the discovery and applications of steam and electricity in the nineteenth century be a reply!

Could the science of geology have been understood and turned to account by simply surveying the surface of the ground? Could the marvellously complex laws of chemistry have been grasped by considering merely the mechanical properties of matter? Can superficial and uncultivated readers appreciate, or even perceive, the literary excellence of Dante or Shakespeare? And are we to imagine that, while human compositions are adapted to the highest intelligence, the book of God can be fathomed with facility by the weakest and most uncultivated minds? That were a conception altogether derogatory to the dignity of inspiration! Ought we not rather to expect in the oracles of God heights and depths of hidden wisdom which shall utter themselves only to those who earnestly seek wisdom, "watching daily at her gates, and waiting at the posts of her doors"? Simplicity of result in nature arises from arrangements of extreme complexity; as, for instance, the movements of the moon or the planets. To calculate the motions of only three bodies in space in accordance with the laws of gravitation and motion is, as is well known, a problem passing human intelligence.

The *result* of the chronological calculations and historical adaptations which we have endeavoured to indicate is simple enough, and may be expressed in a sentence. It has pleased God to order the revolutions of history in harmony with that law of completion in weeks, by which He has ordered many of the revolutions of nature, and according to which He arranged the typical ritual service of the Jewish people. The Gentile dispensation of the four great empires, whose nature, course, and close is revealed in Daniel, is a great week, beginning with the rise of the typical, and ending with the fall of the antitypical Babylon, and bisected by the rise of the Papal and Mohammedan Powers. This great dispensational week and its sections are measured from the different crises of the commencing era on the different natural scales, the longest of which, the solar, alone is final. There is surely no great complexity in this *result*, though to establish it requires study and research. Herein, however, the parallel with nature is too exact to warrant objection.

CHAPTER XVII

The Canon of Ptolemy

"SURE AS THE STARS."

THE uncertainty which attaches to remote periods of secular chronology disappears at the date of the accession of Nabonassar, with whose reign the times of the four Gentile empires commence. From this time forward we are able to verify the chronological records of the past; and the dates of ancient history are confirmed by astronomic observations.

The astronomical records of the ancients, by whose means we are able to fix with certainty the chronology of the earlier centuries of the "times of the Gentiles," are contained in the *Syntaxis*, or *Almagest* of Ptolemy.

In the existence of this invaluable work, and in its preservation as a precious remnant of antiquity, the hand of Providence can clearly be traced. The same Divine care which raised up Herodotus and other Greek historians to carry on the records of the past from the point to which they had been brought by the writings of the prophets at the close of the Babylonish captivity;—the Providence which raised up Josephus, the Jewish historian, at the termination of New Testament history, to record the fulfilment of prophecy in the destruction of Jerusalem,—raised up also Ptolemy in the important interval which extended from Titus to Hadrian, that of the completion of Jewish desolation, *to record the chronology of the nine previous centuries*, and to associate it in such a way with the revolutions of the solar system as to permit of the most searching demonstration of its truth.

Ptolemy's great work, the *Almagest*, is a treatise on astronomy, setting forth the researches of ancient observers and mathematicians with reference to the position of the stars, the exact length of the year, and the elements of the orbits of the sun, moon, and planets. This work was written in Greek, and subsequently translated into Arabic, Persian, Hebrew, and Latin, etc. ; it became the text-book of astronomic knowledge both in the East and in Europe, and retained that high position for about fourteen centuries, or till the time of Copernicus, the birth of modern astronomy, three centuries ago.

The chronological value of the *Almagest* is owing to the fact that it interweaves a series of ancient dates with a series of celestial positions. It contains a complete catalogue of the succession of Babylonian, Persian, Grecian, and Roman monarchs, from Nabonassar to Hadrian and Antoninus, together with the dates of their accession and the duration of their reigns. Its astronomic events are referred to definite historic dates, and by this connexion there is conferred on the latter the character of scientific certainty.

This important feature of the *Almagest* is described as follows in the *Chrono-astrolabe*, by James B. Lindsay, a work published in 1858, demonstrating the authenticity of Hebrew, Greek, and Roman chronology, etc., by astronomic methods :

"The *Syntaxis* of Ptolemy contains an account of

many historic events, and blended with them is a multitude of astronomic observations. The *astronomic* and *historic* cannot be separated, and they must both stand or fall together. *The astronomic can be rigidly verified, and the truth of the historic is a legitimate deduction.*"

In the *Almagest*, "a celestial phenomenon is coupled with a terrestrial event. An eclipse of the moon or an acronic of Mars is assigned to a given year and day of a king's reign. The celestial mechanism, though complicate, is intelligible; the motions are calculable, and we can verify or falsify the recorded observations."

With reference to Ptolemy's Canon, or chronological list of the monarchs of the four great empires, Lindsay says:

"The complete harmony that is to be found in this canon with the dates previously determined by eclipses, entitles it to our highest confidence. That Ptolemy was its author, and not Theon, is confirmed by the fact that it is not continued beyond Antoninus, in whose reign our author dates most of his observations. We have had abundant evidence that he was φιλόπονος and φιλαλήθης, a lover of labour and a lover of truth, and are fully warranted to regard this canon as giving to ancient history *mathematical exactness.* . . . The motions and phases of the luminaries are visible every day, and with these alone we have been able to authenticate the whole of the *Almagest.* Even the errors of Ptolemy augment, if possible, the evidence for the authenticity of the *Syntaxis, and a foundation is laid for chronology sure as the stars.* The external evidence for the text-book is most abundant. It is mentioned in terms of the highest approbation by Greek, Hebrew, and Arabian historians. In the ninth century the celebrated caliph, Al Mamun, caused it to be translated into Arabic. Persic and Hebrew versions engaged the attention of oriental *savants* in our Middle Ages, and at the dawn of printing Latin translations were abundantly diffused. . . . It is to Ptolemy that our modern astronomy is almost wholly due; but those who enjoy the benefits have forgotten the benefactor. The name of Ptolemy, who was certainly not inferior, perhaps superior, to Newton, is seldom mentioned but to be covered with pity or with ridicule. Even men of science have not given to Ptolemy the honour that belongs to him. Delambre has fancied that he was a mere copyist of Hipparchus, and that to the latter the excellences found in the *Syntaxis* are all to be attributed. Far be it from us to deny the greatness of Hipparchus, but Ptolemy was greater. *His account of the ancient eclipses, and of their connexion with historic facts, is more precious than gold, and guarantees a translation of the Almagest into every language.* In the want of modern instruments he may have made an error in the observation of the equinoxes, and all facts then known sanctioned the earth's stability. *Veritas prævalebit,* and the worth of Ptolemy is again appreciated. La Place, *Système du Monde,* has seen his value." The following is his eulogy :

"Ptolémée inscrivit dans le temple de Sérapis à Canope les principaux élémens de son système astronomique. Le système a subsisté pendant quatorze siècles ; aujourd'hui même qu'il est entièrement détruit, '*l'Almageste*' *considéré comme le dépôt des anciennes observations, est un des plus précieux monuments de l'antiquité.* Malheureusement, il ne renferme qu'un petit nombre des observations faites jusqu'alors. Son auteur n'a rapporté que celles qui lui étaient nécessaires pour expliquer ses théories. Les tables astronomiques une fois formées, il a jugé inutile de transmettre avec elles, à la postérité, les observations qu'Hipparque et lui avaient employées pour cet objet ; et son exemple a été suivi par les Arabes et les Perses. Les grands recueils d'observations précises rassemblées uniquement pour elles-mêmes, et sans aucune application aux théories, appartiennent à l'astronomie moderne, et sont l'un des moyens les plus propres à la perfectionner. Ptolémée a rendu de grands services à la géographie, en rassemblant toutes les déterminations de longitude et de latitude des lieux connus, et en jetant les fondemens de la méthode des projections pour la construction des cartes géographiques. Il a fait un traité d'optique, dans lequel il expose avec étendue le phénomène des réfractions astronomiques ; il est encore auteur de divers ouvrages sur la musique, la chronologie, la gnomonique, et la méchanique. Tant de travaux sur un si grand nombre d'objets, supposent un esprit vaste, et lui assurent un rang distingué dans l'histoire des sciences. Quand son système eut fait place à celui de la nature, on se vengea sur son auteur, du despotisme avec lequel il avait régné trop longtemps ; on accusa Ptolémée de s'être approprié les découvertes de ses prédécesseurs. Mais la manière honorable dont il cite très-souvent Hipparque à l'appui de ses théories, le justifie pleinement de cette inculpation. À la renaissance des lettres parmi les Arabes et en Europe, ses hypothèses, réunissant à l'attrait de la nouveauté, l'autorité de ce qui est ancien, furent généralement adoptées par les esprits avides de connaissances, et qui se virent tout-à-coup en possession de celles que l'antiquité n'avait acquises que par de longs travaux. Leur reconnaissance éleva trop haut Ptolémée qu'ensuite on a trop rabaissé. Sa réputation a éprouvé le même sort que celle d'Aristote et de Descartes ; leurs erreurs n'ont pas été plutôt reconnues, que l'on a passé d'une admiration aveugle, à un injuste mépris ; car dans la science même, les révolutions les plus utiles n'ont point été exemptes de passion et d'injustice."

In order to obtain a safe and scientific foundation for his mathematical calculations as to solar and lunar movements, including his valuable *astronomic tables*, Ptolemy compares three carefully selected, well attested ancient eclipses, observed at Babylon in the reign of Mardocempadus, with three other eclipses which he had observed at Alexandria in the seventeenth, eighteenth, and twentieth years of the reign of Hadrian. He similarly compares three eclipses which took place in the fourth century after Nabonassar, referred to by the celebrated Greek astronomer Hipparchus, with three eclipses recorded by the same astronomer, which occurred two centuries later.

In this comparison Ptolemy deals with no less than *four groups of ancient eclipses*, Babylonian, Grecian, and Roman, containing three in each, twelve in all. These eclipses have been frequently verified by modern astronomers, and they combine to fix the chronological dates with which they are connected with the utmost certainty. If a single eclipse is sufficient to attest an

ancient date, how conclusive the concurrent evidence
afforded by four groups of eclipses ! But these are not
all the astronomic phenomena which Ptolemy records
There is a list of no less than eighty-five solar, lunar,
and planetary positions, with their dates, as given in the
Almagest, and as verified by modern astronomers. This
list contains four vernal equinoxes, eight autumnal, four
summer solstices, nineteen lunar eclipses, nine lunar
observations, and forty-one planetary observations, including sixteen of Mercury, ten of Venus, five of Mars,
five of Jupiter, and five of Saturn.

The time of the occurrence of these astronomic
phenomena is measured by Ptolemy from noon of the
first of the Egyptian month Thoth, in the first year
of Nabonassar. The verification of the time of any
of these events is the verification of the *initial date
from which the whole series is reckoned*. Thoth 1 Nab.
1 is thus abundantly determined to noon February 26th,
B.C. 747.[1]

[1] As an illustration of Ptolemy's use of the Nabonassar era as a
fixed and constant epoch from which to measure various astronomic events, we quote the following, from his chapter on the
epoch of the main movements of the moon in longitude and
anomaly : "In order to reduce these epochs to *noon of the first
day of the Egyptian month Thoth of the first year of Nabonassar*, we
have taken the *interval* of time which elapses from this day to the
middle of the second of the three first and nearest eclipses which
happened, as we said, in the second year of Mardocempadus,
between the 18th and 19th of the Egyptian month Thoth, at
one-half and one-third of an equinoctial hour before midnight,
which made an interval of twenty-seven Egyptian years (years of
365 days) seventeen days and $11\frac{1}{6}$ hours very nearly ; and casting
out two complete revolutions in longitude, 123° 22′ and 103° 35′,
if we subtract respectively these quantities from the positions of
the middle of the second eclipse, we shall have for the first year of
Nabonassar, the first day of the Egyptian month Thoth, at noon,

In addition to this primary Babylonian date, these astronomic records fix *directly* the times of the *Babylonian* monarchs Mardocempadus and Nabopolassar, the *Persian* monarchs Cambyses and Darius, the *Grecian* dates employed by Hipparchus, and the dates of the *Roman* emperors Domitian, Trajan, Hadrian, and Antoninus Pius; while *indirectly* they enable us to determine the dates of *all the intermediate reigns recorded in Ptolemy's* ASTRONOMICAL CANON, a list of fifty-five successive reigns, extending over a period of 907 years, from Nabonassar of Babylon to the Roman emperor Antoninus Pius.

This invaluable Canon, representing the unbroken imperial rule administered by successive dynasties of Gentile empires, is divided by Ptolemy into four distinct parts.

1. Babylonian kings, twenty in number.

2. Persian kings, ten in number, terminating with Alexander the Great, of Macedon, eleven names in all.

3. Grecian kings, twelve in number.

4. Roman emperors, twelve in number.

The sum of years given in the calendar is divided into two parts: first, 424 years, from Nabonassar to Alexander of Macedon; and secondly, 483 years, from Philip Aridæus to Antoninus Pius. The striking and important *agreement between the history and chronological outline given in the Canon of Ptolemy and that set forth in the fourfold image of Nebuchadnezzar's vision*, described and interpreted by Daniel, is referred to by Faber in the following words:

---

the main place of the moon 11° 22′ of Taurus in longitude, and 263° 49′ anomaly, from the apogee of the epicycle, that is to say, at 70° 37′ elongation; the sun, as has been proved, being then in 0° 45′ of Pisces."—*Almagest*, chap. vii.

" As the good Spirit of God employs the four successive empires of Babylon, and Persia, and Greece, and Rome, in the capacity of THE GRAND CALENDAR OF PROPHECY, so Ptolemy has employed the very same four empires in the construction of his invaluable Canon ; because the several lines of their sovereigns so begin and end, when the one line is engrafted upon the other line, as to form a single unbroken series from Nabonassar to Augustus Cæsar.   In each case the principle of continuous arrangement is identical. Where Ptolemy makes the Persian Cyrus the immediate successor of the Babylonic Nabonadius, or Belshazzar, without taking into account the preceding kings of *Persia* or of *Media*, there, in the image, the silver joins itself to the gold ; where Ptolemy makes the Grecian Alexander the immediate successor of the Persian Darius, without taking into account the preceding kings of *Macedon*, there, in the image, the brass joins itself to the silver ; and where Ptolemy makes the Roman Augustus the immediate successor of the Grecian Cleopatra, without taking into account the long preceding roll of the consular *Fasti* and the primitive *Roman* monarchy, there, in the image, the iron joins itself to the brass.   In short, *the Canon of Ptolemy may well be deemed a running comment upon the altitudinal line of the great metallic image.*   As the parts of the image melt into each other, forming jointly one grand succession of supreme imperial domination, so *the Canon of Ptolemy exhibits what may be called a picture of unbroken imperial rule, though administered by four successive dynasties, from Nabonassar to Augustus and his successors.*" [1]

---

[1] *Sacred Calendar of Prophecy*, vol. ii. p. 7.

APPENDIX

---+---

THE CANON OF PTOLEMY

PTOLEMY'S CANON OF KINGS OF THE ASSYRIANS AND MEDES

		Each.	*Sum*
1.	Nabonassar	14	14
2.	Nadius	2	16
3.	Khozirus and Porus	5	21
4.	Jougaius	5	26
5.	Mardocempadus	12	38
6.	Archianus	5	43
7.	First Interregnum	2	45
8.	Belibus	3	48
9.	Apronadius	6	54
10.	Regibelus	1	55
11.	Mesesimordachus	4	59
12.	Second Interregnum	8	67
13.	Asaridinus	13	80
14.	Saosduchinus	20	100
15.	Khuniladanus	22	122
16.	Nabopolassar	21	143
17.	Nabokolassar	43	186
18.	Ilvarodamus	2	188
19.	Nerikassolasar	4	192
20.	Nabonadius	17	209

PERSIAN KINGS

		Each.	*Sum*
21.	Cyrus	9	218
22.	Cambyses	8	226
23.	Darius I.	36	262
24.	Xerxes	21	283

	Each.	Sum.
25. Artaxerxes I.	41	324
26. Darius II.	19	343
27. Artaxerxes II.	46	389
28. Ochus	21	410
29. Arogus	2	412
30. Darius III.	4	416
31. Alexander of Macedon	8	424

YEARS OF THE KINGS AFTER THE DEATH OF KING ALEXANDER

1. Philip, after Alexander the Founder	7	7
2. Alexand. Ægus	12	19

KINGS OF THE GREEKS IN EGYPT

3. Ptolemy Lagus	20	39
4. „ Philadelphus	38	77
5. „ Euergetes I.	25	102
6. „ Philopator	17	119
7. „ Epiphanes	24	143
8. „ Philometor	35	178
9. „ Euergetes II.	29	207
10. „ Soter	36	243
11. „ Dionysius	29	272
12. Cleopatra	22	294

KINGS OF THE ROMANS

13. Augustus	43	337
14. Tiberius	22	359
15. Caius	4	363
16. Claudius	14	377
17. Nero	14	391
18. Vespasian	10	401
19. Titus	3	404
20. Domitian	15	419
21. Nerva	1	420
22. Trajan	19	439
23. Adrian	21	460
24. Antoninus	23	483

A FEW CLOSING WORDS

OF the things that we have spoken, this is the sum.

The moral and political history of mankind for the last twenty-five centuries has been working out a programme divinely revealed beforehand to Daniel in Babylon. This grand outline, which includes the chronological relation of the events predicted to the coming kingdom of God, is given in the brief but pregnant sentence of the angel, " Four kingdoms shall arise out of the earth; but the saints of the Most High shall take the kingdom, and possess it for ever, even for ever and ever."

The period in which the saints are destined to do this —fixed from the beginning in the eternal counsels, mysteriously indicated in this prophecy, and made plain in these days by providential fulfilments—is, as every sign of our time indicates, at hand. It will be a day of sore judgment on the corrupt Papal apostasy and on all kindred false professions of the name of Christ, but a day which will bring eternal glory to the true Church, and unspeakable blessing to the repentant remnant of the Jewish people, as well as to the spared nations of the Gentile world. It will come suddenly and unexpectedly, when least looked for by men. With united voice history, chronology, astronomy, and Scripture endorse this solemn conclusion, and bid the Church lift up her head, because her great redemption is now close at hand.

Now knowledge is the guide of action. If we know these things, happy are we if we act accordingly. We do well to learn and to believe; but "faith without works is dead." Let all who believe in the near coming of the Lord show their faith by their works.

TRUE BELIEVERS, hold fast till He comes! Trim your lamps, and be ready; we have not long to wait. "The night is far spent, the day is at hand; let us therefore cast off the works of darkness, and let us put on the armour of light." "Let us not sleep, as do others." "The Lord is at hand." Let us awake, and act!

YOUNG CHRISTIANS, with all your fresh powers, your vigour of mind and body, your attractiveness, your sympathies, your knowledge of the truth, your warmth of first love, what are you doing with your priceless possessions in this closing period before the King cometh to take account of His servants? *Redeem the time*; for the last sands are running in the hour-glass of this evil age, and on every side work in profusion is awaiting willing hands and loving hearts.

UNSAVED reader of these lines, what are you doing to *lay hold on eternal life* before this day of salvation closes? Oh, cease trifling, cease putting off, cease to hide from yourself the certain fate of all unbelievers. How shall you escape if you neglect Christ's great salvation? You may be moral in your relations to your fellow-men, but what are your relations to God? He claims, and justly claims, the first place in your heart and mind; your deepest trust, your warmest love; you are not giving Him these, and hence the day of Christ, which glows with glory and joy to His people, looks dark and dreadful to you. We speak to you in His name. He died upon the cross that all who believe in Him should be justified and saved. His message to you is in your mouth and heart. BELIEVE AND LIVE! Turn. Trust. Be reconciled to God. Take His gift *freely*. Learn, and you will love. Then Christ shall be *in* you—your own, your All.

SCEPTICS, you who reject with a smile of superior wisdom the very notion of inspired prophecy and of God in history, we challenge you to account for the numerous and unquestionable facts set forth in this volume. Here are *proofs* of foreknowledge and prediction which you *cannot honestly gainsay*. The day for denying the true date of Daniel is past. Can you give any credible account of the fore-view of human history contained in his book? Is it within the power of man to discern and delineate the events of twenty-five future centuries, with their times? Yet you are witnessing in the political condition of Europe this day that which was foreseen and foretold in the days of Nebuchadnezzar! What does this mean? It means that the Mind which made your mind is appealing to it. God has not left Himself without a witness! He is saying to you, "Behold, the former things are come to pass, and new things do I declare: *before they spring forth I tell you of them.*" "Who hath declared this from ancient time? . . . have not I, the Lord? and there is no God else beside Me; a just God and a Saviour; there is none beside Me." If the Bible be not Divine, you will lose nothing by studying it candidly; while if it be so, you may gain more than tongue can tell! "Prove all things; hold fast that which is good." Search the Divine word. He who will not *search* shall not *find*.

STUDENTS OF THE SURE WORD OF PROPHECY, let no anti-Christianism surprise you. *Before Christ, Anti-*

christ.[1] Such is the foretold order. We have had the great predicted historic Antichrist in the self-exalting head of Papal superstition; we have now its soul-destroying result and outcome in the existence of modern infidelity. But the darkest hour is that before the dawn. Let us gird on our armour for the final conflict, and strive for the reward promised "to him that *over-cometh.*"

The "sure word of prophecy" was given for the guidance and establishment of faith. The apostasies of the falsely professing Church, its fall into vice, super-stition, and infidelity, viewed as *foretold*, ought to be a confirmation of our faith! The fact that the Jews ful-filled prophecy in rejecting Christ is one reason why we receive Him. The fact that so large a portion of Christendom now in another way rejects Him was equally foretold, and is an added reason why we should cleave to Him in faith.

May we see through this anti-Christianism, tracing it to its roots in the historic past, and to its fruits in the foretold future! May the despairing infidelity, the scoffing unbelief, the Christ-rejecting, God-ignoring blasphemy of these days be seen in their true light, as the natural, predicted consequence of the long con-tinued corruption of the professing Church! It is a question of the rotting of dead branches severed from the true and living Vine, of the mortification of lifeless members. Modern infidelity is the legitimate outcome of the great Apostasy, which, having passed through many and various stages, is now assuming its final form. Long has been the warfare waged by the powers of darkness "against Jehovah and His Anointed"; now the last conflict has set in. Let us not shrink from it!

[1] "Venit Antichristus, sed et supervenit Christus" (Cyprian).

The world has never changed in its rejection of Christ nor the true Church in its faith in Him. The cross is still " a stone of stumbling and rock of offence" to the disobedient, but still also "the power of God unto salvation" to every one who believes. Let us remember the solemn and repeated warnings of the Word of God. Is it not written, "They shall turn away their ears from the truth, and shall be turned unto fables"? Is it not written, "These shall make war with the Lamb, and the Lamb shall overcome them: for He is Lord of lords, and King of kings; and they that are with Him are called, and chosen, and faithful"? Is it not written also, "But ye, beloved, seeing ye know these things before, beware lest ye also, being led away with the error of the wicked, fall from your own steadfastness"? But instead of apostatising thus, "grow in grace, and in the knowledge of our Lord and Saviour Jesus Christ. To Him be glory both now and for ever."

May the spirit of careless security, the popular " peace and safety" cry of these days, which is the foretold precursor of the coming of "sudden destruction," have no power over *us* to lull us into unwatchfulness and unbelief! Let us not expose ourselves to the reproachful question, "Could ye not watch with Me one hour?" May we "be diligent," that we "may be found of Him in peace, without spot and blameless"! May we " abide " in Him, and abound in the work of His service according to His word, " *Occupy till I come* "! May we stir up the gift that is in us, utilise the buried talents, and bring in the precious sheaves of the harvest field! " *Looking for that blessed hope*, and the glorious appearing of the great God and our Saviour Jesus Christ."

"Now unto Him that is able to keep you from falling, and to present you faultless before the presence of His glory with exceeding joy, to the only wise God our Saviour, be glory, and majesty, dominion, and power, both now and ever. Amen."

GENERAL INDEX

Abandonment of Rome by Cæsars, 76.

Abomination, 180.

Agnosticism, 280, 324.

Alexander and Daniel, xii.

Alexandria bombarded, 119, 211.

Alison's *History*, 185.

Allies reactionary, 203.

Almagest, 311.

Alva, 94.

American Independence, 227.

Analogy of fulfilments, 44, 244.

Answers to objections, 285.

Antichrist, Papal, 75, 77, 193, 289, 302, 324.

Apocalypse, date, 238.

Apostasies fall, 262.

— rise, 80, 174, 271.

Apostasy, from Koran, 231.

Arabi and Egypt, 119.

Aramaic, xiii, 214.

Artaxerxes' decrees, 36, 66.

Astronomical cycles in Daniel, 223.

Astronomy and history, 313.

Austria, Sadowa, 108.

Aviation, 282.

Babylon, Romish Church, 19, 21, 27, 87, 167, 252, 273.

Babylonish captivity, 28.

Bagdad taken, 121.

Barricades, War of, 202.

Bastile, 229.

Beasts, cruel rulers, 27.

Berlin Treaty, 118, 195, 232, 306.

Bible chronology, 166.

Bible, power of, 92.

Bisection era, 45, 176, 201.

Blasphemous pretensions, 77.

Blood shed by Papacy, 94.

Bones of martyrs, 108.

Books, study of, 13.

Bourbons, 203.

Bush not consumed, 133.

Calendar year, 40.

Camisardes, Cevennes, 98.

Canon of Ptolemy, 311.

Capitalists, Jewish, 152.

Captivity, era, 49, 60.

— gradual, 14, 15, 43.

Carlowitz peace, 111, 178, 185, 306.

Charles X., 306.

Chastisers chastised, 43.

Chrono-astrolabe, 312.

Chronologic, signs, 283.

— prophecy, 4, 38.

Chrytæus, 302.

Cleansing of sanctuary, 180.

Closes and commencements, 41.

Closing, dates, 245.

— words, 321.

Collins, x.

Commencements and closes, 41.

Concealed yet revealed, 38, 293.

Constantine and Jews, 130.

Constantinople, Fall of, 111.

— and Russia, 118.

Crete lost, 212, 244.

Crimean War, 115, 306.

Cromwell and Jews, 143.

Crusades, 131, 133.

INDEX OF CRITICAL DATES

—◆—

This Index will enable readers at once to turn to the pages where a given date is explained. It is easy to see, from the number of references, that certain dates are of special importance.

CPSIA information can be obtained
at www.ICGtesting.com
Printed in the USA
BVHW02s0232271217
503702BV00004B/215/P